GOD'S FIERCE WHIMSY

GOD'S FIERCE
W * H * I * M * S * Y

Christian Feminism and Theological Education

THE PILGRIM PRESS
New York

Library of Congress Cataloging in Publication Data
Main entry under title:

God's fierce whimsy.

Bibliography: p. 214.
1. Feminism—Religious aspects—Christianity—
Addresses, essays, lectures.   2. Theology—Study and
teaching—United States—Addresses, essays, lectures.
I. Mud Flower Collective.
HQ1394.G63   1985   305.4'2   84-26561
ISBN 0-8298-0546-X (pbk.)

3d printing, 1988

The Pilgrim Press, 132 West 31 Street, New York, NY 10001

C·O·N·T·E·N·T·S

P*R*E*F*A*C*E

In naming ourselves Mud Flower, we claim the yet unrealized vision of solidarity reflected in the poem by Delores Williams we have included at the end of our book. We are a collective of racially and ethnically mixed women in theological education. Together, we have told stories, read books, and analyzed what has been happening among us as well as elsewhere in theological education. We have laughed and we have cried more than we had anticipated in our collective effort to learn and to write an honest, constructive essay on Christian feminism and theological education. Together, we name and identify ourselves:

Katie G. Cannon is an ethicist, minister, and feminist of faith rooted and grounded in the black religious tradition. Currently on the faculty of the Episcopal Divinity School in Cambridge, Kate is working on a book on survival resources in the black women's literary tradition.

Beverly Wildung Harrison teaches Christian Social Ethics at Union Theological Seminary in New York and works as an ethicist with many Christian/postchristian feminist and liberation groups. She loves her work and her life but does not recommend emulation of the workload that falls on feminist professors as theological education moves toward or away from the feminist challenge. Over the years, Bev has been a mentor to all of us in Mud Flower and has become also a best friend/soul sister. She has just published a collection of essays in feminist social ethics, *Making the Connections* (Boston: Beacon Press, 1985).

Ada Maria Isasi-Diaz, a Hispanic feminist, lecturer, activist, and organizer, works from a faith perspective on both women's issues and Hispanic issues. Currently finishing her M.Div. at Union Seminary in New York, Ada is grounded in liberation understandings and methodology, and is busy working toward a new world/new order of relationship in which oppression will not exist.

Bess B. Johnson is an artist, theologian, and mother of five who has been involved in theology and ministry in several institutional settings, and is currently involved in research and writing.

Mary D. Pellauer, weaver and theologian, has taught courses related to women and Christianity in various theological schools over the last decade. Currently in vocational transition, Mary and her family live in St. Paul, Minnesota.

Nancy Richardson is codirector of the Women's Theological Center in Boston, where she is working with a group of women to build a Christian feminist program of Theological and Ministerial Education. She is a UCC minister and an ethicist, and has been a consultant on Women's Programs at Episcopal Divinity School.

Carter Heyward, theologian, writer, priest, and activist, returned recently from studying liberation theology and Spanish in Nicaragua. She teaches Anglican theology and feminist theology, and delights in some magnificent students and colleagues at the Episcopal Divinity School. She has recently published *Our Passion for Justice*, a collection of her essays, addresses, and homilies (New York: The Pilgrim Press, 1984).

Among our learnings: that the forces of male gender superiority and homophobia, white supremacy, and economic injustice in this society are so powerful that we could not produce this book without serious cost to several of us and to the project itself. Consequently, we have lost and gained members along the way.

Flowers do not grow easily in mud. In the midst of the hope and solidarity, which the very publication of this book affirms, stand our alienation and pain. While much of it is not of our own choice or making, but rather that which we have inherited, it is still ours. We have tried in this project to name as our responsibility the points of bitter continuity between ourselves—our attitudes and actions—and the lives of those who have gone before us in a racist, sexist, classist world. Our words reflect the fierce intensity of broken lives and promises.

It is not all bitter. Among us there has always been time/space to play and, moreover, a spirit of whimsy which will find its way invariably into the work and witness of women who celebrate strong women. We have been learning to recognize and enjoy the particular sweet blessings that have come to us from our foresisters. Their heritages, their people, and their gods have become our legacy. To the extent that each of us in Mud Flower has been able to share with the others something about her own story as a woman of creative/redemptive power, all of us have been strengthened.

Reflecting a bruised but irrepressible, angry and utopic, womanspirit-bonding, *God's Fierce Whimsy* is meant to elicit your response—your yes's, your no's, your me-too's, your not-me's. We invite your participation in these rituals of our common and separate lives. We ask you to move with us into our places of alienation as well as onto our commongrounds. Come with us into our remembering, our naming, our silences, and our speech. Join us in holding and withholding. Be with us in our affirmations and our denunciations, our mourning and our raging, our laying to rest what we must and our lifting up what we can. Think with us critically about where we have been, what we have done, where we are going, and what we are going to do.

In addition to the seven coauthors who carried *God's Fierce Whimsy* full term to its birth, many women joined in the work that produced it. Our thanks go to the following participants in a series of consultations with U.S. and Canadian women during the 1982–83 academic year.

The Racial/Ethnic Clergywomen of the Presbyterian Church,

U.S.A. Also, in *Rochester, New York:* Lucy Brady; Toinette Eugene, PBVM; Gratia l'Esperance, RSM; Rosalie Muschal-Reinhardt; Marilyle Sweet Page. In *Cambridge, Massachusetts:* Elisabeth Schüssler Fiorenza, Rita Rainsford Rouner, Shawn Copeland, O.P., Alison M. Cheek, Sheila Briggs, Rosemary R. Ruether, Nancy Hughes, Sandra Hughes Boyd, Suzanne R. Hiatt, Cheryl Giles, Connie Parvey, Delores Williams. In *Banff, Alberta:* Judith Tansley, Susan Sorensen, Belle Callier, Gwen Davis, Ellen Wood, Barb Elliott, Vicki Obedkoff, Laura Jo Bell. In *Toronto, Ontario:* Ruth Evans, Shelley Finson, Mary Thompson Boyd, Mary Snyder, Marsha Sfeir, Ann Naylor, Wendy Hunt, Kathy Turner, Elizabeth Wensley, Judy Morkep, Janet Silman, Anne Woods, Mary Rose D'Angelo, Marilyn Legge. In *Oakland, California:* Chris Smith, Nadean Bishop, Gloria Soliz, Susan Lyon, Edwina Hunter-Snyder, Patricia Schecter, Diane Weddington, Barbara Brown Zikmund, Cyndy Adams, Helen Tanner Colman, Gloria Smallwood, Debra Houston, Sandee Yarlett, Carol Hepokoski, Sandy Park, Barbara Smith-Moran, Lynn Rhodes, Jane Vennard, Martha Ann Kirk, Clair B. Fischer, Sarah Barber-Braun, Antoinette Wire, Til Evans, Mary Cross, Barbara Roche.

Thanks also to these folks for discussing the project and its purpose with Carter Heyward and/or reading parts of the manuscript and making suggestions once we began writing: Adair Loomis, Connie Buchanan, Fredrica Harris Thompsett, Barbara Wheeler, Alison Cheek, Joan Martin, Mary Glasspool, Drorah Setel, Virginia Mollenkott, Ardith Hayes, Janet Walton, Ruth Ann Clark, Dorothee Sölle, Sidney Brown, Robert McAfee Brown, and Mary Hunt.

Carter Heyward served as coordinator of the project. Jane van Zandt helped Carter with this work by taking on assorted tasks, from dog-walking to reality-testing. Ada Maria Isasi-Diaz put the book on her word processor, thereby enhancing the speed and economy of our work. Anne Gilson and Sara Layton Adams assisted with the typing, research, and editing of the manuscript. Sandra Hughes Boyd compiled the selected bibliography. Marion Meyer worked as our editor at The Pilgrim Press. For these various contributions and the women who made them, we give thanks.

The Mud Flower project was funded by a Basic Issues Research grant from the Association of Theological Schools (ATS) in the U.S.

and Canada. Our appreciation to ATS Executive Director Leon Pacala for having been supportive of our work from the beginning. Our special thanks also to Harvey Guthrie, Dean, and Edward Stiess, Director of Degree Programs, of the Episcopal Divinity School for having encouraged Carter Heyward to spend her sabbatical in the fall of 1982, and one fourth of her teaching time during the spring of 1983, on *God's Fierce Whimsy*. Both these men believe in our work, and we delight in their collegiality. A supplementary grant was made to us by the Episcopal Church's Conant Fund, for which we are grateful. We also wish to express our appreciation for a grant from the Gregory Book Fund—administered by the American Missionary Association and the Division of Higher Education of the United Church Board for Homeland Ministries—which helped to make possible the publication of this book.

Mud Flower has begun to name and examine some of the fundamental implications of Christian feminism for theological education. Much remains to be done if theological schools are to become educational arenas in which women's lives, work, and faith are accorded deep respect. The next volume should be, perhaps, a detailed feminist study of curricular development or of pedagogical possibilities. We are suggesting to the ATS that it enable a continuation of the project begun in this book by making a grant to another group of women interested in theological education from different racial, ethnic, and possibly religious perspectives. We do not know who the women are, but we know they are there.

We offer *God's Fierce Whimsy* as a sign that—like a mud flower— women's power in the world/church grows only with difficulty and then only when well nourished and absolutely determined to grow sturdier and bigger and ever more beautiful.

¡GRACIAS A LAS MUJERES!
Katie G. Cannon
Beverly W. Harrison
Carter Heyward
Ada Maria Isasi-Diaz
Bess B. Johnson
Mary D. Pellauer
Nancy D. Richardson

xiii

GOD'S FIERCE WHIMSY

Chapter One

IN SEARCH OF COMMONGROUND

From a feminist perspective, theological education is in serious trouble. We simply do not look at the enterprise and see it as healthy and thriving from any adequate criteria of human intelligence, or commonsense, or human relationships.

—Beverly Wildung Harrison

OUR TASK[1]

At the outset what the Mud Flower Collective had in common, besides working in Christian seminaries, was a shared commitment and a shared complaint: Each of us is immersed in theological education, broadly conceived as her life's work, a personal vocational commitment. Each of us perceives also that Christian seminaries, in which the church's ministers and teachers often receive their formal theological education, are arenas in which lukewarm faith and uninspired scholarship are peddled. And we do not exempt ourselves

3

from this charge. To the extent that we join regularly in this educational venture in bad faith without mounting protest, we are in complicity with pushers of theological mediocrity. Our critique of seminary education involves our self-assessment as students and teachers of Christian faith.

The purpose of our book is to show what theological education can be and, from our feminist points of view, must be if we Christians are truly interested in human well-being and in knowing how to serve this common good. We are writing not only to suggest some ways in which, we believe, seminary education needs to be foundationally restructured but, even more basically, to demonstrate theological education: how we learn and what we learn. We think these lessons may be as valuable to people in local parishes, church and community organizations, activist groups, women's task forces, and others doing theological and/or educational work as to professional theological educators.

OUR COMMUNITIES OF ACCOUNTABILITY

We are all educators and learners. Among us, one is Roman Catholic; the others are Protestant. One of us was born and raised in Cuba; the rest, in the United States—South, North, Midwest. Our various backgrounds continue to shape our foregrounds, our communities of accountability in the present. We speak in special relation to different constituencies in theological education: some of us, as black women, are mindful in what we say of all black people, male and female. In this project, we are especially mindful of black women whose voices are often muted by the separate choruses of black men and white women. One of us, whose people are Hispanic women and men throughout the Americas, works in relation to other Hispanic women as her primary focus of accountability.

We who are white live in a historically shaped relation to our sisters of color.[2] While several members of this research team were friends across racial/ethnic lines prior to our work on this book, personal affection does not negate the grotesque effects of white supremacy. This historical structure of oppressive racism is a pattern of social organization in which prejudice is organized and institutionalized against people whose physical traits, cultural back-

4

grounds, and values differ from those of the dominant culture. In this society, racism is evidenced, for example, in patterns of economic distribution and employment opportunity. Contrary to what we would wish, friendship between members of dominant and subordinate races does nothing in and of itself to eliminate racism. Friendship can enable us, however, to risk seeing and naming the barriers that divide us and our people so that, in facing the reality of the social order we have inherited, we can participate more effectively in its transformation.

Racism is a real and ugly constant, a burden and a problem for women and men of all colors. The white women in this group understand that our position here is one of racial privilege. When asked to which people we are especially accountable, who our people are, we, like most white people of goodwill, are tempted to say that our people are all people. The ruling class in any social situation, especially those who are concerned about justice for all, can assume easily enough a Big Mamma posture of trying to be "for everybody." And so it is that white women can fall into believing that we have no particular people; and rather that we, as feminists, are advocates of a universal justice, and especially justice for all women—black, Hispanic, Asian, indigenous, white, lesbian, straight, old, young. With our white brothers, we are apt to find ourselves looking and reaching and speaking in many directions, attending conferences on everybody's causes, allying ourselves with people everywhere who need advocacy. And we do not mean to imply that this is necessarily wrong or superficial. It may be an important dimension of the collective vocation of people of social privilege who desire that justice be done.

But people who pursue institutional change can do so only on behalf of particular people, because oppression only comes in specific, concrete forms. Furthermore, each person is effective only insofar as she acts honestly on the basis of her own life situation, interests, history, and goals as these dimensions of who she is intersect the lives of particular people.

White women must realize that we, no less than women of color, need to be clear about to whom, in particular, we hold ourselves accountable. Who needs, wants, and trusts our voices, specifically in relation to this project? Whose experiences and language do we know? From whom can we reasonably expect candid response, affirmative and critical? Who are our people, we who are white North American women? We believe that our context of accountability is shaped largely by other white women who are struggling against injustice—women who, like us, lead mystified lives, often unaware that our skin color is an indelible mark of worth in this society; people who, like us, are troubled, and more or less puzzled, by the interplay of economic forces with racial and gender status; those who, like us, are tired of living in response to men's definitions of, opinions about, and authority over our lives as members of the human family.

In accountability to these people, we offer this book as a resource. We hope that what we say may be of use to women and men of all racial and ethnic groups who find themselves ill at ease with many of the prevailing assumptions in theological education about human and divine life. But we are reasonably certain that what we say can be valuable to those black, Hispanic, and white sisters who assume with us that theological education should be a process in learning and in doing the work of liberation.

Our work and involvement with women has been an abundant wellspring of our professional interests and theological convictions: our having come to see, hear, touch and be touched by the lives of women with whom we have participated in a variety of tasks relating to women's ordination; procreative choice; political campaigns; battered and abused women; denominational and ecumenical projects; ministries in local parishes; campus ministry; the National Organization for Women and other women's groups; civil rights, peace, and liberation movements for people in Latin America, Asia, Africa; antinuclear work; office work—secretarial and administrative; litigation on behalf of women; lesbian/gay projects; seminary teaching and counseling; liturgical renewal. The women with whom we have worked continue to teach us much of what we have learned over time to appreciate: the inestimable value of women's lives.

OUR DIVERSITY AND OUR LIMITS

We take with utmost seriousness our racial and ethnic differences as fundamental to our work. We will attempt to lift up rather than

6

gloss over our various perspectives and priorities. Among us, as should be the case throughout theological education, cultural pluralism is critical in examining the value of what is taught and what is learned.

But we need as well to acknowledge immediately the limits of this small group and, therefore, those women whose interests we cannot represent directly, if at all. Given the multidimensional composite of peoples and cultures in the world and in this society, our team's mixture of colors and heritages is barely a beginning of "representation." There are, for example, no Asian women among us and no indigenous women. There are no Jewish or Muslim women; no one from any religion other than Christianity. None of us at the time of this writing has left the church. None of us is currently living in any nation except the United States. All but one of us are based professionally in the Northeast; we cannot speak with authority, therefore, of the special interests of women in theological education in the West, the South, or elsewhere. All of us are, or are headed toward being, by training, professional theologians and educators. None of us is a parish minister, a chaplain, or otherwise fully involved in the work for which most women seminarians are preparing. Among us are members of only four Protestant denominations—Episcopal, Presbyterian, Lutheran, and United Church of Christ; together with our Roman Catholic teammate, we hardly represent the spectrum of the church in the United States.

All of us have been associated, though not exclusively, with schools that, among seminaries, have been commonly held to be on the progressive edge of liberal Protestant thought and practice. For this reason, too, our working group cannot pretend that it is speaking universally about women's experiences in Christian seminaries.

In our primary relational commitments, our team includes married, single, divorced, and celibate women; straight and lesbian women; women with children, women without children of our own. In age we span from early thirties to early fifties, and we cannot speak, in the first person, of the current situation among women in seminaries who are either our juniors or our seniors.

Most of us, through our own life experiences and intellectual pursuits (primarily in the disciplines of systematic theology and ethics), have come to comprehend the world primarily in terms of

7

structures—that is, of how power is organized on the basis of many factors (including gender, race, money) in such a way that certain groups of people are expected to play powerful, or powerless, roles in social institutions such as marriage, church, and education. This structural perspective differs, for example, from the view that an individual can "make it" if she tries; or from the opinion that certain groups of people have innate traits which enable them to play certain powerful roles in institutions (such as the man being the natural head of the family or church); or from theories that present psychological or spiritual wholeness and integration as the source of social well-being. We do not believe that "exceptional women" can succeed at less than great cost. We do not believe that any gender or race of humanity is naturally suited to particular roles in social organizations. And we do not believe that a sum total of well-integrated individuals at prayer, or at work in the world, is necessarily synonymous with a just society, so deeply pervasive and historical are such cruel structures of our lives as racism and sexism. Our team is committed to structural analysis and institutional change as fundamentally necessary.

While this perspective informs and has become the basis of our feminist commitment, we know that not every woman who cares about justice shares the primacy of this world view in her work. We have women colleagues in seminary whose concerns for women's well-being are apparent and whose first allegiance is to their academic disciplines, for example, rather than to institutional change. Our first allegiance may derive from our sense of how each of us can contribute most creatively to the education of our people—in our case, to the needs and interests of black, Hispanic, and white women who are wrestling with structures of injustice in churches and seminaries. We admit that our first allegiance—intellectually and professionally—is to changing structures of theological education so as to benefit these sisters. We recognize that not all women who are interested in the education of women share our priority.

In the course of our work we have talked with and asked for reflections from women in theological education whose priorities—in terms of where they put their energy—we have not always shared, yet whose work we value. We have tried to hear and address what we have been learning from these women, as well as from other women from across the United States and Canada.

Still, we must share the responsibility for this book: its themes and emphases; what is told, what is left untold. What has emerged among us is, in the first instance, our perspectives and our interpretations. Realizing our limits, we make no attempt to define "woman's" situation—much less "the human" condition. We would like to imagine that, in part because we realize that we do *not* speak on behalf of everyone, what we say may ring true in some way to all who share a hunger for justice and who bring this hunger to theological education.

OUR USE OF THE TERM FEMINIST

Many who hold with us that Christian seminaries should be educating men and women to live and work knowledgeably and creatively in the world find the term feminist annoying. To many it denotes distraction from the real concerns that Christians should share. With the exception of a small number of white women, and many fewer women of color and men, most who otherwise would share a number of our perceptions about theological education are likely to be put off by the title and focus of our work. No doubt we lost some potential readers when we decided to call ourselves Christian feminists rather than Christian women. What does the word feminist imply that related terms, such as justice and women's well-being, do not? What feelings does the mention of "feminist" evoke?

The contemporary feminist movement has philosophical and political roots in the Euroamerican Enlightenment. As such, it is a continuation of the work of such liberals as Mary Wollstonecraft and John Stuart Mill for legal recognition of women's full citizenship and moral realization of women's full personhood. Neither of these goals has been reached in the United States. And the latter—as manifest acknowledgment that for women to be the subjects of their own lives is *good*—is a vision unrecognized or unrealized globally, in all malestream religions, both sacred and civil. Women are not perceived by rulers of state or religion as appropriate subjects of their own lives. This fact cuts sharply across racial, religious, national, ethnic, and class lines. Hence, we believe the moral implications of feminism are universal, although the limits of particularity do not license an attempt on our part to determine, for example, what women in Iran should be doing.

Like many theopolitical movements, feminism has a morally ambiguous history. At moments, it has been a courageous movement—radical and deeply moral. It has been a racist, classist movement—superficial and blatantly immoral. The Enlightenment that helped generate it, as so many others' efforts toward social reform, was essentially a philosophical venture of, by, and for the benefit of white upper-strata men in Europe and the still young United States. Slogans hailing "liberty, equality, fraternity" as revolutionary goals referred specifically to a vintage liberal, and utterly naive, credo, held by idealistic white men of goodwill, that "all men are created equal." What has, in fact, been the case is that some white males with access to economic resources can make it if they try. Neither people of color (male or female), nor women (of any color), nor, increasingly in the twentieth-century United States, wage laborers or the very poor, have intrinsic rights in enlightened societies.

Zillah Eisenstein, Angela Davis, and other contemporary feminists discuss the rise of the women's movement in the context of an Enlightened, liberal society run by white men with economic power. It is in this context that feminism's history is morally muddled. On one hand, the U.S. feminist movement that began in the mid-nineteenth century was predominantly, though not exclusively, a white middle- and upper-strata women's movement. It was also a vital abolitionist force, the chief spokeswomen for women's rights and abolition being frequently the same people, such as the Grimke sisters and Sojourner Truth. On the other hand, as the feminist movement grew and began to divide into different groups on the basis of philosophy and/or strategy, some of the most vocal proponents of women's suffrage were white racist women who had turned their backs on black men and women in an attempt to salvage "women's rights" (read: *white* women's rights).

Contemporary feminism has inherited both the courage of the feminist abolitionists and the racism of the white women who sold out black people in a futile attempt to climb the ladders of success put in place by white men of privilege.

Mud Flower believes that feminism, to be worth anything at all good, must be rooted even more deeply in the soil of abolition. Only then can black women, other racial/ethnic women, and Anglo/ Northern European women in the United States act together to rid this society of white supremacy, gender injustice, and economic suffering in their various racial/ethnic and class-based communities.

It is within this historically ambiguous and morally utopic sense that Mud Flower understands feminism as conveying an intense interest in *all* women's lives. Here many people in seminaries make a frantic and irrational leap to an assumption that a feminist is a woman (of course) who is more concerned about women's needs than about men's; or, in extremes, a woman who hates men, a woman obsessed with "women's issues" (read: white women's issues) and who, in her self-inflated preoccupation, is more or less oblivious to the interests of people of color, poor people, and the critical global survival issue of our time—nuclear disarmament.

If the feminist theologian is white, she is characterized as narcissistic. If she is a woman of color, she is thought to have been co-opted by white women; she has bleached herself and might as well be gone—because there is no place in the black community, or the Hispanic community, for white women's narcissism, white women's racism, and white women's competitiveness with men of color. Whether white, black, or Hispanic, the feminist woman in the church or seminary is often caricatured as the epitome of bourgeois womanhood, hardly a sister in the work of liberation. When a woman of any color requires that her male colleagues, her compañeros, her brothers take her and other women as seriously as they take themselves, the woman's feminism is labeled counterproductive to the important business at hand. Put simply, in our Western United States part of the world/church, feminism conjures up images of hostile, selfish "white women" (regardless of their color) who have a dry, worthless bone to pick. At best feminism is trivial, a leisure-time activity like golf or bridge; at worst, it is an impediment to any serious movement toward a better world.

But we must push harder here against the forces of masculinist sanction and suggest that, among our colleagues in Christian theological education, the main objection to the word feminist is that it is often heard as a byword for lesbian. And lesbian is a very

11

bad thing to be, because it is the kind of woman who neither likes nor needs men—or so the popular myth goes. We hear that a lesbian is not only a woman who enjoys sex with women, but moreover a woman who—because she does not need a man in bed—does not need men, period. So closely knit is the male-female relation with genital titillation that for a woman to choose not to have intercourse with men is tantamount, in the minds of many men, to this woman's rejection of men. Thus does the lesbian become a man-hater.

We are persuaded that all the pejorative connotations of feminism are related to the lesbian onus: a feminist is, thus, a selfish, bitchy, hostile broad "in need of a good——." We return in our work to some discussion of the ways in which the fear of lesbianism keeps women separate. For now, we will say simply that heterosexism renders lesbians the focus of extravagant fear, anger, and projection. To the extent that feminism is assumed to be synonymous with lesbianism—a false equation—all feminists (single, married, mothers, grandmothers, celibate, lesbian, straight, bisexual) can expect to receive the harsh blows dealt systematically to "castrating bitches/man-hating dykes" in a male-dominated society.

Why then do we choose to call ourselves and our work feminist, realizing as we do that even the word makes lots of men and some women in the realm of theological education very angry? We do so to sharpen the awareness of the actual situation of women in this society. Those Christian teachers and students who are angry about feminism are those who have some sizable investment in holding the power in place in prevailing patterns of social organization—often those who are already holders of institutional power; sometimes those who aspire to holding and using power as already defined in structures of work, love, politics, and religion.

Anger about feminism in theological education must be understood as anger about power in theological education. This anger must be acknowledged and examined if women and men are to be educated to use power creatively, surely a basic task of theological teachers/learners. To avoid or camouflage conversations about feminism in today's church and world—including theological seminaries—is a transparent refusal to examine the phenomenon of power as it pertains to either human or divine action in the world. Such a refusal is tantamount to gross failure in both theological and educational tasks. Thus, we employ the term feminist in an effort to call theological educators to a professional mandate: to examine how power is experienced in human life and how it is structured in the methods and content of what is taught and learned in seminaries.

We use the word feminist also, of course, as a sign of our commitment to women. We suggest that there are at least two interrelated reasons that those who have, desire, or support institutional power are often angered by feminist caucuses, feminist courses, and feminist language in seminaries. The first is that the feminist challenge carries, irrefutably, a demand that those who accept it must begin to examine their own lives, which more often than not means looking at the ways they live in relation to those closest to them—spouses, children, students, teachers, colleagues, friends. This demand for self-assessment is hard to take, to the extent that people do not want to, or are afraid to, change the ways they live and relate. The second is that the demand is heard as woman's complaint (even if a man voices it). That it is heard as woman's insistence on behalf of herself tends to exacerbate the annoyance, because this incarnation of womanpower suggests that women can assert themselves, take care of themselves, and tend their own needs—that is to say, that women can stand alongside men as equally able to be for themselves. And this possibility—that a woman can be interdependent with rather than dependent on men—is shocking, even offensive, in a social order in which all of us have grown to expect that woman should be dependent upon man. Racial/ethnic women and white women have different collective histories with regard to sex-role expectations, but all women and men in this society have picked up the message that *all* men of *all* colors ought to have authority over *all* women of *all* colors—however benevolently or deceptively it may be exercised. This message, together with our common resistance to changing our own lives, makes it easy for many people to hear "feminism" as a slogan for tearing apart the fabric of how we "ought" to live our lives in society, beginning in the home, between spouse and spouse, parent and child. Accordingly, to be feminist is tantamount to flying in the face of the "ideal" human community.

This is especially true in black and other racial/ethnic communities, in which solidarity between men and women is critical to the survival of our people. The perceived threat that feminism poses to oppressed communities must be taken seriously. Not to take it so (and white feminists are often guilty of this) is to ignore the genocidal dimensions of white supremacy as it moves against our survival. At the same time, we black and Hispanic women ask our people to consider the possibility that our corporate strength and power as a people may rest finally on the quality of the respect, trust, and friendship we women and men have among ourselves—for each other, and for ourselves. Our solidarity cannot be constructed on the bodies of women.

The dangers that many fear feminism brings to our life together—regardless of our color—need to be named, and the anger acknowledged, if women's lives are actually to be valued as highly as we have been taught men's lives should be valued. We employ the term feminism as shorthand for our commitment to the infinitely deep value of women's lives.

OUR PROCESS OF DEFINING FEMINISM

During our first meeting, we asked the question: What *is* feminism for each of us?

Mary: I think it's simply the struggle against sexism.
Carter: I agree, but I'd have to add that this involves a stubborn insistence, a refusal to compromise the well-being of women.
Kate: For me it doesn't have anything to do with women; it's the commitment to end white supremacy, male domination, and economic exploitation.
Ada: For me feminism and feminist are different. Only the person can say if she's feminist; but feminism has to do with understanding sexism as the paradigm of all oppression. And I agree with the refusal to compromise women's welfare—both women's rights and women's well-being.
Bev: I'd have to say that it begins in a woman's assertion of her power. It's not, in the first instance, a theory, but a very personal act.
Bess: For me it always has to be preceded by the word black, and it means the creation of inclusivity and mutuality, which in-

14

volves struggle against what I call the trinity of sexism, racism, and classism. But you know, these words . . . I always think in images.

Nancy: I believe it begins with the "experiencing of your experience" and that it means insisting on the well-being of women, all women, which is why racism must be examined in any feminist analysis.

Each of us defined it differently, in most cases building on what others had said; in several cases adding a previously inarticulated insight, with which others in the group might or might not agree. It is important for us, and for our readers, to look carefully at what was happening among us: In fact, our entire team, including its white members, understands, with Nancy, that "racism must be examined in any feminist analysis." In fact, no one on our team—including Ada who spoke of sexism as the "the paradigm of all oppression"— believes that male domination is a more significant or more problematic structure of injustice than white supremacy or economic exploitation. Our team was called together, in large part, because Carter, who convened the group, believed that each of its members is manifestly concerned about the trinity of sexism, racism, and classism. We are not at odds in our common vision, and yet Kate's suggestion ("It doesn't have anything to do with women") and Ada's ("[It] has to do with understanding sexism as the paradigm of all oppression") are assertions that appear to flag disagreement among us. Moreover, the two black women in this conversation were the first to state explicitly that feminism involves struggling against racism. In this one brief round-robin exchange among us, at least two of the most perplexing and painful tensions in the contemporary women's movement were voiced: between women who understand sexism to be the paradigm of oppression and those who do not; and between women whose commitment to end sexism is inextricable from their commitment to end racism and those women who frequently either do not see or do not name racism as a critical feminist issue.

Early in our work we realized that we might not ascribe to sexism (the oppression of women of all colors and classes) the same gross weight in its interaction with race and class. But we agreed that our

15

candor—and the integrity of each of our commitments and convictions—needed to be heard and respected; and furthermore that this—rather than any attempt to agree conceptually—might be a key to our work as feminists, as theologians, and as educators. We began to hear ourselves saying that we need not compare the value of our experiences in order to take ourselves and one another seriously, and that our different experiences are mutually instructive. We began to see that our diverse, possibly conflictual, perspectives shape our common praxis, and that, in fact, our diversity is basic to whatever creative work we are able to do collectively.

As women with often disparate definitions of what is what, we came together to a common task. This tension, intrinsic to pluralism, pushes us into listening harder, speaking more clearly, and moving toward fresh insights and new words that we can frame as ours. Good education, real education, involves dialogue, and dialogue is predicated not upon oneness, sameness, or unity, but rather upon a willingness to relate in a praxis of diverse life experiences.

Even among us, women whose politics and theologies are rather compatible, feminism has no uniform definition. Rather, we agree that our feminist commitment is the dynamic that draws us together. As we work, our feminism emerges as the energizing force in our work; our raison d'être as a working group; the spark that ignites us; the vision that inspires us; the heartbeat of our corporate body. Feminism is the ground upon which we stand and from which we draw our nourishment to think and write and celebrate together. Whereas we would not define feminism the same way were we, individually, writing systematic theologies, all of us affirmed spontaneously that our feminism is pervasive and thoroughgoing in our work; and that, as a concept, feminism could best be defined in the course of what we do together—that is, in our praxis. We affirmed that feminism may be understood as a vision of a different reality that can only be seen as it is brought into being.

Thus, we are contending that theory is formulated in the course of activity—specifically in our examination of feminism and theological education. Our definitions (of feminism, theology, education) cannot be brought to our work as a priori: the defining—a process of clarifying, owning, and communicating—cannot precede the conversations, analyses, and writing. Ideas, words, theories, and symbols

16

must always be re-created and re-invented in the process of studying their meaning. Nothing can really be learned or taught outside praxis—in which all definitions, concepts, and knowledge are born.

OUR UNDERSTANDING OF PRAXIS

Ada: [Paulo] Freire says that praxis is that in doing the theorizing, you're doing the practice, which I think is very important in education. The analyzing itself is a praxis.

Bess: Are you saying that the mere act of reflecting—in my office, wherever I am—is praxis?

Ada: It is itself a praxis.

Bess: I'm afraid of that.

Ada: Because reflection comes from your experience, and leads to strategizing.

Nancy: It's also a collective process.

Ada: Yes.

Bess: Well, if you didn't say "collective," we could get into that individual thing and perpetuate what we've got, and use that concept [praxis] to say, "This makes what we're doing valid." And we're really not getting out there doing anything.

All people live and act in praxis, all the time, although the term praxis—as currently employed in liberation theology—is meant specifically to denote the context in which liberation theology is done. Theologians such as Gustavo Gutiérrez and Juan Luis Segundo contend that a collective praxis—the ongoing dialectic between theory and practice, or the constant interplay of reflection and action—is the only arena in which a theology of liberation can be done. They recognize that most European and North American theologies have been the brainchildren of individual white men who have spent their lives thinking about the nature and activity of human and divine life.

These Euroamerican men have their praxis no less than the rest of us have ours. All people live and work in an ongoing dialectic between theory and practice. No one's ideas fall full-blown out of the sky. Everyone's concepts of reality are informed by how, where, and

17

with whom they engage the world. The significant difference between the claims made by liberation theologians and those made by theologians who presume themselves to be theologically objective—those whose ideas are "unpolluted" by ideology—is that the former admit readily the extent to which their daily lives provide the substance of their theologies, while the latter seldom do. Put simply, liberation theologians claim they theologize in praxis; most other theologians fail to acknowledge explicitly that they have a praxis, as if their doctrines somehow float free of the contingencies of human life.

Given the current Latin American usage of the term, it would be misleading for us to attach ourselves to the term liberation theology without saying something about how we understand our relation to this theological movement, which took root among revolutionary Christians in such places as Nicaragua, Peru, and Argentina over a decade ago. Several of us would place ourselves closer than others to the liberation theology movement among Third World Christians. In her work as a Catholic Hispanic feminist, Ada Maria is the only one among us who has been immersed over time in the political and theological efforts on behalf of the poor in Latin America, but all of us have been connected in one way or another with Latin America and/or the theology that has grown out of liberation struggles in Latin America. We have participated in the Theology in the Americas projects or worked in the United States and Nicaragua on behalf of the people of Central America; or sought connections between what is happening theologically in Latin America and what is happening and being shaped theologically in the United States, Canada, Europe, Africa, and Asia.

We have been influenced by Latin American liberation theology. Most of us have learned much from this theological movement about praxis as context of theology; about choosing to side with the poor; about the incarnate, material character of beauty, truth, and goodness in the world as the actual redistribution of food, clothes, love; about God's movement among us on behalf of justice and our opportunity to participate in this movement; and about the analytical tools of Marxism in helping us understand and transform history.

While much of what we are doing flows with the currents of Latin American liberation theology and with theologies being constructed

18

by black men in the United States, we have two points of serious disengagement from them.

First, we note the failure of nonfeminist liberation theologians to take sexism and heterosexism seriously as fundamental political and theological issues. Despite the fact that illegal abortions claim the lives of more women between ages fifteen and thirty-nine in Latin America than any other cause except murder-by-death squads, most men who are writing liberation theology in Latin America pay little attention to the particular plight of women in these repressive and revolutionary situations. In this country, relative to white women and all men, women of color continue to be the least financially secure; the most responsible for nurturing children; and the most likely victims of violence. Even so, few black male theologians discuss the liberation of women as a serious justice-issue. While Latin American and black male liberation theologians emphasize the incarnate character of spiritual value—the concreteness of truth—few demonstrate strong interest (if any at all) in the lives of women or gay/lesbian people as a praxis of liberation.

The refusal to deal with women and lesbians/gays as intrinsic to the work of liberation reveals, we believe, a flaw in the vision, theology, and process of liberation espoused by these theologians. Unless people who are committed to liberation seek and find systematic connections between racism, sexism, heterosexism, classism, and the many other variations of oppression built on the dominant-submissive social relation, the revolution cannot be won. The characters may shift, but the plot remains the same: some people suffering under the control of others. In such a way, the power is held in place and little is changed for the common good.

No one with an adequate understanding of the dialectical and dialogical processes of liberation will attempt to block out certain people and issues as unrelated or unimportant. All social relations, between and among groups and individuals, are related politically to all other social relations. One does not change without affecting others, for better or worse.

Moreover, all persons, collectively and individually, actually live their lives as members of various groups on the basis of race, gender, sexuality, religion, age, class, nationality, and so on. We cannot be liberated—become free, whole people, alive and well—in one area only of our lives. Although masculinist theorists and organizers

19

may think in this piecemeal fashion, we do not live fragmented lives. We cannot be affirmed as women and put down as black or Hispanic and consider this liberating. We cannot be lauded as fine, strong women, and rejected as lesbians and experience this as anything but oppressive.

We who struggle for justice need to be clear that we cannot remove simply a single form of oppression from our backs, nor can we work with such fragmented vision on behalf of sisters and brothers. Those liberals who remind us "how far" blacks have come since the Civil Rights Act of 1964 and the Voting Rights Act of 1965 seem unaware that, still today, most blacks in the United States are poor women and children, victims simultaneously of sexist, racist, and economically exploitative practices. Furthermore, we do not transform simply by legal fiat, critical as that may be, the structures of white supremacy, male domination, and economic injustice that have served as base points of our common life for centuries, playing no small part in the shaping of our faith, values, and the ways we live our lives.

Sexuality and the reality of our sensual bodies, which women and gay men represent on behalf of all persons, is accorded no greater value as theological praxis among Latin American and black North American Christian theologians than among their white male colonizers in the United States and Europe. Most black and Latin American men, like most white North American men, have not reflected honestly or clearly enough about sexism and heterosexism to know whether or not, and relative to what, these issues are important to theology. We contend that people generally have a sizable stake in holding in place whatever power they experience; and that especially among oppressed peoples, the power most clearly accessible to men is that which they can wield sexually over women, a power most men are loath to relinquish.

Our second and related point of departure from Latin American and black North American malestream theology is that most male theologians of whatever color, culture, or continent tend to overlook the "small places" of their lives as theological praxis. "The personal is political." This has become a feminist motto of considerable truth. Nothing that we do, alone or together, is unrelated to our well-being and to the lives of others. As Mary asserts:

20

Actions I undertake in my bedroom are hardly what the conventional [Marxian] understanding of praxis means, but they are very important to feminism. Feminism always takes account of what is going on in a woman's own backyard, not just in front of the house.

Suggesting that the masculinist view of women and sexuality is related to the relegation of these "smaller" issues to the realm of privacy, Carter writes:

To make a "private" matter public—such as in "coming out" as a gay man or lesbian or in acknowledging that one has had an abortion—is to unveil the political dimensions of what is commonly and naively held to be strictly personal. To speak publicly at all of one's sexuality is to lend recognition to what has been for generations an important economic and political issue among shapers of social value and policy. Sexuality has never been a private matter.[3]

But the Euroamerican ruling class has attempted to contain women within a private sphere. Women, sexuality, bodies, feelings, and children have had no place in the public world of economics, politics, and "matters of consequence." Insofar as black men in the United States and men who are acting and writing on behalf of the poor in Latin America or elsewhere are paying lip service or lending silent complicity to this credo of white male culture, they reveal a dangerously superficial comprehension of the struggle for racial and economic justice, as well as of the movements for sexual liberation.

Our own lives are changing in many ways, most often in small places. The ways we live our lives, individually and together in our work, are constantly and mutually interactive: Our ideas are shaping our relationships, our actions, our interests; our lives are shaping our ideas. The written work that we are doing and you are reading reflects this fluid process of interaction among us, with others, and within each of our persons. Each of us becomes different in the course of our corporate work from the person she was before we began. To the extent that we are learning, we are changing—so too our ideas, theologies, senses of commitment.

21

OUR UNDERSTANDING OF THE PRAXIS OF
CONCEPTUAL LABOR

Even for those of us for whom, via the influence of liberation theology, praxis has become part of our theological vocabulary, it is difficult to grasp and take seriously the very act of our conceptual labor as praxis. As Bess notes, there is danger in assuming that, in sitting around talking or writing, we are actually doing the work of justice or contributing anything whatsoever to anyone's well-being, except our own in only the most superficial and short-lived sense.

We need to call attention to the difference between an individualistic praxis, which characterizes the bulk of Euroamerican theology, and liberation praxis. It is the latter we are attempting to embody and examine here, although we must admit that—like everyone schooled in Euroamerican educational and theological traditions— we fall easily and unaware into privatistic assumptions about the ultimacy of the individual mind in creative thinking.

Let us be emphatic that, in praxis, the dialectical poles (theory/ practice; reflection/action; thinking/doing) are not separate moments or enterprises. Ada proposes that the best way of explaining praxis may be by using the binomial *reflection/action* as one word. Praxis is not meant to convey a back-and-forth movement between the streets and the classroom. To work in praxis does not mean that we go out and act and then come in and think about what we have done so that we can go back out and do it better. This presumed split between theory and practice reveals a mistaken epistemological understanding of how we learn. This misunderstanding is widespread in theological education.

Obviously, praxis can be dualistic, split, just as it can be individualistic. Beverly alleges, "We're so used to the split between theory and action that we don't even see it." We are used to assuming that when we are thinking, we are not actually involved in ministry. To compound the quandary, we are usually not involved in anything creative, because we have been taught falsely that "scholarship" is something the individual does in her head.

As feminist theological educators, we must cite what we believe to be an urgent need for clear, honest, and creative thinking in seminaries. Nearly every woman seminarian or alumna who has discussed this project with us has decried the abysmal intellectual climate she has found in seminary.

We see this as a problem of individualistic and dualistic praxis. Honest intellectual achievement is never, under any circumstance, an individualistic enterprise. Everyone works in relation to others' lives and work, whether or not she acknowledges this. Moreover, our mental faculties are not, in fact, disembodied. The brain is in the body. Thinking is bound up organically in feeling and sensation, just as the life of the thinker is involved, inextricably, in the lives of those who comprise her social world. We do not think only in the head or feel simply in the heart any more than we work merely on our own apart from the lives of others.

But more often than not in educational systems, including theological seminaries, we have been taught to believe that we are very much on our own when it comes to real scholarship and academic excellence; and certainly, that the intellectual enterprise is, or ought to be, separate from the world of mere experience. Here let us state emphatically our contention that the finest scholarship, the most powerful intellectual work, and the most creative thinking is done always by those whose hearts are in their work; those who acknowledge this to be the case, and admit gladly the subjective bias of their scholarship; and certainly those who understand that what they are doing has some bearing on the lives of others, for good or ill.

Thus, we submit that the very act of reflecting—story telling, conceptual analysis, research and writing—can be a praxis of liberation, but only under certain conditions.

CONDITIONS OF OUR PRAXIS

What conditions are necessary to an intellectually honest praxis? We suggest that there are at least five, which we are attempting to take seriously in our work.

1. *Accountability*. We have noted that we are working on behalf of our own well-being in relation to the interest of our people— certain particular people: black and Hispanic women and those

white women who are struggling against racial, sexual, and economic injustice. If, as the context of theology, praxis is to be anything other than a person's or a group's thinking about interesting abstract ideas, there must be at the outset of the conceptual effort a sense of to whom, in addition to ourselves, we are accountable. Otherwise, even at our personal best, we are laboring under the assumptions of a liberal epistemology, in which each person authorizes herself to idealize her subject matter—whether feminism, theological education, God, or the world—and for which she is accountable to no one but herself.

2. *Collaboration.* Not only does each of us come to this work on behalf of certain people, we come together. As Nancy points out, this distinguishes us from the classical model of the lone researcher as think tank. As our short dialogue in which each of us defined feminism suggests, the fullness of what we can learn together and teach one another is not merely the sum total of each person's opinions. Collaboration is not a matter of stacking up insights; rather, we are moving into an emergence of new learnings that affect our lives. Regardless of subject matter, a conceptual task undertaken in the mind of a solo scholar lacks the dialogical power and educational value of those theories conceived in a spirit of collaboration, theories not only meant to be confirmed or critiqued farther down the road but also conceived in the praxis of such engagement.

3. *Beginning with our own lives-in-relation.* We believe that this is where all research, teaching, and learning should begin. This sets us in marked contrast with the intellectual claim and theological methodology of malestream scholarship, in which to be academically excellent is to be objective (a matter of personal disinterest). Such a claim is not only pretentious, it is a sham. In order to have responsible and creative dialogue, in such a way that each participant actually learns, we must begin with the study of our lives.

Our social situations are so fully the arenas of our becoming that we cannot lift ourselves, as individuals, outside our communities in the exploration of who we are. In this fundamental sense, we begin with our lives not as isolated individuals (although we may feel alone) but rather as members of particular communities of people—women, black people, Christians, mothers, single people, lesbians, whatever. All that we learn and all that we teach is shaped by a constant, double-edged sense of accountability to ourselves as we experience our commonalities with our people and to ourselves as we experience our uniqueness, our individuality, that which makes us different from many of our people.

How then do we both move with other sisters and brothers as folks who hold all things in common, and at the same time remain alert to the beat of a different drummer that may call us to step out of line and make our own way? To take our lives in community seriously as the basis of all we learn and teach is to seek not a resolution of this problem but rather the wisdom and courage to bear constructively the tensions shared by all who experience the authority of their experience as unique persons in relation.

To begin with our lives is to make a pedagogical and epistemological claim. Rather than presuming to possess a universal knowledge of what feminism or theology or education is, we assume that the most honest—and therefore most intellectually sound—contribution we can make at the outset of our work is to name and examine our experiences of feminism, theology, and education. In so sharing we begin to realize that our knowledge is both relational (born in dialogue with others) and relative (contingent upon the difference it makes to our lives and the lives of others).

4. *Diversity of cultures.* In asserting that we must begin with a study of our lives, we incur the danger of turning inward, even when the inwardness is toward our people and not only into our individual selves. In terms of accountability, feminist theory and feminist theology cannot merely be the weaving together of a person's, or a group's, experiences.

White feminists have been challenged to show in what way feminist theologizing is not just this sort of navel-gazing enterprise. Insofar as anyone, or any group, theologizes solely on the basis of its own experiences of reality—and takes no care to listen to anyone else—its theology ought to lack credibility. We who are white have been guilty at times of this approach. We are well advised by our racial/ethnic sisters to open our lives and theologies to serious engagement with the lives and theologies of our racial/ethnic sisters.

We white feminist theologians do not accept, however, a similar sounding but very different critique when it is voiced by white male theologians. White male critics often dismiss feminist theology because it is done simply on the basis of women's experience and, therefore, lacks the "universal applicability" of classical malestream theology. To such critics we point out, first, that we do not operate on the assumption that *any* theology can be applied universally; and, second, that there is an arrogance implicit in the assumption that theology constructed on the basis of *men's* experiences has a universal significance lacking in theology constructed on the basis of *women's* experiences.

We note further that our most vocal critics, white Christian academic men, have modeled for a couple of millennia a kind of incubator theologizing—theology that is nondialogical, untouchable, and nonsensual. These men have done this truly narcissistic theologizing, as if in a mirror, with less candor, on the whole, than their contemporary white sisters.

Beginning with our lives, we must do so in as diverse a cultural situation as we can find—if not face to face with people of different cultures, then at least through engagement with their books, art, music, and rituals. Educationally, this pluralism requires that we learn to listen more astutely; that we suspend the urge to idolatrize our own perceptions and beliefs; and that we challenge one another, rather than acting like passive receptors. Ada maintains, "I don't want my diversity simply to be respected. I want it to challenge you, to rub against you."

5. *Shared commitment.* Our praxis is a collaborative arena in which we see both that our own lives provide the primary data for our work and that we are accountable to people outside this circle. The purpose of our work—which requires experiential candor, accountability, and collective effort—is to participate in the reshaping of theological education to benefit our people. We share a commitment, which brought us together in the first place, to participate in the transformation of theological education in such a way that the needs and interests of black, Hispanic, and white women are

realized as basic to the methods and content of the enterprise. As such, our praxis is strategic and action oriented.

TO WHOM, IN PARTICULAR, WE ARE WRITING

Our foremost desire is to reach other feminist women of different colors and religious traditions in theological education. You, like us, black, Hispanic, white . . . and you, unlike us, Asian, indigenous American, women of other colors, ethnic groups, cultures. You, our feminist sisters, know who you are, and we take heart that you are who you are.

As players with us in the grandiose games of misogynist academic gymnastics, you have been involved in a lose-lose situation. Scorned as mush-brains and as strong wills, as touchy-feely and as distant and aloof, you have been objectified simultaneously as attractive and repulsive. The more compelling your work, the more likely you are to have been branded heretical, animus-ridden, hostile, dyke. The more creative your scholarship, the more deceptively encouraged you have been to believe that your interests, your passions, yourselves are trivial, irrelevant, or counterproductive to the important business of God and man. The more competent your ministry, the higher risk you have run of being chastised, called on the carpet for all manner of imaginary complaints harbored by supervisors, professors, and employers whose senses of self are undone by your very being.

After all this, occasionally one of you emerges, with the support of your sisters, as a Force with whom your colleagues must contend if they are to be taken seriously by those whose approval they need (their own professional peers, or their students). You become the Model, the Exceptional Woman, set apart, singled out, she who is deemed superior to run-of-the-mill womanhood. Thinking they compliment you, those who would make you uncommon women heap upon you gross misogyny disguised as respect. And sometimes, out of nowhere, the very colleagues who have turned their backs on you and us when we needed their solidarity now court our camaraderie as their entree into a professional credibility they seek but do not understand. And they seek to employ our competence as reliable institutional workhorses—women to man the machinery of theological education, since feminist women tend, almost invariably, to be among those theological educators who not only value the work of theological education, but also know something about how it should be done.

Surely every feminist woman in seminary has had well-meaning, progressive professors (usually men) and clergy (usually men) encourage her not to get carried away with "ideologies" or "fads" like feminism. If you, like some of us, are racial/ethnic women and have been the least bit open about your feminist commitment, you have no doubt experienced some derision from the brothers, a callousness that thrives in the soil of a fear too deep for words. Regardless of race or ethnic group, you have had to combat massive efforts to discredit your interests and diffuse your passion, all in the name of greater causes. You have been told that racism comes first; that economic exploitation is more important; that imperialism and the threat of nuclear genocide are the most pressing issues. These words reveal that those who make such simplistic charges understand neither the problems nor the solutions of racial, economic, sexist, or militaristic oppression; and furthermore have not grasped the simple, devastating truth that no form of oppression can be sifted out from any other, that no "ism" stands independently on its own, not when one is concerned about real human beings, most of whose lives are blighted by double, triple, quadruple oppressions.

We are writing to you, our sisters in bodysoul, because we know how badly you and we need resources in which our lives are taken seriously. Our lives are bound up with yours. You have given us community, supported us for years, a decade or more in many cases, as we together have stumbled through life in seminary, fearful of opening our eyes, knowing that once we shed our naiveté, we would never be the same again, ambivalent about this, yet knowing we had to change in order to be. You have been with us in this, and we with you. And we offer you this book because it is time for all of us to ask hard questions about where we go from here, what we do now. You know this book before you read it. Not that you will agree with every dot and comma; none of us does. But it is ours, and yours.

We write also for feminist men in theological education. We know some, and it is likely that any man who has read this far is either a feminist or well on his way to being one. Like feminist women, feminist men know who they are. Like their sisters, these men have suffered in a sociotheological climate in which gender roles are drawn tightly to stymie the intellectual and theological potency of both women and men. Our feminist male readers

- do not find our work strident, antiintellectual, hostile, or unimportant;
- are not concerned about whether any of us, its authors, are lesbians;
- do not assume that this book is about "the women's cause" and therefore of only derivative interest to men;
- do not assume that we are all white women and that the book is about sexism *instead of* racism, classism, and other structures of injustice.

The most engaging men we know understand well that men have as much creative power to gain from the women's movement as women do, and that feminist women and feminist men must continue to work on behalf of justice for women of all races and ethnic groups. We who seek justice need to focus our energies on helping to loose the bonds of oppression from those who have been kept under historically. Otherwise those put down do not rise up. Feminist men will expect no apology for our strong interest in *women's* lives. These brothers are aware also that the work they must do has to begin with an honest assessment of their own lives.

In addition to feminists, we speak to those who hold the power in theological education, most often seminary administrators, faculties, boards, and church leaders. These people are empowered, officially, to set and reset policy, to construct and reconstruct theological educational priorities and agendas. In this project we make a conceptual case for structural changes in curricula, in pedagogy, and in the very assumptions that undergird much of the work done in theology, ministry, education, church, and seminary.

We doubt that many theological educators with authority to effect significant institutional change will choose to do so, especially to enhance women's lives. We say this on the basis of data already in. Since the early 1970s, the number of women students in U.S.

29

seminaries has increased 222%.[4] During this period of time, the structural changes in seminaries have been minimal. Women's courses have been added to some curricula, women teachers have been employed here and there, women's programs have been launched around the edges of seminary life; but few curricula have been reconstructed, few female professors have been promoted and tenured, and, as far as we know, none of the learnings from such a venture as the Seminary Quarter at Grailville has been actually incorporated into the theological educational policy of Protestant or Catholic seminaries.

Furthermore, we believe that racial and cultural diversity is indispensable to education. This awareness was born among feminists—not simply that it is a good idea to have racial, ethnic, and religious pluralism in theological education, but that high-quality education cannot occur outside the context of diverse life experience and commitment. It is not enough to tag on an urban program, a field ed requirement, an antiracism workshop, to help meet requirements in practical theology. Either the whole of the theological enterprise (biblical, theological, historical disciplines included) takes place amid cultural diversity, or theological educators miss the point of the inclusivity and universality of the love of God and are, in fact, peddlers of impractical theology.

During the last fifteen years, women in seminaries have come more and more to realize the wholistic, noncompartmental character of theological education at its best. But few seminary curricula have reflected this. Thus, we must not expect much from seminary administrators, boards, and faculties. And yet, today between 40 percent and 50 percent of the Master of Divinity students in many liberal Protestant schools are women; and a number of the more conservative Protestant seminaries and Catholic seminaries are approaching the same large number of women students. Increasingly, these women are being dumped into a job market in which, still today, the mediocre man is more often than not hired over the outstanding woman. All the while members of admissions committees in many seminaries seem ever more delighted by the personal integrity, intellectual facility, and professional promise of the majority of women applicants as well as of those men who present themselves as serious advocates of women's liberation and all struggles for justice. Something must change if seminaries are going to continue to draw and keep intellectually powerful, creative students—female or male.

We understand the relation between the well-being of women in particular and the common good, or the well-being of all people, to be at one level very clear and simple: the common good is distorted whenever anyone—women, people of color, gay and lesbian people, anyone—is not empowered by the community to participate proudly and publicly in the naming and shaping of the common good. If seminaries are to be places of empowerment for anyone, the needs and interests of women must be taken to heart.

Even many women students and women faculty who do not identify with feminism are becoming frustrated by the lack of support they receive from church and seminary in finding work, receiving support in their work, coping constructively with family issues (especially around children and shifting gender roles), dealing with problems of professional isolation and personal loneliness, and learning how to handle various vocational problems that the theological tradition cannot answer on its own—e.g., questions about clerical authority; gender and sexuality; what it is to be pastor and prophet. These questions are exacerbated if the minister is a woman, because just being female constitutes an invitation to a skeptical voyeurism, a watching over that seeks to criticize or condemn. If the seminarian, the professor, the dean, or the minister is a woman, she need not be a feminist to experience being looked over, picked at, harassed in low-key fashion, as if somebody out there were biding their time, waiting for her demise. The feminist is the woman, or man, who *experiences this experience*—knows that it is happening—and who is coming with others into a shared power to say "No more!"

A woman does not have to be a feminist to notice and care about the preponderance in Christian worship and doctrine of masculinist symbolism, language, and assumptions about both divine and human life. While such a woman can maintain earnestly that the words do not bother *her*, most sensitive women and men are troubled that the words do bother lots of *other* people. This sensitivity to what

31

bothers others, if not oneself, is on the rise in many liberal seminaries. For increasing numbers of seminarians and professors, there can be no return from this concern.

Theological educators will have to deal with sexist language and theology; with cultural chauvinism, racism, and myopic theologizing; with training women for work in a world/church (especially church) that does not know what to do with women in authority—or with authority, period. On it goes: issues connect with other issues, interactive, complicated politically, theologically, educationally.

We are concerned that liberal Christian theological education is headed toward financial, as well as theological and educational, bankruptcy. We believe that the possibility of its deliverance is rooted in a praxis-based transformation of theological and educational assumptions that have undergirded the enterprise for a hundred years.

Feminism offers redemptive gifts to our various cultures, races, ethnic and religious heritages. In this spirit, we offer this resource as a gift to theological educators. We trust that what we have to say may be valuable in helping you—and most of us count ourselves among you—live into the crisis being sparked in theological education by feminist questions: about how our common life is ordered; about who teaches what and who learns what; about how we teach and learn what we do; about what constitutes excellence and competence in our work; about ministry and scholarship; about the goals of seminary education and how these may relate to justice; and about what any of this has to do with the value and quality of our relation to that which we experience as divine.

Finally, we are interested in reaching any people interested in theological education. Whether you agree with much of what we propose is not important to us. The issue between us and our readers—especially those who may take exception to what we say—is whether dialogue is possible between us. We think it is, but only if we are willing to speak and listen honestly, which means giving voice and ear to what we love, fear, believe, know, seek. We value such candor not only because it means we can try to take ourselves and others seriously, but also because all real education is steeped in honest communication.

OUR VISION: A COMMONGROUND

So strongly do we believe that justice is the foundation of human life well lived that we understand the primary theological and educational task of the churches to be the work of justice in the world.

This does not mean that all of us must be political activists in order to be involved in the work of justice. It does mean that no seminary teacher or student, regardless of his or her discipline, interests, or skills, is excused from an accountability to human well-being. It means that the scholar who is indifferent to justice is not an excellent scholar. It means that the pastor who is unconcerned about all persons' dignity in his or her work is not a competent pastor. It means that no academic field or practice of ministry falls outside the realm of accountability to the common good. And it means that all of us—professors, students, pastors, priests, employers and employees, colleagues and friends—are responsible for calling one another to account for whatever apathy toward justice may be apparent among us. It means, for all practical purposes, that insofar as theological education benefits primarily those persons who have institutional power or who are heirs to power by "virtue" of race, gender, or class, it is bad education.

In the work of justice those whose voices need most critically to be heard and taken seriously are those who are themselves victims of injustice, people who have been deprived of the power to effect creative change in their own lives or on behalf of others. Liberation theologians argue rightly that these people have an "epistemological privilege" in education—the right of naming the reality to be studied and of leading the way. It is the privilege of people of color to put racism high on the theological agenda. It is women's privilege to insist that sexism be taken seriously as a fundamental theological problem. And it is imperative that white people and men heed these calls if we are to make significant headway toward life lived abundantly and humanely as sisters and brothers.

Bess said that, for her, the term feminism must always be preceded by the word black. We white, black, and Hispanic women affirm that black feminism images well our vision of justice for all as our commonground. The vast majority of the poor in the world are people of color and, of those, the majority are women and children—people who are put down because they are people of color; done in because they are poor; kept under because they are women and children. A commitment to women's well-being that does not take into account the complexity of women's oppression is not, to our understanding, a feminist commitment. An analysis of sexism that is not also an assessment of racism, ethnic prejudice, and economic injustice is not, in our opinion, a feminist analysis. We do not have to be economists, anthropologists, or sociologists to know that race, class, and gender are critical, even determinative, forces in the ordering of human life and religion. We do not have to have worlds of specialized knowledge to be sensitive to gross injustice or to assert our understandings of what is good and what is evil in our common life.

We in theological education have a special mandate to do just that: to develop and deploy our knowledge and the tools of our trade—beginning with an informed and active commitment to human well-being—to do what we can to eliminate (or where that is beyond our power, to diminish) human suffering. This allegiance is not simply something we prepare students to take into the world later. It must be the immediate basis of what we teach and learn and of how we teach and learn. In the larger historical praxis of a racist, classist, sexist, and heterosexist world/church, there is no way to teach or learn justice except by studying the generations of our conflicts, the intersections of our pain, and the roots of our corporate dilemma and hope.

Chapter Two

CAN WE BE DIFFERENT BUT NOT ALIENATED? AN EXCHANGE OF LETTERS

I will flow, not censor or edit, but let the innermost part of me speak.

—Katie Cannon

I'm pulled between excitement and anxiety over what you say.

—Carter Heyward

Often candor is born between friends who already share a bond of assurance that speaking the truth of one's life will not be futile. In this spirit, Katie, a black woman, and Carter, a white woman, corresponded after our first meeting in the fall of 1982. On the basis of the original outline we had drawn up for our work, Carter had asked each of us to do some thinking about particular issues that had been of special interest to us. The correspondence between Katie and Carter grew out of this request. The rest of us did not know about the letters until after they had been written. During our second weekend meeting, in the winter of 1983, we shared what Katie and Carter had written. We offer it here with few alterations, because it reflects teaching/learning in the praxis of particularities.

A little background: Katie refers to *The Color Purple* by Alice Walker.[1] At Kate's suggestion, Carter had read this novel, and the two of them had discussed its theological value as a narrative of a rural black woman who is cut off from all love, relationality, and God until she has a friend who takes her seriously.

October 31, 1982

Dear Carter,

I will respond to the parts of the outline you've asked me to think about by writing a letter much like Celie in *The Color Purple* wrote letters to God and Nettie. By this I mean that I will flow, not censor or edit, but let the innermost part of me speak.

Can we be different but not alienated? Only if there is mutuality in our relating. The analogy for me is the difference between the miracle of dialogue and bilateral conversations. When two parties, people, races, nations, etc., are dialoguing, they respect whatever their intellect, spirit, culture, and traditions tell them is sound in each other, with an attitude of openness for growth and change that comes with the moving of God's spirit. The open-flowing energy between the two removes alienation. But when one of the parties tries to listen only long enough to tell the others what to do, to control, to obtain power or superiority, the result has to be alienation. It is like what Alice Walker says about Church. We come to Church to share with others the God we have found in ourselves, not to find God.

When we, as various people, can claim the beauty of our innerselves, then we do not have to exploit, oppress, disenfranchise other people in some kind of hierarchical, vertical, sadomasochistic pecking order.

Racism, sexism, class elitism are all false, institutionalized systems of the abortive search for somebodiness (meaning). Therefore, in such systems there cannot be acceptance of difference. Difference is interpreted by those in power as *less than.* Conformity is the norm, and anyone who cannot be bleached out and neutered has to be isolated, alienated, and eventually exterminated. It is no mere coincidence that hard and destructive drugs flow freely in our black communities. The self-defense that comes from the side of the oppressed is to maintain the alienation that is already in place, because history bears out that whenever any of us try to heal the breach, they either get co-opted and become a token pet in the system or they get assassinated as a threat to the status quo: academic excellence, national security, etc.

As Zora Neale Hurston says, our survival in the black community is to let those researchers probe—but *not* to give them the information, because the very data shared will be used as the boomerang to destroy us.[2] The beauty of living is appreciating the various differences in God's creation, but, for those in power and control, that very difference is the seed of negation that demands a spontaneity in relating which they refuse to give. Race/class and gender oppressions are based on removing the intelligence, the source of feelings, aspirations, and achievements of those who are different by closeting, categorizing, burying, and cremating them, so that those who reap the privileges of superiority and supremacy do not have to confront their futile and anachronistic gestures of success, progress, or their inability to live any other way.

The particular relation between white and black women. My mama always says that black people must remember that all white people have white mamas. She makes several points with this proverb.

First, the hand that rocks the cradle is the hand that rules the world. We may question the validity and truth of such assumptions, but we cannot deny the impact that racist child-rearing practices have had on sustaining and perpetuating white supremacy.

Second, the volatile relationship between the majority of white women and the majority of women of color has to do with the pedestaled position that white women allow themselves to be placed upon, always at the expense of other women. When white women buy into the privileges of white supremacy and the illusive protectiveness of their superiority, women of color are forced to pick up their slack.

Third, white women are the only ones to guarantee the purity of the white race. They are the white man's most important treasure. George Frederickson makes a strong historical case for white supremacy in South Africa and in the United States, with the bottom-line motivation for the oppression of people of color: white men protecting the virtue and virginity of white women, resulting in the objectification of white women and all others.[3]

Fourth, white women in particular are always seeking blessings of assurance from women of color. By this I mean that, even as a teenager when I worked as a domestic, I was asked by the white kids that I tended to, who were sometimes my age and sometimes older, for advice. (My confusion was always about the injustice of why, if we were the same age, I was their caretaker.) They would sometimes ask me what I thought about washing their hair with beer and other white folk phenomena. Learning, knowing, and remembering my place was critical to my job security. If I responded "What in the hell do I care?" or any milder version of that feeling, I would have been written off as uppity and therefore disrespectful—and fired. If I dumbed-up and numbed-out, ignoring them completely, just continuing my menial, low-paying work, such silence would have been read either the same way or as reinforcing my so-called inferiority and ignorance. It really was that precarious situation my mama describes: when you have your head in the lion's mouth, you have to treat the lion very gently.

Economic/work relationships cannot be minimized in discussing and understanding the relationship between white women and women of color. Also this same kind of blessing of assurance has been manifested in my experience with white women when they don't want to participate in an equal, reciprocal process of give and take.

I remember once at a party lots of folks relaxing and having a good time. Black and white together. My conversation with a white woman appeared to be fairly open and honest. She said that she had always been taught that black people had a foul odor and asked for permission to smell me. (I didn't even flinch. I just registered the request in my category of weird-things-white-people-do.) After she sniffed and smelled and got her nose full of me, she concluded that all that time she had been living with a racist myth, which, as far as she could tell from her experiment with me, was not true.

I then reciprocated the experiment by saying that I, too, had heard some smell-myths about white people. I had been taught that when white people wash their hair or get wet, they smell like dogs. I then proceeded to smell her. She jumped back, appalled, infuriated. How dare I have the audacity to smell her. This is when I was shocked. It was good enough for me to be the object of her examination, but it was not OK when the tables were turned.

And that white woman, huffing and puffing, got up and stormed out of the party. This is often what white women do when they're not in front of the line, calling the shots, or in charge of the dynamics between themselves and women of color. They take their toys, their funds, their programs, their printing press, and go home, where they can perch on a ledge and not have their boat rocked. This in itself is privilege.

My relationship with white feminists and women of color, who may or may not be feminists, is radically different. White feminists are aware of racism. White feminists are aware of their own subjugation and oppression as females. White feminists are beginning to claim their biases, their elitist values, and their assumptions about life. And not only are they aware; they are engaged, actively, in justice-making. This, to me, is the hope. White feminists and women of color are changing the directions and the quality of their relations to each other.

White women who are not about the above, even if they call themselves feminists, are not feminists to me, but only white women with white mamas perpetuating systems of oppression by continuing to participate in them.

I believe that, as women, we need each other. We need to cross race lines and class lines, join forces to stop this messing up of lives by the racist, patriarchal systems and structures steeped in a greed for power and domination, all toward the maximizing of profits.

White feminists are standing over against their privileges inherent in an oppressive system to be in mutual relation with others. Women of color often need to test and retest the authenticity of white women's willingness to relate. The question before us is whether our timing and tolerance will sustain the processes of change.

I wholeheartedly believe that "godding is relating."[4] I only know the essential nature of God when I as an individual, and my people as a race, are not permitted—but command by the respect of our very being—space to engage in the most rigorously honest confrontation. When we confront and are confronted so that all might have life and have life more abundantly—this is what it's all about. And this is why, when I hear of "postfeminist" movements, I quake and shake.[5] The hands that rocked the cradle now cradle the rock, so that, together, we can change the powers and principalities of this world.

Studying our lives in relation to the lives of other women. I respond to this by adapting a metaphor of Amari Baraka:[6]

A black woman is locked up in one room of a large house by an oppressor (white male/female and/or racial/ethnic male) who never enters that room. When the isolated woman finally comes out, she is able to talk about the whole house, whereas her oppressor who imprisoned her is not.

Women who are in touch with their oppression may be more fit to handle the totality of the ethical ambiguities in their lives than their oppressors. Since the oppression of women is the oldest oppression, and since no anthropologist, feminist or otherwise, has ever come up with convincing evidence of a culture in which some form of male dominance does not exist, we, as women, have a wealth of wisdom in our stories, many which have never been told.

The metaphor about the woman in the locked room depicts the "epistemological privilege" of *women of color.* Langston Hughes sums it up in his book *The Ways of White Folks.*[7] The class and economic location of women of color affords them the inside scoop on the nemeses, the jugular veins, and the Achilles' heels of those in power. But the catch-22 is that by the time they get through slaving, with no reflective time for analysis, they don't know how to fight, only how to stay alive. The privilege to reflect in order to prevail beyond survival is not granted to them, so their epistemological privilege either lies dormant, in some kind of state of denial or self-delusion, or it is acted out in ways that get black women beaten up, incarcerated, mutilated. How to channel this wisdom is the essential concern of the ongoing survival of women of color.

Do black women and white women experience a common dilemma? A common possibility? I wholeheartedly respond, Yes. The difference is that white women tend to have more layers of veneer with which they deny our common bond. Racism as idolatry teaches them that they are somebody in spite of the violence in the home, the beatings, rapes, incest, conspiracies of silence, because their white skin makes them better than any black person. The "culture of inequality" teaches them that if they obtain certain material objects, they are far superior to those who have not obtained them. Not until white women and women of color are aware and willing to accept our common dilemma can there be any possible common action for liberative change.

A demon that divides us. You asked about these demons. I've mentioned some, but one that we have to name is the hidden injuries of class.[8] The more economic security one has, the more one can buy illusive myths and distance herself from reality. In other words, money can give those who have it the false security and illusory worth that their personhood is more valuable because of their finances. They then set up and

41

manipulate systems to undergird their uniqueness so that those at the bottom of the pyramid also get on the treadmill of wanting that same shallowness always available in the shadows of the golden ghettoes. A case in point is professionalism. The more one goes to school, the more elite one is supposed to be. The farce of so many of our systems cannot be exposed because those of us struggling for upward mobility, once we see the light, cannot speak; or else we have nothing to sustain our energy and effort after the sacrifices that have put us where we are. So many of our class locations are based on the story line of the emperor who has no clothes. But who will dare name this?—because the namer will be discredited either as a liar and a fool, or as a failure who has a bone to pick, or as a traitor to the guild. A few of us marginated people are tolerated to show the equality of the system, but only a limited quota can survive.

I'll stop here because my brain needs to rest.

Kate

November 2, 1982

Dear Carter,

I haven't heard from you, so I will continue this dialogue in my head, assuming you have asked me to elaborate a little more about my mother's statement that all white people have white mamas. Whether this is your question or not, I think it is where a little more clarification is needed. My line of reasoning is not to establish white women or women of color either as the evil ones or as the victims of patriarchal oppression and exploitation but to lift up the rape of the psyche that causes all of us to internalize our own destruction so that "if there is not a backdoor our very nature will demand one."[9]

Rosa D. Bowser, an outstanding black woman of the late nineteenth and early twentieth century, coined the words my mother used to accept her accountability: "Men are what the women make them."[10] One of Bowser's contemporaries, Sarah Dudley Pettey, said: "Men go from home into the world to execute what women have decreed."[11] George Jackson in *Soledad Brother* drove this point home for me.[12] Reading his life story about how his mother made him a black man/child, I was struck with my own reality, which is—if I were to choose to bring forth a child from my womb or raise a child as an adoptive parent, I would have the responsibility to teach that child the rudiments of surviving a racist world. The only way that can be done is to set up a schizoid, push-pull, give-take child-rearing pattern, wherein I rape the psyche of my own off-spring or immerse the child in the bleaching-vat process myself. Parenting is difficult in a racist patriarchal capitalist society.

Maybe I am totally off target in holding white women accountable for their role in white families in the same way; if so, I think there needs to be some honest communication with me and other women of color about the paralyzing nature of oppression of white females. I do know that black women have a sayso in child-rearing and the goings-on in the black family, and I believe white women have some sayso too, for perpetuating white privilege. Black women are not solely responsible for pathology in the black community. Poverty, drug abuse, low educational achievement, prostitution, and unemployment are real. But we are, like Bernice Johnson Reagan said, holding up the wall of society so that it doesn't crush the next generation—and simultaneously taking from that wall the essentials of survival. Black women, therefore, have neither the privilege nor the leisure to analyze the changing reality and the changing needs of the very people they claim that they are accountable to. If I don't accept some of the responsibility for the perpetuation of my own oppression, I can never be free. Whether I use the analogy of holding up the wall with my back, or the rape of my psyche, once the violence has happened, and even when it becomes routinized in well-documented, insidious institutional systems the people in my community and I have a responsibility to the God who has created us in God's image to face and explore the terror, so as to militate the radicality of our own rebirth.

43

My commitment to finishing my Ph.D. degree comes from owing the black female community all that I have obtained and been exposed to in this privileged process. Since the masses cannot have reflecting and reading time to analyze, those of us who do are indebted to the very ones who called us forth "to discover books, desks, a place for [those] who know nothing of these things themselves."[13]

Now to pick up again on the demons that divide us.

Co-opting and rendering invisible our contributions and histories. The most devastating reality of writing my dissertation is having to face the fact that black women have been omitted from the writing of black history. As I try to reconstruct the "Black Woman's Moral Situation," the glaring vacancies make my endeavor extremely difficult. The oral tradition and its validity sustain me, however. My grandmother, who lived from Reconstruction until 1975, told me many of the tales that I have pieced together like quilted patchwork. The literature on black women in American history is so sparse (Noble, Lerner, and maybe two others) that one can establish only a skeletal framework of the past. Gloria Hull, Patricia Scott, and Barbara Smith hit the nail squarely on the head when they titled their book *All the Women Are White, All the Blacks Are Men, but Some of Us Are Brave.*[14]

Now to respond to the white privilege of co-opting and rendering invisible black experience: There is one scene in the Broadway musical *Dreamgirls* that dramatically depicts this kind of co-optation, when whites rip off the black musical tradition. This also relates to what I shared in the first letter about so little tolerance and appreciation for differences. Those in power tend to render things "universal" in a cloning fashion or else to define their worth, value, and quality out of existence by assessing them as liabilities and inferior. It has to do with superiority and arrogance again, wherein dominant oppressors structure life so that they are always taking control, never appreciating the color purple. Sometimes I hear people in the black community talking about not trusting white folks because they (whites) just want to study us enough to write

44

about us, continuing the exploitation of our very lives by monopolizing the publishing of our history and experiences.

In essence what I am asking, given these systems of inequality, is how do we maximize them for a more equitable distribution of wealth in society? Well, we can begin as feminists by understanding our interconnectedness, our interdependency, and therefore lifting each other as we climb.

Another demon: marginalization of women's studies and interests. To marginalize is to disempower, to push to the outer edge of the hub of the life-decision-making-center. When one—as an individual, a group, a race—has to hang on to the edge, white-knuckling all the way, there is little time to confront authorities and demand change in the system. It is to the advantage of those who maintain the power in society to keep those who think differently about themselves and their rights engaged in all kinds of cliff-hanging activities. It is very much like a crushing wall that's caving in on the sustaining forces of life. Marginality also means that one is removed from the nurturing and sustaining sources of life's energy. It can render one docile, ignorant of self and therefore willingly susceptible to whatever comes down the pike. Marginality places women's communities and racial/ethnic interests in throwaway, expendable positions, diluting our potency.

Another demon: exceptional women as tokens. Depending on which side of tokenism one is on, one can either lose by losing or lose by winning, but all the time losing just the same. When strong, positive, God-centered women confront their male counterparts, they are usually afforded a subtle, institutionalized option to conform to whatever those in power have defined as normative or to become a slightly "deformed" one of the boys. I was quite successful in seminary because I knew how to behave in men's space so as to not threaten them. My stance was primarily that of the fly on the wall—a fly with many privileges granted to me as long as I remembered my place/space. Sometimes I was permitted to soar like a mighty eagle and at other times I sat quietly like a bump on a log. Knowing the difference made me constantly feel as if I was driving with one foot on the accelerator and the other one simultaneously on the brakes. This meant that even though I was producing at top quality on one side of my brain, my soul sagged and ached with the heavy load of the precariousness of my tokenism.

Another one of my mother's proverbs is that if you let people make you at will, they can break you at whim. Martin Luther King, Jr. said that all a token is good for is a one-way ride on a subway. I have tried to keep myself sensitized to this so that, when in token positions, I understand that it is a place to bring about change for a few until the revolution comes. The privileged inside circle can serve as a vantage point for some change only if those who are allowed into such holy-of-holies stay mindful of our call, our commitment, and our community. What happens so often is that tokens behave like doorkeepers. The system uses the token, like the main character in Sam Greenlee's novel *The Spook Who Sat by the Door*, to screen out whoever is unacceptable to the functioning of the status quo and, thereby, to nullify the legitimacy of calls for justice.

Well, Carter, I think these responses take care of my thoughts for now. If I have anything to share on the other theme you asked about—embodied learning—I will drop it in the mail. Take care.

Kate

November 18, 1982

Dear Kate,

I've reread your letters many times, and only now, having had them with me for several weeks, can I begin to try to articulate a response, and not only a response to you but to myself. Responding to my own feelings, questions, confusions, and delights. Even now I'm pulled between excitement and anxiety over what you say, what I read, what we're doing, especially as women of different colors. You see, I find that I want to be a color! I'd always, even as a little girl, thought there was something weird about the implication that white people have no color—unlike "colored" people. White seemed to me to be a color, but then someone told me that whiteness is the absence of color—sort of like evil is the absence of good? I have serious reservations about whether this is true ethically and politically. Isn't it crucial for white people to own up to our whiteness (read: privilege in a racist society) and to acknowledge the difference our color makes?

I don't think this is nitpicking but rather that it's one more example of racial privilege looked at through the lens of liberalism—color doesn't make any difference and shouldn't matter; we shouldn't even notice it—because, in the world of God, color (like sex, etc.) is transcended, a nonissue, a nonreality. That sounds to me like the sort of logic that could only bounce out of the brain of a race/a people that thinks of itself as "colorless," folks like my people who distance ourselves from the difference color makes.

I'm excited to be writing this to you, Kate, because I like you and I know you like me, which makes it a little easier to speak my mind. But I would be lying if I said that I'm comfortable discussing race—even with you, or maybe especially with you. My fear is that you'll leave; that you'll notice my racism—which I certainly notice—and that you'll leave, close the door.

Surely I've told you about Bessie. Bessie was our maid. I was about four years old, living with Mamma and Daddy; at the time still the only child. Bessie came every several days, maybe once a week, to clean the house and cook fried chicken, my favorite food, and look after me. And I adored her. Sometimes she'd take me to the movie theater in Hendersonville, North Carolina where "colored" people had to sit in the balcony and white people downstairs. I can remember begging her to let me go with her to the balcony! And I remember asking Mamma and Daddy why we never went to Bessie's house, except to drop her off at the end of the driveway; and why Bessie's house looked so poor, like a shack, and ours didn't. My memory is fuzzy, but I think I recall both my parents' very pained and strained expressions as they tried to explain racism to a four-year-old white child. I will go to my grave grateful that they told me racism was wrong and that it was not God's will and that we, all of us, were living in a sinful society. Those were the lessons my parents tried to teach, and they were, even then, considered by most folks who knew them to be moderate to liberal white southerners.

But they didn't try to teach me, explicitly, that we should do something about ending racism. I suppose, like most, they didn't know what to do. They felt powerless. They did tell me that I must always be kind to colored people and respect them as God's children. And they also told me that I should never ever call a colored person a nigger—that this was a bad word that only ignorant and racist white people used (notice the class bias of dominant white culture here—white folks' sense of "poor white trash").

But one day my friend Elliott (a white girl) and I were playing jump rope in the front yard and Bessie was watching over us. And I began that infamous little jingle: "Eenie, meenie, miny mo, catch a nigger by its toe." I still to this day have no sense of whether I knew what I was saying, whether I was making the connection between "nigger" and "colored person" or between "nigger" and Bessie; but Bessie walked into the house, got her coat and walked out again, slowly down the driveway. I never saw her again.

That was 1950. Mamma and Daddy explained to me that I had hurt Bessie's feelings and that it was wrong for me to have done it, but that Bessie shouldn't have taken such offense at a five-year-old girl. Recollecting this story is still painful for me, and I haven't fully unloaded it. I do know that it represents my fear—but of what? Of someone leaving? But who? Necessarily a black person? Or might it be anyone? And as I've gotten older, the story has begun to make me angry—to put me in touch with my feelings of having been betrayed—by Bessie. My fantasy now is not to watch silently as she walks down the driveway, but to run after her and ask her to stop, turn around, come back—even demand—that she tell me why she's going, what she feels like, and that, even at age five, if I could do something about it, I would. I also want her to know that I'm sorry, that I am ashamed, that I didn't know what I was do- ing—at least not consciously or willfully.

It is almost more than I can bear to imagine that Bessie didn't give a damn about me, and yet now, over thirty years later, I can say, for certain, that if I were black, a black woman, I would be burning with an unquenchable fire of rage against white people—including the five-year-old girls and boys I had been expected to nurture at the expense of my own.

As I've told you before, sexism makes racism all the more complicated for me to try to sort out—especially my own attitudes and actions. Sometimes I think that if there were only black women and white women in the world (and of course women of other colors too), racism wouldn't be a problem—for *me*, that is. I don't mean to be idealizing womanhood, because I don't believe women are morally superior to men. What I do mean is that, for me, it's in relation to black men that I get confused about the ways in which I am or am not racist. I do not like for any man of any color or ethnic group to harass me sexually. My experience has been that in relation to most (not all) white men who've come on to me sexually, when I brush them off or say no, they back off and rather quietly get out of my way. In relation to black men (again, not all of them) who've come on to me, when I say no or brush them off, there's usually a big scene about my being racist or about chocolate being better than vanilla—"if only you weren't too hung up to taste it"—and on it goes.

Furthermore, since I came out as a lesbian, I've felt (paranoid or not) that a good many black men have wanted to do to me what the guys in Brewster Place did to one of "The Two."[15] I'll never forget the contemptuous look in the eyes of Mr. —— when a gay man and I gave a five-minute speech on behalf of lesbians and gays at the Theology in the Americas Conference in 1980. He and a dozen or so other black men, together with the men in the Native American group, were the only people, out of some six hundred, who chose to sit there with stone faces after the gay/lesbian presentation rather than to rise and applaud. I understand this from a sociological, historical perspective, of course. But even to write about it makes me angry. And I find that at times—much to my chagrin, actually—my image of black men is of people I cannot trust, people who scare me, people who'll use me—whether physically, professionally, whatever—to bolster themselves. It's really clear to me that these feelings of mine combine simple truth-telling (black men and white women have at best a strained relationship historically that none of us individually can transcend absolutely) and flashy remnants of my own racism (really believing that black men are more violent than white men; being afraid, for example, that a black male mugger would kill me whereas a white male mugger would simply take my money . . .).

I didn't mean to go on about my relations with black men—that's not exactly the point of this correspondence. And yet, it does relate to us, you and me, does it not?

Can we be different but not alienated? I agree totally, Kate, that the answer lies in the quality of our relation; whether real dialogue, the "miracle of dialogue" as you say, is possible and desired between us and around us, among our sisters, black and white. The problem with white liberalism (I don't know about black liberalism) is that liberal white men and women do not advocate real relation, not mutual relation, but rather a patronizing sort of relation based on hand-me-down affections. White liberals "love" black people; white liberal men "love" all women (white women and women of color)—as long as we're not threatening to change the name of the power game. There's really not much difference between white liberals and white conservatives when it comes to race relations or any relations. There may be a different attitude or worldview—but the actions seem to me, when all is said and done, pretty much the same.

I would distinguish between conservatives and reactionaries. Conservatives are very much like liberals—it's just that their patronizing is attached more explicitly to the value of the past. But both liberal and conservative white people (and I suppose their black clones) really don't want to see things shaken up. Change? Maybe, very gradually, very cautiously, and very amicably. No disruptions, no riots, no violence. Whereas reactionaries in white communities are today in this country very much an incarnation of fascism. They do want to see things change and they do want to see things shaken up—and all in the service of what they believe either once was (the American Dream) or what ought to be—because it's God's will (Moral Majority, for example).

The point of this little digression is that, in my opinion, among us white people, we have very few models of mutual relation—people helping show the way. Most of the white people I know (myself included) grew up as more or less liberal—and, as such, really not very relational in any authentic sense. Even our primary, most intimate relations—parent-child, spouse-spouse, lover-lover, friend-friend—have been characterized more by a "let me give you what's good for you" attitude and less by a "let's try to see what's good for ourselves and then work together for what we see" way of being together. As far as I am concerned, the former is destructive of human well-being, whether between two lovers or two races of people. The latter may be redemptive, or so it seems to me. And it seems to me that that's exactly what we need to be about, we white women and women of color.

Women of color and white women need to own up to our own respective situations, getting ourselves together *as white* women or *as black* women or *as Hispanic* women—so our racial/ethnic womanness and particularity is clear. We need to be clear about who we are *as a people*—which is why white people like me have to own up to our whiteness and not be always bouncing ourselves off people who are black or brown or yellow, as if somehow we are looking to you for our definition—which could only be a sham.

We have to work together—as we are doing right now on this project. I don't believe these two steps of being separate, and also working together, follow in any neat sequence. Rather they can go on simultaneously under the right conditions, sometimes in crisis situations in which solidarity becomes mandatory; or through friendship when solidarity has become thinkable or at least a common dream.

51

It seems to me that we can work together only if we are willing to risk being candid with each other—about what we need, how we affect each other, how we experience the difference our race makes even in the instant we are acting together for what we believe is our common good.

As you know—I've heard you discuss this—being candid is more difficult for white liberal women than for just about anyone else, because (1) liberals don't like conflict; (2) whites don't like to get in touch with the difference our race makes; and (3) women, white women at least, have been cultivated to be reconcilers—although I should add that such attitudes are also class related. The sort of candor that involves conflict is especially hard for white, upper-middle-strata, liberal women like me raised to think that we must be "ladies." I thought a lot about this when Grace Kelly died. When I was a child, she was my role model of what a "lady" should be; in recent years, I had grown to find Grace Kelly a rather dreary archetype of passivity, a woman who did not interest me in any way, except that once upon a time I had wanted to be like her.

And so what is it I'm afraid of? What do I fear my candor may unleash or cause? Several things: I've already mentioned my fear that you, rather than struggling through issues with me, will simply walk away—not because you won't want to have anything to do with me but rather because I will have become a source of great pain for you, a pain you won't feel that you should have to bear. I'm also afraid that you'd be right to leave, to say "To hell with you," because I'm afraid that my own racism is deeper and more pervasive than I realize, and such that no black person would really want to be with me if ever she were to see this nasty wad of remnant racism, from generations past and present, which I have swallowed, and which, like a giant furball, has infected my gut.

And why am I afraid that I'm the most racist person in the Northeast? Because it's clear to me that racism is far more pervasive, far more odious, far more sinful and outrageous than any of us white children were ever taught to believe or imagine, even those of us who had white "ladies and gentlemen" for parents. Racism is so obnoxious, so unspeakably devastating to each white personality and psyche, that I, no less than any white sister or brother, must surely have been infected by this gross malaise in ways that I still cannot comprehend.

Yes, indeed, every white person has a white mama—and a white papa too. And while I do hear the particular poignancy and responsibility in the black mama-child relation you articulate, Kate, it's the white daddy/white papa/white father image, symbol, and reality that cuts to the core of what I see the problem to be in the white world I know. It's interesting, isn't it, that a white woman would say, "But let's talk about the white father instead"? Interesting to me—in that it may have something to do with some of the tensions between black and white women. Something we need to sort out?

You see, for me, in my white culture it's the *father* who's been responsible for a kind of headship of family, which the mother simply passes on, passively. She is to nurture and coddle the father's values—including racism. This sounds simplistic, if what I am saying is interpreted on the basis of individual personalities, because, within lots of families—including my own—individual white mothers are as assertive and strong as white fathers. But among white folks in my world, the prevailing, *public* assumption is that father does indeed know best—and even in families where there is no father at home, or in which the mother personally rules the roost, there looms large this image of "the man"/"the father"/ "God," in whose service this life is being lived. Which makes for a complex and often intense relation between the white mother and the white child.

Often this means that the white mama must be manipulative if she's ever to have her own way, because wives and mothers do not live for themselves. To be manipulative is to be indirect, circuitous. It means that the mama must never let the daddy think that the children love her more, even if they do. Because, in fact, she is simply the channel through which the children's feelings get passed to daddy. Which means, again, that the mother must be coy, mysterious, enigmatic when it comes to appropriating the child's feelings for her;

moreover, it means that she seldom ever really feels loved by the children—even though they may adore her. What this means is that many white mamas live frantic emotional lives in relation to their children—trying always not to love them too much, but at the same time desperate to feel loved by them. And so it is that white mothers "hang on" or "won't let go"—or so the stories suggest, and I think, to be honest, it is often true.

And while black mamas have to teach their kids how to survive in a racist world, white mamas—if they are women of goodwill—have to teach their kids something similar: on one hand, how to reject patriarchal values of racism, sexism, and economic greed; and, on the other hand, how to pretend to accept these values in order not to be destroyed. So white mothers, if they believe in justice, and white fathers too, if they advocate justice, find themselves in the roles of teaching schizophrenia to the kids in order to help them learn to cope humanely and responsibly in—and still survive—a racist, sexist, classist, warmongering situation.

I'll probably write to you more later. Right now I'm spent. Your words bear witness to some deep and abiding truths—and I don't often speak of "eternals." Thank you for the gift of you.

Carter

November 20, 1982

Dear Carter,

I feel so grateful for the honesty of sharing that is occurring in these letters. It reminds me of my childhood, when I habitually watched Red Buttons on TV. I gathered a host of imaginary friends around me for comfort, all named HiHi, HoHo, HeHe, based on the characters I remembered that Red Buttons talked about a great deal. My sister, Sara, who is twenty-three months older than I, refused to play with me because I insisted that my imaginary friends be allowed to play too. At that point she announced to the world (which consisted of my younger sister, Doris, and the neighborhood children, all blood relatives) that I was crazy. But I didn't really care, because my imaginary friends were with me through thick and thin, they never left; and when I raised questions about the fundamental order of life, especially as to what the curse of blackness was all about, they (the imaginary friends) raised the same question. I knew in my heart of hearts that they knew I wasn't crazy, just extremely delicate and sensitive.

I feel that you are one of those imaginary friends who is now present in the flesh. The bond between us has been there before we were born. I just remembered I wrote a poem about such a bond on the day that the Feminist Theological Institute came into existence—November 22, 1980.

> *Strolling down the sidewalk*
> *   a woman-pair*
> *Holding quadraphonic conversations*
> *   in our heads*
> *Sure of words*
> *   not sure of the genus of our souls*
> *Agonizing the same truths*
> *Embedded in the common womb*
> *   of wrestling supplications*
> *Posing difficult questions*
> *   with piercing X-ray vision*
> *   inherent in the friendship*
>
> *   before the beginning.*

The poem goes on, but the point I am making is that the covenant of relating is mutual. I know that if I tried to lift or erase the fear you have about your racism hanging out that I would be trespassing on God's territory. However, I do believe that only in experiencing the new heaven and the new earth do we develop convictions about what is really possible as well as renewed commitment to keep the covenant alive and ever-expanding.

I don't know whether you are familiar with Lillian Smith's book, *Killers of the Dream*, written in the 1940s and revised and reissued in 1961.[16] I urge you to read it and add it to our book discussion for the collective, along with *The Colo. Pur-ple*. We discussed Smith's book in the RSAC (Race, Sex, and Class) meeting yesterday.[17] I only wish that more women in my age group had been present. There was such a need for reality checking with counterparts of my generation, and maybe that day will come soon. What you talked about in your last letter resonated exactly with Lillian Smith's discussion of her child-hood. For instance, she says:

> The mother who taught me what I know of tenderness and love and compassion taught me also the bleak rituals of keeping Negroes in their "place." The father who rebuked me for an air of superiority toward schoolmates from the mill and rounded out his rebuke by gravely reminding me that "all men are brothers," trained me in the steel-rigid decorum I must de-mand of every colored male. They who so gravely taught me to split my body from my mind and both from my "soul," taught me also to split my conscience from my acts and Christianity from southern tradition.[18]

I need to respond to another issue you raised. Carter, I ask that you separate your experience of black men from every-thing else right now because as long as those two (men, plus all else) stay tangled inside you, we cannot get on with the con-versation that will take both of our lifetimes, and then some, to complete anyway. You and I have shared with each other the experience of being molested as children.[19] It just dawned on me that when you shared your experience with me, I identified so readily with what happened to you that it may be that only in my imagination did I share my experience with you! Do you recall my telling you about being repeatedly molested by an older boy when I was about five years of age? If you don't recall it, then it is probably because I told it to you when you still existed only in your "imaginary" state!

Your fear, feelings, and responses to black men are not ab-stract racist ideology and doctrine but come from that place inside of you that has not healed from violation. I say that from my own space/place. The teenage boy who molested me several times died soon afterwards and I believed, until my early adulthood, that God did that especially for me, that I was special and that if someone hurts Kate, I could ask "Friend-God" to zap that person—and in seconds my will would be done. That theological narrowness of imagining a controlled/controlling God has changed for me, but it sustained me through some of the abuse I endured from men, including that childhood violation.

Think about the incident with your heart, not your mind. Here's a little white girl who shared what she thought was harmless. Then when she spoke of it, she had to endure the response of angry, frightened parents and the retaliation by the white community to the black man. And, all along, Carter gets lost in the shuffle, denying the good feeling, feeling unclean, having confused-as-hell feelings, assuring everybody that she is okay, and remembering we must love "those" people. No wonder your fear of black males is deep and still confusing to you: but it is like I said in our discussion of *The Color Purple: rebirth is only possible when we face terror face to face.* That experience was terror in your life, just as my experience of being molested was. It wreaked havoc in our psyches. What I have learned in facing terror, sometimes day by day, is that I don't go to certain people for affirmation, especially to those who remind me of the boy who molested me.

I hope that the challenge I am presenting to you is not too threatening. I hope that it is simple and clear to you. I think of the pain of violation like the woman in the scriptures who had the issue of blood for seven long years. (Remember all that the number seven symbolizes in the Bible, especially that seven means "complete.") Think of the woman as bleeding away her life energy and life substance, that they flowed from her in wasteful ways. The story affirms that the woman was healed by her awareness of her situation, an acceptance of the help that was available, and the courage to take the action to touch God in the person of Jesus. And even though Jesus was being pressed by the crowd, he knew that he had been touched by this woman in a significant way.

It is like all the healing-touching between Celie and Shug in *The Color Purple*. The people who hurt you in all kinds of ways cannot do the healing. Nor can those who act like our violators act today. For you still to worry so much about black men or the Native American men who did not stand in support of the lesbian/gay presentation at TIA meeting is to long for and look for healing from the source from whence it will not and cannot come. To focus on the walking dead means that you may miss out on the powerful healing touch and touching healing of the six hundred people who stood with you in love and commitment and cheered.

I want to say more about this healing at some later date. For now I will close with a story that I heard recently. Before doing that I affirm that I enter this covenant of friendship with you because I am thoroughly convinced that I cannot be all that I can be as a black woman if I dismiss you from the community of humanity just because you are a white woman. I cannot be in an I-It relationship with anyone and call myself Christian. And the more I-Thous in my life, the more I feel, experience, and know the Eternal Thou who lives and breathes in each one of us in beautiful and unique ways. (I never thought I would reach the day when I'd say that I need white people in my life, just like I need black people and the other people in the world because we are all part of the whole!) On with the story.

As a child, I was a lover of baby dolls. I yearned to the point of experiencing physical pain in my body for a black doll. I always got white dolls because they were more plentiful and cheaper. But my sister, Doris, who is thirteen months younger than I, got a beautiful black doll one Christmas, and the next year we used it for Jesus in the Christmas play at the church. Back in 1956–57 that was a revolutionary, radical thing to do, but we did it, and it felt so good to me, to know that this little black female doll symbolized the boy Jesus. After that point I didn't care whether I got a black doll, because if the baby Jesus was black, then the boy Jesus and the grownup Jesus could also be black, and it all started to make sense in my little ever-churched Sunday school mind. Of course I only acknowledged this radical truth to HiHi, HoHo, and HeHe, and they, of course, agreed with me. (Believe it or not, this is not the story I started out to tell. The above story is the one that flowed from the miracle of dialogue. Now, for the story I heard recently . . .)

A woman was asked by her therapist to imagine that she was a child in a crib who had pushed her favorite toy onto the floor so that it rolled out of sight. When no one came to return this beloved object of pleasure to her, what, she was asked, would she do? The young woman started crying, saying no one had ever been there for her. She insisted that people, places, and things had rolled out of her sight and life repeatedly, and, as a result, she was now terrified to trust anyone to be there with and for her. When we have been intentionally or unintentionally hurt by others, it is not enough to have had someone there to return our lost toy on several occasions, randomly, at their convenience. It would not be enough to assure the wounded child that there is somebody who cares. The sexual abuse against you and me, Carter, caused a part of us to roll out of sight. Even though we have done a lot to put ourselves together again, the healing only happens for each of us, I believe, when we embrace God in ourselves and each other. When I touch other individuals, they feel touched by me, and in a miraculous way the healing happens, slowly but surely. The issue of blood stops flowing out of me. Instead it flows through me, in new and invigorating ways, so that I can be present when the next touch connects with me. When my blood stays inside me, flowing in me, I am more sensitive to the press from the crowd, and I am also in tune with myself to know when "somebody has touched me. And, oh, what joy floods my soul, something happened, and now I know, somebody touched me and made me whole." (This is a paraphrase of a popular gospel song in the black church tradition.)

Have a great Thanksgiving.

Kate

CHAPTER THREE

IN MY VOICE YOU WILL HEAR PAIN[1]

Como mujeres no tenemos un sentido de clase. A pesar del hecho de que yo pienso en términos políticos y comunitários, cuando una mujer logra algo yo no lo considero un éxito en el que yo participo. Cuando una hispana triunfa, para mí es una alegría porque entre nosostros hispanos si hay un sentido de clase: pero esa mentalidad todavía no existe entre mujeres.[2]

—Ada Maria Isasi-Diaz

OUR BROKEN BODY

The empowerment of women is key to any significant change in theological education that will benefit women, since structural change will come, if it does at all, out of our insistence as women that our lives be taken seriously. Our capacity to insist effectively depends on our solidarity as sisters. And we are aware, as are surely all women in seminaries, that we do not experience this solidarity except in fragments here and there. We are here addressing this dilemma head on: What might it involve to be in solidarity with one another across the lines that divide us? What might such a community of women look like? And what about the lines that divide us— are they drawn permanently? And are the lines, our differences, necessarily divisive, destructive to the possibility of community? Or are there ways we can live and work with one another not in spite of, but because of, our differences?

Community does not come easily. Our questions and intellectual passions do not unfold automatically. We do not, maybe we cannot, tender beings that we are, begin our work with the critical candor in which our energies and interests will be sparked. We talk and we make damned good sense, and we enjoy finding points of agreement—theological education is in a bad way; most white male professors are obtuse around issues of race and sex; seminary rhetoric about competence and excellence is employed in inverse proportion to its actuality; white women have not dealt with our racism; men of color have not dealt with their sexism; black women and other racial/ethnic women live always in the jeopardy of at least a double oppression; the most difficult issues for us to try to discuss—even theoretically—are heterosexism and classism (is this true, as we think it is, of theological education in general?).

And Nancy talks about feminist resources in theological education always being "add-ons," pointing out that while graduate students in Christian ethics are often required to read John Rawls, they are seldom required to read Beverly Harrison.

And Bev elaborates the dilemma of feminist professors who are expected both to teach *the tradition* [sic] and to provide special resources for all women (and men) interested in feminist studies.

And Ada decries the out-of-touchness of Hispanic male theologians with their actual daily lives as a critical theological praxis.

And Mary is angry that theological scholars who operate on the assumption that white male culture is all of reality would dare call their work excellent.

And Kate recalls that Lucy Brady of Rochester said recently, "What happened to Joan of Arc was that she was burned at the stake, and what's happening to us is that we're burnt out."

And our irritations mount, and our insights sharpen, and we realize we have our work cut out for us.

We proceed to outline our project. We are working well, and we can begin to detail a collaborative analysis of the problem—the imperialism and mystification of white male culture in theological education. We can begin to envision feminist proposals for pedagogical and curricular change in theological education.

And yet, the difficulty in our work, in giving it voice among ourselves even more than in writing it, needs to be underscored, because the process of giving voice to our lives is essential in theological education.

Yes, we could gather as a small, compatible group of reasonably intelligent, articulate women and shape the outline of a Christian feminist theology. Adhering to the conditions of good theologizing we suggested in the first chapter, we could write a book about feminist theory, feminist theology, feminist education. And such work has its place, even here in this book.

But soon into our work, we detect a restlessness among ourselves. Our collective ability to examine feminist theory is facilitating an evasion of the more fundamental work we must do in order to illuminate the theory our task demands. It is one thing to say that all good theology and education begins with the study of our lives and quite another thing actually to study our lives as participants in theological education.

Carter had convened our group because she holds to the theoretical assumption that all theology is done, acknowledged or not, in the praxis of human experience, the context of our daily lives. Moreover, she had experienced each of us as women who share this assumption and who, therefore, would be willing to join in a process of studying our lives—in particular, as black, white, Hispanic feminists. The others of us had agreed with Carter that there is no more pressing issue among women in seminaries than racism. We concurred that theological education suffers in fundamental ways from the failure of teachers and students to acknowledge, much less deal with, racism in theology, in the church, in education, and in our lives.

Thus we find ourselves, as we knew we would, unable to do much of anything worth our time or anybody else's unless we leap beyond the defenses we have worked so long to construct (a major one being our facility in theological discourse) and open ourselves to the possibility of actually learning something about ourselves, the world, and God.

And it is hard for us, anxiety-producing for us theologians/ professionals/strong women: opening up, shutting down, holding and withholding, rarely able to see in the moment what our learning adventure might mean or where it might fit in the seminary courses we are teaching or taking back to our schools or to our work and relationships beyond this group.

It is tedious because our body is fragmented by the diversity of our cultures, our experiences, and our commitments. But not only do we come with these variations; we know we do. Each of us takes care to harbor herself from the tumults she has been educated, throughout her life, to watch out for, lest she be torn from the anchor of her own identity—in which her sense of personal and professional worth is fastened. And although each of us may be racked by any number of failures to adjust ourselves well to this or other social situations, the fragmentation we have described cannot be relegated, validly or constructively, to the realm of our personal problems. Much to the contrary. More often than not in theological education, our individual wounds can be tended, sometimes healed, in the context of our common acknowledgment that we are all members of a broken body.

Ours is, in this sense, a typical theological body, representative of all theological educators and students. What may be atypical about Mud Flower is that we know already that we cannot, in good faith, make the same vows to the same creeds or the same gods. Or that, if we do, we are simply coping as best we can with the ecclesial and academic structures in which we intend to work. We know, moreover, that only insofar as we face and name and pay respect to our broken places can we even hope to catch glimpses of our body as One.

ACKNOWLEDGING OUR HISTORICAL PRAXIS

As a broken body of women, we confess the pathos of our very concrete historical limits. Like all people, we continue to be shaped by sociopolitical factors and dynamics. There is much to be celebrated about each of our lives and certainly about our life and work together in theological education—and there is also much sadness and much evil into which we have come, and in which we live despite our goodwill. White supremacy, male gender superiority, economic exploitation, homophobia, anti-Semitism—these forces constitute the destruction of human well-being. These are evil forces that mar our common life and our possibilities of community. We are persuaded that dialogue—a sharing of our lives that seeks justice-based relation—is the only means we have to transform, even in the smallest ways, the history that renders us separate and unequal.

A racist world-order does not support the possibility of mutual relation between white people and people of color. For that reason if no other, we who are committed to racial justice must push for a mutuality of respect and opportunity and power, beginning in our lives, aware as we do that we pose a threat to every racist person and principle still operative in our world/church. Only as we attempt to relate as peers, equally able to give and receive, to learn and teach, can we even fantasize well what it would be like to work, play, and enjoy ourselves as a community of women.

Especially in the praxis of theological education and the history of Christian thought, the large majority of white male theologians have been educated to regard only their own experience as normative in the making of Christian doctrine. And the content of the "great" theological systems confirms this methodological assumption. To do theology, so we are told by these men, is to assess the nature and character of universals, to sweep with broad strokes the particularities of personal and specific events; to bypass the nitty-gritty pains and problems, whims and fantasies, of the common folk in an effort to direct us away from ourselves toward that which cannot be known in human experience. The concept of God has become virtually synonymous with a goodness and a power that transcends us, an elusive, often static spirit beyond our reach, ontologically uninvolved with us.

These assumptions continue to prevail even in the various modern and contemporary patterns of Christian thought in which God is said to have been crucified, and in the incarnation to have become like us, willing to suffer and be subjected to common human experience. Even in the work of those theologians who acknowledge the truth and the value of God's participation in human life, there remains a refusal to acknowledge an experiential and philosophical

64

need to re-image and reconstruct what it may mean to speak of God at all in terms of such traditional theological concepts as transcendence and omnipotence. This refusal seems to us rooted in a failure to comprehend our own lives as theological praxis, the arena in which God is encountered, valued, studied, known.

Happily for us, women of all cultures have a headstart on men when it comes to appreciating the value of their own lives as the starting point in community-building and theologizing. Throughout Christian history, women have been socialized to seek and know God in the context of our daily lives. The very factors that have accompanied our subservience to men—our "place" in the home or in the fields, in the bedroom or with the children, in the kitchen or in the steno pool, with the dustpan or arranging church flowers— have constituted a womanspace in which to love is to serve both man and God. We should not take lightly the assumptions about ourselves-in-relation-to-God that undergird our spiritual cultures, as evidenced in our journals, prayers, art, and music. Among those of us who are black, we note especially our spirituals, jazz, and oral and literary traditions. People of color in this country, and white women too, know what it is to do theology on the basis of our daily lives. Our problem, as theological educators and students, is to take this as seriously as it needs to be taken.

God knows, we know, all of us know that we are all tokenized, trivialized, and set over against one another in the church, in the world, in theological education. And we are set over against one another in this group—white vs. black and Hispanic, black vs. Hispanic, lesbian vs. straight, etc. We are set in opposition not, in the first instance, because of who each of us is, nor because of how we feel about ourselves or one another, but because we represent certain various proximities to the interests of white male theological academic culture.

From the perspective then simply of what is real—the actual conditions of our lives and work—we women of different racial/ethnic communities do not stand on commonground, not in the seminaries and not in this group. Our ground as women of different colors will be even less common if *God's Fierce Whimsy* serves the interests of the holders of power in the establishment of theological education.

The divisions between us are cemented, historically, in the ways we are related to those white male guardians of power, privilege, and prestige in the world/church. As Bell Hooks contends,

> Animosity between black and white women's liberationists was not due solely to disagreement over racism within the women's movement; it was the end result of years of jealousy, envy, competition, and anger between the two groups. Conflict between black and white women did not begin with the 20th Century women's movement. It began during slavery. The social status of white women in America has to a large extent been determined by white people's relationship to black people. It was the enslavement of African people in colonized America that marked the beginning of a change in the social status of white women. Prior to slavery, patriarchal law decreed white women were lowly inferior beings, the subordinate group in society. The subjugation of black people allowed them to vacate their deposed position and assume the role of a superior.
>
> Consequently, it can be easily argued that even though white men institutionalized slavery, white women were its most immediate beneficiaries. Slavery in no way altered the hierarchical social status of the white male but it created a new status for the white female. The only way that her new status could be maintained was through the constant assertion of her superiority over the black woman and man.[3]

We cannot understand our present situation apart from our past. The situation described by Hooks has evolved over the last hundred years in different, concrete sociopolitical forms. The most public form, legal segregation, has served to perpetuate the historical dynamic between black and white women. As a racial group, white women have benefited in various ways from the subordinate racial status of black women. In examining the roots of our divisions, we need always to pay careful attention to the ways our relations, as women to women, have been set in place—structured—according to where we fit in the world of white male social and economic relations.

It is one thing to say that our problems are, historically and structurally, the products of what white men have expected from us (more often than not, simply done to us), regardless of our color; it is another thing to complain that men are to blame for the difficulties women have in relating to one another. However true this may be politically, it is no less true that, as women, we are going to have to find the solutions to our own problems—if, indeed, we expect any transformation in the structures of our lives. To expect that men of any color will, in great numbers, change their attitudes toward women and become less sexist, simply because they are nice fellows of goodwill, is farfetched. Education is never a matter simply of teaching ideas. It always involves struggle between and among what we perceive to be competing interests.

The control of society by the dominant culture group will not change until women and people of color no longer tolerate the injustice and oppression of sexual, racial, and economic exploitation. What this means is that all men of color and all women will continue to be rewarded and punished on the basis of where we stand in relation to white male interests. Consequently, women of all colors and all people of color will continue to find ourselves at odds with one another—women vs. women, black vs. black, Hispanic vs. Hispanic, as well as white women vs. men and women of color and men of color vs. women of color and white women. Our divisiveness is a social structure that benefits white male economic interests. And nobody has any stake in changing this situation except those whose lives are marginalized, trivialized, co-opted, disvalued, and often rendered null and void by it.

The situation that has set us against one another will not be changed—and women will continue to hate, distrust, or fear one another as much in the twenty-first century as we do now—unless we ourselves are willing to struggle for the transformation of this debilitating dynamic that keeps us apart and, in so doing, holds the unjust power in place. To struggle to this end is to involve ourselves in revolutionary work. For us to become woman-identified (and we do not use the term here as the equivalent of lesbian) in our social relations would bring down the sacred canopy of male culture. To the extent that in speaking of women, we are speaking emphatically of women of all colors, our solidarity as women would surely signal the death of white culture as normative for all people. The domination by white male culture depends on "keeping women in their places"—white women in one place, women of color in other places, women separate and alienated from one another.

We seek to become woman-aware, woman-identified. And so we ask ourselves what educational risks we incur if we dare to speak our faith and doubts, our rage and alienation, our dreams and fears candidly—perhaps offensively—enough to drive sharp wedges between us. This is a false question, because the impediments are between us already, long before we came together to teach and learn, driven in mercilessly by generation upon generation of forces and attitudes we have inherited and which we, naively and faithlessly, have chosen to believe that we can avoid personally by right thought, right belief, and right behavior.

We know this. Either we work in this predicament as our educational/theological praxis or we will not work at all.

TRUST-BUILDING

As women, the possibility of building community among us is contingent on our capacity to value our lives as the beginning of relating to one another across the chasms that separate us. It is no wonder that much of the most exciting, inspirational relating between women of different cultures takes place among artists, such as Audre Lorde and Adrienne Rich, women of different racial/ethnic cultures whose wellspring of creativity is the value they accord to their own life experience in relation to other women's lives. These women represent to us the possibility of women working together across racial/ethnic lines, because each treats the other and herself with such respect. These women tell their own stories with integrity, candor, and the expectation that they will be taken seriously because they take themselves seriously and because they understand that the meaning of their own lives is stretched and deepened in the relational interaction between their lives and the lives of others.

A good artist/theologian is able to envision the interactive dynamics of human experience and to see the essential connectedness between her life and the lives of other women and men. She knows that her words, or the strokes of her brush, convey not simply her own truth. At the same time, she knows that unless she speaks her own truth, she will fail to make the connections with the lives of others. Her relating will lack integrity, and others will know this. It is the kind of relating none of us can afford to trust, because either it wastes our time or it rips off our own relational needs and energies.

Black women, Hispanic women, white women, Jewish women, Christian women, postchristian women, lesbian women, and straight women have much to gain in sharing our stories. But we do not propose for a minute that this can simply happen. Yes, the sharing of our lives is indispensable to community, which in turn is fundamental in the doing of constructive theology. We believe it is imperative that we move in this direction with one another. Yet such sharing, such revelation of both oneself and one's God, is not easy work.

It presupposes at least two conditions. First, we ourselves must know our own stories. We have, after all, been educated in white male culture, in which to forget oneself is to reap reward. We must learn to remember our own lives, to tell ourselves about ourselves. This may be especially difficult for most white women, certainly white women of the upper social strata, whose experiences have been dulled by the false lessons that race, gender, and class are irrelevant to our lives and our relationships. For women of color and for poorer white women, the capacity to remember, to repeat the tales of where we have been and what we have felt and what has happened, has been a key to our survival. We find it less difficult to remember what we might say about ourselves. But sharing our lives in this way requires, second, a sense of trust that is by no means automatic, even among women who genuinely seek community. Among us white women and racial/ethnic women, sharing our experiences requires a willingness to be vulnerable and to risk saying things that our friends may not want to hear, which means risking a rupture in whatever good feelings have characterized who we are together. And this means risking a coming-apart of even the barest fragment of community we have shared to this point.

When women who have existed on the underside of history risk speaking, the anxiety that grips us all is formidable. The risk is that we who are white will withdraw, sucked into a guilt-induced catatonia, unable or unwilling either to receive or to give, to appropriate what our sisters of color are trying to tell us about themselves or to speak to these women about our lives as "lioness" or as consort with "the enemy." And the risk for those of us who are black or Hispanic is that we will be, yet again, disappointed, subverted, unheard, co-opted, trivialized, done in by white women who, however unwittingly, do not comprehend the gravity of our presence and our words and who fail to see how costly the premium is that we put on the possibility of trusting white women.

What is at stake for us racial/ethnic women is survival, not being politically correct. We have to trust white women colleagues to understand this even if they do not fully comprehend in what sense their survival is, finally, also at stake. As Ada says, "The Anglo culture only turns to us for our food and our music, and I'm tired of being a circus!" She elaborates.

> Something that is true about Hispanic women in relation to Anglo women and men is the enormous sense of worthlessness one feels. Even when they are telling me that they respect me and I'm good, the fact is that the way we are, the way we do things, our values, are never good enough for Anglo women to consider adopting them for themselves, for them to become normative or at least acceptable by society at large. We are invited to participate, to share, but never to help define.

Whenever we racial/ethnic women open our mouths around members of the dominant race and ethnic background, we risk coming up once more against feelings of worthlessness, as if our words are silence and will be heard, recorded, and read through white sensibilities, which have been manifest historically toward racial/ethnic people as narrow and self-serving.

In this project, we risk having our names attached to a book that will be read by many as a white women's book. More exactly, we risk pooling our lives—our stories and our time, what we fear and what we hope for—with those of white women, who—in the final analysis, when our project enters the arena of public scrutiny—will be the most likely recipients of professional reward and the least likely victims of professional punishment for what we have shared. Such is the character of racism and ethnic prejudice in theological education.

70

This racism is a constant specter, looming large over our attempts to share our lives, to trust white women, and to experience the utopic possibility of the women's community we write about. All of which is to say that we know how enormously difficult it is to begin with sharing our lives in the building of community. We also know that, unless we can muster the courage to do so, the courage that grows in our self-confidence as black, as Hispanic, and as white, we might as well throw in the towel and quit paying lip service to love, justice, the world, or God.

Each of the women in Mud Flower experienced some tension with at least one of the others during our work. Some of these tensions are evident in what we are presenting; others are not so apparent. In one case, the strain experienced between a member of the collective and the rest of us was so severe that this member withdrew. In other cases, our tensions did not result in a loss of membership but rather forced us to alter the shape of our project— our words, as well as the way the collective is organized. All the tensions between and among us have required trust-building, an easier process for certain ones of us than others. In most instances, where we have been able to name the difficulties together and explore them, our trust has grown stronger. At this point, it is our choice, each of our choices in relation to the group as a whole, what we do, and do not, reveal about ourselves and our relational dynamics for public consumption.

We say this for two reasons. First, we want to suggest that it is always the choice of each person in the educational situation to determine how much is enough in terms of self-revelation. We do not bring a let-it-all-hang-out mentality to our work here or elsewhere in theological education. Rather we bring conviction that we must realize enough and share enough about ourselves to literally inspire the learning process and the theological adventure. Second, we tell you, the reader, that we are choosing, for the purposes of publication, what to say and what not to say, in order to tell you also that we have struggled in some ways that are not apparent or explicit, yet which do, in fact, inform our work. This seems to us likely to be true in all liberation theological processes, and in the best educational experiences. What can be passed on, via publication or other public testimony, is always only an image of the real thing. We believe this also is an important theological confession and affirmation.

BARRIERS TO OUR SANITY, SISTERHOOD, AND SALVATION

Because many of our relational dynamics across racial/ethnic and class lines, as well as across the other chasms of our lives, are so painful and complex, we have thus far only hinted at the specifics of our brokenness. Even that much has been copious. But here we move more particularly into some of the difficult places of our work together. We do so because we believe that the dis-ease in our body, as Mud Flower, as well as in the larger theological body within which each of us works, spreads to spoil the possibilities of constructive theologizing among us. Our capacities to teach and learn are blocked unless we name the demons, thereby enabling ourselves to loosen their stranglehold on our lives and our learning.

We present here a few of the dynamics operative among us. We recognize them as steady-flowing undercurrents in the seminary classroom, discussion groups, refectory, faculty meeting, search committee, chapel. None is unrelated to the others. All are pieces of a whole and ugly cloth, stapled together over time by white men in power and those who help hold this power in place. Insofar as our lives reveal these vicious dynamics of control, this abuse of power, we ourselves are servants of The Man who is hostile to human well-being and contemptuous of the whole creation/creative process.

DYNAMICS OF WHITE SUPREMACY, ECONOMIC EXPLOITATION, AND MALE SUPERIORITY

Whom do we worship with our lives? In whose service do we study, act, re-act, and aspire to shape our lives, relationships, and work? Every day, in the smallest, most minute ways, whose interests have we been taught to respect and to bow before? Whose ways have we learned to appreciate as most in keeping with whatever is true, excellent, competent, deserving of an A / a "High Pass" / a

"Credit with Distinction"? As whose servants are we assured of getting ordained, getting a job, getting a raise, getting promoted, getting tenured, getting published, getting a man, keeping a job, keeping a man, keeping our reputations as excellent students, master teachers, loving wives, good mothers, fine priests, competent ministers, able pastors, brilliant scholars, outstanding blacks, exceptional women, distinguished Hispanics?

We confess to you, as we do to ourselves, that we must be on the alert every waking moment of our lives not to succumb to the incalculable pressures to bend and break ourselves in the service of this idol. To succumb would be perpetuating with our lives the worship of the color white, the elevation of men above us all, and the adoration of material gain as it represents our moving up, having value, being able to feel and act like we are worth something.

We name these demons, these structures of evil.

Racism. We are afraid of the dark, or so we have been taught that we must be—for our own good—regardless of our race. People of color are not responsible for white racism. White people brought white racism into being and white people are responsible. White racism is a white evil. But all people, of all colors, are affected by racism—its destructive internal consequences (such as self-hatred among racial/ethnic people), as well as its more publicly conspicuous manifestations (such as the anti-affirmative action movements currently abroad in the land).

No one needs to convince any of us that racism is a fundamental theological problem, an impediment both to living life in the world of God and to articulating the approximate conditions in which this life can be lived fully. All of us are acutely aware of this problem, and yet we heard ourselves voicing feelings and insights that surprised us.

Beverly speaks with intensity of how hard it is to move beyond liberalism. She discusses

> this business of getting into the pain of what white people have done to black people; of sitting here in this room realizing that even so, you don't hate me so much as to write me off. Realizing that you women of color take me seriously, and knowing how much it has cost you to get to that point. And then I recall

the good society I was raised to believe in. And that's a painful process—not the same pain for me as for those victimized by the society, but the pain of having to own lies. The pain of knowing that much of my life has been built on lies. And this, to me, is very hard. It requires me to recognize that my mother's liberal idealism wasn't good enough; my mother's real fine values were untested and hadn't been worked out in a realistic awareness of what society really is. It means saying that the best of my own past wasn't really deep enough and honest enough.

Picking up on this theme of expectation—of what we white women grew up believing the world ought to be, and therefore, *is*— Bess responds:

I was the only black woman in my feminist issues class. White women began talking about what the church had done to them, and this whole business of women seeming shocked at the way men are treating them. I shook my head at first and I think I asked the question, "Oh, did you really ever think you were included?" And then somebody said, "Yes." And I remember being stunned for days, because I was looking at it from my experience. And I've always known I'm not included. I guess I'm just beginning to realize this real difference between women in white and black cultures. Just realizing how terribly painful it must be for white women to be so shocked, and so trusting, you know. The fact of exclusion comes as no surprise to black women.

White women trusting. Racial/ethnic women suspicious. Difficult as it may be for white women to hear and see and believe ourselves excluded from ordination, jobs, professional affirmation, we black and Hispanic women do not expect to be heard or seen or taken seriously by members of the dominant racial/ethnic groups, male or female.

And so it is harder for us black and Hispanic women to expect as much from the white women here in this group as they probably expect from us, in terms of how much of great value can be shared and taken to heart. Often it is not a matter of what is actually given, but rather of what people expect to receive and, therefore, of what we are open to receiving. And a question that every racial/ethnic woman brings into every racially mixed group of women is, how open will I be? Because when white women and women of color get together in white racist society, we women of color know it is in the interest of our survival, simply that, to be no more open to receiving, no more open to the possibilities of personal transformation, than the white women with whom we now share this opportunity.

All of us tell stories of when we first became aware of racism in our lives. For the black women, knowledge of racism as a reality comes with being born.

For Ada, the realization of racism in her life has evolved. In Cuba, as a member of a middle-income family, the interplay of race and class factors bestowed upon her opportunities that translate into privileges. But when she came to the United States at age eighteen Ada began to experience, firsthand, life on the underside of racial/ethnic privilege.

Here in this country Hispanics are on neither the top nor the bottom of the racial heap. But political and economic power in the United States is not only white; it is a power fastened, historically, in the roots of Anglo imperialism. In relation to the dominant Anglo culture, Ada's Hispanic world is perceived by the holders of power to be "outside," a culture and a people of less value than the lighter skinned, lighter eyed representatives of the English crown. Unlike the rest of us, Ada speaks alone, by herself, as a member of an ethnic group that is in our society the recipient of gross trivialization, stereotyping, and racial prejudices, harbored and perpetuated by both whites and blacks.

For the white women, awareness of racism came gradually, for each white woman, in a different way. For Nancy it was through the riots on college campuses in the 1960s as well as in her work with the YWCA, in which she was first asked the questions, "For you, what does being white mean?" and "For you, what does being black mean?" For Carter, it was through her early childhood experiences with maids and yardmen, and later through the civil rights movement in the sixties (a formative experience for all of us). For Bev, it was through her mother's respect for the one black woman who lived in Luverne, Minnesota—but also through her religious tradition and culture's "virulent anti-Semitism." For Mary, her thinking about racism grew in her awareness of the Great Sioux Indian Reservation, which, in her white Minnesota culture, represented worthlessness. Later, her consciousness was sharpened in higher education, the civil rights movement, and antipoverty work.

In our discussion of racism, most of us were mindful also of something we had learned about lighter shades being "better" than darker shades of blackness. Katie recalls:

> This was very real for me. If you looked at *Who's Who* or who went to professional college, they were all very light complexioned. And if a man was black, he'd make sure he married a light woman so that the children would be lighter, or so he'd think. And even in dating, you had to be careful, because you wanted the children to have straighter hair. And it was talked about. Even if you were born a low class black, you had a better chance for mobility if you were lighter. At least in my community you did.

Bess concurs:

> Think of the slave woman, and the high and mighty money the mulatto slave woman brought on the market. I think it has to do with the value men, white men, put on the white woman; and the lighter skinned black woman is put in competition with the white woman.

Carter nods, recalling her own white southern heritage.

> I grew up hearing the assumption voiced that lighter skinned black people were more acceptable—more intelligent—because they had white blood. For that matter, even if they weren't light skinned, if black people were intelligent, it was because, somewhere, there was some white blood.

And Bev adds,

> I was thinking just now that when I was growing up in Minnesota every light-skinned black person I knew was a professional. These are the people that mediated the meaning of

racism to me. I noted them and I would have to say that I think
I could hear them because they were light skinned. That realization has never really hit me before.

Not only among blacks and whites in the United States does this
perception function to divide people from other people, but also, as
Ada points out, among Europeans and people of European descent.

If you're from a Northern European background, you're pure.
I mean, that's a pure Aryan race person. But if you're from one
of those more spontaneous, boisterous, colorful places in
Southern Europe . . .

Lightness, whiteness, purity, goodness, God. Please be very clear
that we do not, in any conscious or intentional way, love or pray to—
open ourselves to—a white god. But this is the deity to whom we
are expected, by most people who hold power in the world/church,
to pay our respects, to give our lip service, to offer our life service.
The bottom line is that regardless of race, ethnicity, or gender, we
are expected to live in the economic structures built by white,
privileged men. The word God has become a symbol of the aspirations of these white privileged men in Western culture. This white
privilege is racism, one of the surest foundations upon which all
mainline Christian theology and Christian education is constructed
and maintained to this day.

Classism. Nothing has been as difficult for us to talk about as
economic injustice, especially as we attempt to understand our own
lives in terms of class. This is because racial/ethnic oppression and
sexism are constitutive elements of class dynamics in the United
States. Dark-skinned immigrants to this country who were considered of the privileged class back home because of their economic
status are not allowed to move in class circles parallel to those they
frequented in their mother countries. Likewise, male privilege in
the sex-segregated labor market and in the sex-stereotyped roles in
the home give men access to wider economic opportunities. Therefore, one of the effects of racial/ethnic oppression and sexism on

class is to create a permanent underclass. Attitudes that denigrate minority groups and women ensure that however low men or white women fall in the economic order, they will always have someone under them.

It has also been difficult for us to talk about class because in the United States no single sociopolitical (hence, psychological) force is as thoroughly mystifying to us all. Not only are we not taught economics, except the obsolete and impractical theories of most college texts; we are trained not even to want to learn anything about the meaning of wealth in this society—except how to get it, as if this were within the realm of possibility for 98 percent of the population, which it is not.

But we know that no analysis of either sexism or racism can be adequate without the realization that the hidden realities of class contribute to both in often confusing and contradictory ways. Do an upper-middle-class woman and a poor woman have something in common that can unite them despite their different economic strata? Or is that merely a pious hope? Does the experience of economic oppression in any way parallel that of racial/ethnic prejudice?

To be able to do certain things requires access to levels of money, leisure, connections, and resources that are not available to all and that are, more often than not, taken for granted by those who are privileged to have them. For example, few of our male colleagues have reflected about their class position in fundamental relationship to the theological enterprise in which they have been engaged—another way in which the particularities of experience have been erased from our theological consciousness. But scholarly work costs money. Consider, for example, how often in book prefaces we see thanks expressed to foundations, grants, and wives for "making possible" the work that follows.

This very project on which we now work is a case in point. It is happening because the Association of Theological Schools has given us money for our travel, phone calls, typing, mailing, and fees. Few, if any, of us could afford to do this on our own resources—although all of us have found the money to move through long and expensive processes of higher education. Few, if any, of us have simply "had" the money we have needed for our education. Like the vast majority of college and graduate students, we have shaped our formal educational journeys around our employment opportunities. And, in every case, we have been able to work, and able to go to school, because we have had access to employment, scholarships, financial aid, admission. This access—whether by means of friendship, or family ties, or personal references who are respected, or whatever—has been the ticket of entry into the places where we now work.

The concrete average salaries of most women and men are among the reasons we feel so passionately the need to discuss this issue. The average salaries for 1983 (U.S. Census Bureau) were $21,077 for men and $13,014 for women.[4] This is why men have a greater ability to pay expensive tuition bills in theological schools and greater chances of earning more when they complete their theological degree. (Currently a woman clergy's salary is two thirds that of her average male colleague.)

To have no money and no access to money is to be disempowered in our capacities to contribute to the world/church. Most people of all colors have to cope with this debilitating factor in their lives; but among women of all colors and all men of color, the incidence of economic disempowerment and, thus, disability in creative possibility is of staggering proportions.

It is hard for us even to know, much less discuss, the ways our own lives have been shaped by money, by having or not having access to it and by what significance it has had for us. It is tedious— and embarrassing—to try to articulate the sense in which, in relation to our gender and to our racial/ethnic cultures, money has gone into the formation of who each of us is, what we value, what we seek, what we do.

It is confusing because we can feel the differences in our experience without having reliable and critical ways to express and understand them. Anyone who has walked into a social occasion—or into a church—to find that her clothing is either significantly richer or significantly poorer than the clothing worn by others around her knows the feeling of not belonging. And every community has churches where the more affluent go and where the less affluent

79

go—naturally, of course. These distinctions in society and church embarrass us enough that we rarely talk about them out loud or honestly. They embarrass us because we sense that the size of our paychecks signals something about the way our work, our contributions, even our very selves are valued by those around us. And there is little, if anything, in our educational system or in our churches—in spite of their teaching that everyone is a child of God—that helps us see the danger of attaching our sense of self-worth to our ability to earn and enjoy financial resources. Nor are there readily available resources in theological education—or elsewhere in our society—that help us see the fallacy of connecting the size of our paychecks with real wealth. The fact is, in the United States, 2 percent of the population controls the wealth. The multinational corporate network shapes both our foreign and our domestic policy and, in so doing, the form of our daily lives.

Such issues become dazzlingly complicated when we connect them as black women and white women. Usually significantly underpaid in comparison with our male colleagues, we have few realistic expectations about the level of reward appropriate for our work. We may have wildly varying notions about how the economic world really works—as, for example, whether raises and promotions come automatically to those who deserve them because the system rewards merit that is obvious to those who have the power to give them; or whether you must constantly push, assert, demand. Even in this working group, we use different language to understand our economic situations. Some of us use Marxist-feminist analysis perhaps too glibly, reducing personal dynamics to theoretical generalizations. Others struggle to articulate our concrete experience and express misgivings with this sometimes tedious, technical language. All of us agree that we must challenge our dominant economic system, capitalism.

We have talked about class, specifically our memories of when we were first aware of class reality in our own lives. We share here two of our stories and an encounter, in our group, between these two women—one black, one white, both from poor families—as it illustrates the powerful, complex interplay of racial and economic oppression.

"Most of my father's brothers married much lighter women than my mother. So my mother was determined that we were going to be just as good as our first cousins. We were one of the few families in our community with a telephone, a television, and a streetlight in front of our house. Everyone who could not read or write came to our house for assistance.

"My mother was a staunch leader in the PTA; she conducted much of the business that had to be transacted between the white community and the black community; she was always speaking up, advocating. My mother, an Avon representative for more than twenty-eight years, also served as a champion of culture and decorum in my hometown. As a matter of fact my home church, which will be celebrating its twenty-fifth anniversary this year, was started in our kitchen.

"Class has always been a reality for me. Everybody in the community was poor. Everything was segregated. I didn't know we were poor, because we were all situated in the same place. But I did know I was going to college. I had known it since the beginning. Some of my cousins knew that college was outside their realm of possibilities. A college education was something my mother always believed in.

"During my senior year in college I did my student teaching in Rochester, New York. It was an exchange program between black southern colleges and the Monroe County school system. I volunteered to go because I had come to realize that it was a wide, wide world out there of which I knew nothing. I wanted to expand my horizons, to experience new realities. At the same time I applied to teach in upstate New York I signed up for a summer in Africa.

"I had a militant black nationalist pan-African consciousness which my mother identified as 'ultra black.' I wanted to go to Africa so badly I could taste it. I had no money or capital resources to make either of these dreams come true.

"A friend gave me a wardrobe of clothes so that I could do my student teaching. Some Presbyterian friends, who believed in my human potential, invested money in my trip to Africa. So after I completed my student teaching, I packed my bags for Africa. When the plane touched down on the West Coast of Africa, I experienced an ecstasy I had never known before. All of us screamed, hollered, cried and shouted. It was the most wonderful feeling I had ever known. We believed that we had returned to Africa in honor of our ancestors who wanted to but never could return home.

"Every Sunday while in Liberia my work team went to the beach. The most beautiful beaches I've ever seen. The water was pure blue. The coconut trees grew right to the coastline. Every Sunday I would walk for miles along the shore and collect sand dollars. They would often crumble and break, but I loved picking them up and seeing how many I could carry back to the village in one piece. In 1976 I found a place I could order a sand dollar made out of pewter. I bought it because I knew it wouldn't break. The memories of the mother continent are here to stay. And so I bring my sand dollar to share with you."

MARY'S PHOTOGRAPHS

"I found some old photographs in a box, and I bring them along because I'm very fond of the struggle I see in these pictures. The first one with my mother in it was taken in a place called Starvation Corners, for very good reasons. Here are my aunt and uncle and my mother dressed in their flour-sack dresses. And some others that show what it was like to be a person on a farm in the 1910s and '20s and '30s. Some of these less-yellow ones are coming into the later decades, sort of ending up there with me and my brothers. They are painful because that family got off Starvation Corners and significantly bettered itself eventually by moving into a small town, into what they all thought was a wonderful way to live, near the poverty line in rural Minnesota. Here's this house, which I hated. Let's see, they put plumbing in when I was about nine. It had the occasional light bulb hanging from the ceiling. My mother thought the house was absolutely wonderful because it didn't have the rats of the little shanty we had lived in before. So property is relative, which I didn't know until I was well out of there. I began to know, when we started school, that we didn't have the money other people had. That came out mostly in going on welfare, eating lots of baloney and cornbread. For about eight years after I ran away from home, I couldn't stand cornbread.

"My father retired in 1963 at the age of sixty-three and went on social security, and it was as though he had gotten a raise. We lived better between 1963 and the time when I ran away to go to college in 1968 than we ever had before. We had lots of screaming fights about money. My parents largely had their fights in the front yard, rather than quietly in the kitchen like everybody else's parents. In small-town Minnesota, the police often came in the middle of the night because my parents were disturbing the peace. What I later learned to treasure was the fact that I hadn't learned to hide conflict or pretend that it didn't exist or sweep it under the rug, like so many of my friends who grew up middle-class, whose families were concerned about appearances.

"I went to college against my father's will. He wanted me to be a typist because, as he used to say, typists earn as much as $60 a week. More than he made. But I knew I didn't want to type. And in college I discovered all these movements. I frequently say that this was the turning point in my life, because up until that point, I believed very much as you did, Katie [reference to an earlier conversation], that my family had done something which God was punishing us for. There had to be some specific sin, on the part of somebody, or some lack of merit that was the reason we were poor and other folks weren't. It was the antipoverty movement that taught it was not a question of merit but rather that this is just the way our society is structured. That was the beginning of my having some serious concepts about class. I remember reading Marx avidly in the sixties and being absolutely blown away, because he was describing the situation I knew very well.

"Now there is a corollary in this story about race, which is also very painful. I sometimes say, to express the racism of my hometown, that I had to leave Granite Falls and go to St. Paul in order to realize that I was living on the edge of the Great Sioux Indian Reservation. But that's not exactly true. That covers up the seamier side of my understanding, which is that I knew the Great Sioux Indian Reservation was there, because one of the things I felt was seamy about my father's drinking was that, among his drinking companions, were Indians from the reservation. That seemed to me at the time another sign of my family's worthlessness. And my own.

"And then in the sixties when I met black people, I thought that all black people were poor. Because of my own poverty, I identified with them. And I think also because of my birthmark, of not being an entirely white person myself, because of the bright pink spot on one part of my face. I immediately overidentified with every single oppressed group in this country.

"The last ten or twelve years of my experience of all this have been partly my trying to understand the ways in which I have overidentified with oppressed people and not stopped to see where structural differences in our experiences mean that my overidentification has been inappropriate."

In a subsequent session of our work, Carter remarks that, for her, racism and sexism were forces she actually became aware of before having any conceptual words or analyses to make sense of her experience. With classism, however, her intellectual understanding came first, and only then—very recently, in fact—has she begun to be aware of economic forces in her life and around her in the world. To this, Mary responds that her experience was quite different. The facts of economic injustice and male gender superiority were real to her long before she had any conceptual handles on them. But with white supremacy, her conceptual clarity, as it grew through her work and education, opened her to an awareness of racism in her own life. "My personal awareness of racism has come later," she says.

"I'm grateful for what you just said," Kate says to Mary, "because I've always had this feeling that, for you, racism always comes in third, behind gender and class. And for me it's always first. And I've never understood before why, for you, it's third."

"I hope you didn't hear me saying it's only a concept," replies Mary, "but I do think the directions of our learning make a big difference. Somehow, I think, we trust more deeply those things we experience first. Understanding racism experientially is very important to me, but I have to work very hard at it, and I try to do this."

"Well, I'm glad you illuminated for me how it works for you. That's helpful in my understanding you," continues Kate.

"I'm glad you brought this up," Mary says, "because I've had enormous learnings from you and yet I've always had this sense we weren't friends or that we didn't understand each other or that I was doing something that was offending you and that you were overlooking it. So I'm grateful too."

The conversation ends with Mary and Kate both stating again that they've felt this tension between them and that they've never felt close to each other, even though they've been working together in various groups, and at the same seminary, for years. Both reassert their relief that this dialogue may have enabled a somewhat more comfortable and creative working relationship.

We are grateful to these women for their candor. But what moves us, what is so striking here for us—besides the integrity of these women—is the lesson in how complex our interactions are as women, each with a story to tell, so strong, so fragile, each groping to understand her own life and those of others struggling with her in the tangles of class, race, and gender.

Sexism. We might assume that, among us, in our work on this project, there would be no sexism, no elevation of men to a place of privilege above us. Certainly, in one respect this is true. We are an all-female group, and one of the reasons we are is that we know how surely the entry of even one man into a feminist group (or any group of women) changes the dynamics. This happens because in a sexist society, no man and no woman can think and act entirely free of gender-role expectations, no matter how liberated any of us is.

Put the most feminist white, black, or Hispanic man—or feminist man from any racial/ethnic group—into Mud Flower and imagine how differently we would act. For a beginning, most of us would shut down, censoring ourselves. Some of us would, unwittingly, "play to the man," bond with him, not so much out of a need to be with him for our sake but rather out of our socially induced inclinations to try to make him comfortable, help him feel wanted, assure him it is OK to be here. All of us would be aware of the man in whatever we chose to say or not to say. To that extent, all of us would be male-aware, rather than fully female-aware, in our work. This is, in a microcosm, how we live our lives in a sexist society: aware of the man and, as often as not, playing to him—for his approval (in our nonfeminist consciousness); or to make him feel OK (despite our feminist consciousness).

We do not have to worry about this dynamic in the immediacy of our work together on this project. And yet, to what extent does our male-awareness—our knowledge or fantasies of what men will think when they read this book—affect what we are saying and writing or even what we are able to remember about our lives? Male theologians are watching over our typewriters. Our Father/God may be bending our capacities to feel and think. We are concerned about our own professional/relational futures. Is the Great White/Hispanic/Black Sugardaddy deciding even now—as we sort out our reflections and analyses, our lives and the meaning of our lives—which of us, if any, will pay the price or reap the reward? To the extent that these concerns are pushing any of us, consciously or not, to speak less than honestly or to spend our time on agendas that are not really ours, then sexism is alive and well here and now among us. In that case, what we are writing will more likely serve the interests of men rather than of women.

We do not believe this is the case, at least in any major way. But we realize that assumptions about male superiority can be operative among feminists and can weaken immeasurably the value and integrity of our work on behalf of ourselves and one another.

DYNAMICS OF DISEMBODIMENT, INVISIBILITY, AND LACK OF PARTICULARITY

As we have noted, these dynamics are related structurally to race/ethnic privilege, sexism, and classism. Often we experience them as consequences of white, male, and/or economic privilege. We detect a durable thread running through the dynamics of disembodiment, invisibility, and our failures to realize our particularities. The connecting link is body, the incarnate, visible, tangible substance of who we are. For anybody of any race or class, the first liberating act is slipping, or leaping, into an awareness that she, or he, is *somebody*. Not a no-body, a somebody. Not a no-name: "My name is Ada—and I give you my hand." At the close of one of our sessions, we participated in a wicca ritual, in which each named herself and offered her hand to the woman beside her. The power to name ourselves, the world, and God is especially critical for us to find and claim as women, because we have not been the namers. We have been named, labeled, categorized, and branded—we, and all that we have felt and thought and done. We have not understood the specific value of who each of us is—the value of what we do, feel, think.

Ironically, because the body is not valued by most men with social power, one of the names women have been given is "body," and another name imposed upon us is "bad." For that reason, in order to believe that we are not bad, in order to feel good about ourselves, we have learned to feel as if we are not *really* bodies. In "truth," in "essence," in "spirit," we are good because we are no-body. No bodies with no names of our own choosing. And what we may feel or think, dream or desire, do or refuse to do, means nothing in particular.

In servitude to a Spirit whose being is said to be the antithesis of body, we have been stripped of our bodies/ourselves, deprived of our names and our histories, and appreciated to the extent that we have played our gender roles gladly and efficiently under the veil of men's lives.

We name these demons with a vengeance.

Disembodiment. Related closely to gender oppression, illusions of disembodiment are constructed by men in power in order to protect themselves (that is, their minds) from contamination by feelings (that is, their relational needs). In this context we women have learned to be no-bodies in the most literal sense. Positioning themselves above us as our spiritual head, and projecting their sensuality and their sexuality onto us (women = body = sexual being), white male theologians have functioned historically as disembodied agents of abstract ideas. The less a theological idea is a turn-on, the more profound it is; the more dispassionate a theology, the more brilliant. And we have learned well that, if we are to be considered excellent theologians, we too must act/think/write as if we are no-bodies. Or so these masters of control think. In fact, most white men do not have any idea, even an abstract notion, of how transparently phallic their language and behavior are—driving, penetrating, one-upping each other, and constructing cosmic systems in which their gods act the same way.

The double effect of our education in these systems is to have created no less a schizoid self-image among women than among men. We are both theological no-bodies and, potentially, the warm, receptive incubators in which men's ideas about God, world, themselves—and us—can be shaped. In both cases, women cannot experience our own sensuality—our creative juices and sexual power—without incarnating the very God/ess who will dance on The Man's altars and bring Him tea and honey and make Him very nervous.

And this, we affirm, is exactly what is happening among us. This knowledge of our intellectual/spiritual power as rooted in our feelings and passions is new among us white women from the traditions of Northern Europe. It is a way of being in touch with our bodies/ourselves that we black and Hispanic women have never entirely lost, to the extent that we have never been completely out of touch with our people.

Not that black or Hispanic male theologians will own up to it. When it comes to the beauty and holy power of sexual being as actually creative and as a resource of potent theological insight, most black and Hispanic males, like their white counterparts, have blocked themselves up and cut themselves off. Sensuality, after all, is too much "like a woman." Too antiintellectual. And most surely an arena of nonspiritual fantasy/activity.

This is where straight men and closeted homosexual men have bonded together, clinging to the top of the pyramid. Failing to feel any movement below the neck as sacred, these brothers of all colors have one thing in common: an ability to look down on women and gay men as, at best, trivial (touchy-feely, emotional, irrational, etc.), and, at worst, debased (dirty, pagan, whores, dykes, fags, etc).

And we have not escaped this cursed perception of ourselves and one another. We are no strangers to this disembodied sense of ourselves. And we are no strangers to one of its most egregious corrollaries: homophobia, currently one of the most commonplace and devastating diseases besetting theological education. People hate queers because we embody what is, from traditional cross-cultural Roman Catholic and Protestant perspectives, a "queer" embodiment of sexuality: We embody and embrace our sexuality as good. And this is an odd thing to believe, much less to demonstrate in one's life.

Along with classism, sexuality—our own, including our homophobia as both lesbians and straight women—has been the most difficult topic of conversation among us. We have been able to discuss and analyze sexuality as an issue, but we have avoided talking much about our own experiences as sexual beings. Each time we have begun to discuss our sexualities, we have immediately preempted our conversation with lunchtime, or time-to-move-on-to-something-else time, or just plain silence. We are, in this sense, a remarkably typical body of theological educators and students. When it comes to sexuality, we shut up.

Certainly this reflects our experience in church and seminary. With few exceptions, whenever the silence around sexuality is broken—as it is being broken by both the women's movement and the gay/lesbian movements—the response of ecclesiastical and academic authorities has been to hustle the lid back onto the cauldron, which, they fear, will bubble over and contaminate the general moral character of the institutions—or, at least, its public relations.[5]

But we know as well as we know our own names here in this group that this conspiracy of silence is, quite simply, a conspiracy to cover up the truths of human life as it is being lived throughout the seminaries and the churches and the world. It is a conspiracy to avoid any actual knowledge or love of God/ess and any theology or education that would actually serve the well-being of either human or divine life. We denounce emphatically the antisexual out-of-touchness with self and other that characterizes nearly all theology being done by straight men and closeted homosexual men of whatever color/culture. This seems to us an outrageous way to teach and share a religion of incarnation.

Invisibility. As we continue to learn among ourselves, we are the victims of what is done to us—in this instance the rendering invisible of white, black, and Hispanic women's lives, histories, and contributions. We are, however, not only victims; we are able to do to one another what is done to us.

Well into our work, Ada wrote to Bev and Mary, her professors in a feminist ethics class at Union Theological Seminary. As the only Hispanic among black and white women in this course, Ada had felt invisible, as if her own particularity and that of her people had fallen between the cracks of white and black experiences. She had been a vocal participant and had spoken of her life and work, but the cross-cultural interests and emphasis in the class had seemed consistently to be exclusively on black culture. Mary and Bev acknowledged that, for each of them, their desires to do some justice to the ethical dimensions of black women's lives had been a priority.

As it was, Ada's experience in the class reflected the ambience of the seminary itself, from a Hispanic perspective.

> I've never felt as invisible as I have been at Union as a Hispanic. I mean, in the Roman Catholic Church, well, they have to deal with us because we're about 33 percent of the church. But at Union, there's five of us. And I've never felt so little. It's really like you're just lying in this cage. For me, it's been the most blatant sense of racism I've ever suffered. Usually that sense comes and goes; but at the seminary, it's been constant. I have felt myself consistently dealt with on a racist basis, because it has been as if I were not there. Feeling as if no one, or very few, can see you, or hear you, or even knows that you're there. And this is in spite of the few blessings, I mean, like you, Bev, and Mary.

Ada's experience in this project reflects the invisibility she experiences at Union. She has reminded us white and black women a number of times that her life has been shaped by neither white nor black U.S. culture. She has repeatedly indicated the need to talk not only about racism but also about ethnic prejudice. Ada has felt that she continuously has to remind us of the particularity of her experience and the need for such particularity to be considered an intrinsic element of this project. Her experience represents acutely the distress each of us has felt, time and time and time again, in our work as seminary faculty and students.

In many of our schools, we have come to a point at which women's courses and black courses, Third World courses, and offerings in such subjects as Latin American liberation theology are taught and taken around the edges of basic theological studies. Hispanic courses are hardly ever found. We have entered a period in which feminist, black, Hispanic, and other "special interest" resources are listed somewhere in the bibliographies of certain courses and in which the most progressive professors might include a session or two at the end of the semester on feminist, black, or other liberation perspectives. None of us has ever had a session or two specifically on Hispanic perspectives.

But for women's lives and history—women past or women present—to be regarded as essential to theological studies? For black history to be regarded as indispensable to any understanding of the church in the United States? For Hispanic, Native American, Asian, and African cultures to be regarded as critical forces in the shaping of Christian thought, practice, and politics?

We have barely begun the theological/educational conscientization process necessary to open the eyes and the minds of those who teach and learn. As it is, we remain invisible, or, where we have broken through in small places, we stand at the edges of theological education, barely visible, and then only to those who are looking for us.

Avoidance of our particularities. The most odious and most simple device by which male theologians blot out the lives of women and by which white theologians wipe out the histories of racial/ethnic people is the universalizing away of our particularities. As Valerie Saiving suggested, pride may not be a sin among women, at least in the same way as it is among men.[6] Similarly, when Martin Heidegger made his case for "being towards death," he seemed oblivious to many women's experience of being towards birth.[7] Saiving called into question the tendency of such theologians as Reinhold Niebuhr to generalize their experiences in doctrines that do justice, they assume, to all people's experiences. The Heideggerian assumption is another example of what feminists perceive to be the implicit arrogance of much malestream theology. Such terms as the human condition, the absolute, and the truth, are likely to convey a failure on the part of theologians to recognize the diversity and relativity of cultures, conditions, and experiences that constitute the vast array of human life. This strange claim to know what is

91

true for or about everyone is akin to the tendency of "intelligent" men, as the old adage goes, to "learn more and more about less and less until they know everything about nothing." And this is precisely our grievance: To trivialize our particularities and diversity of experiences is to come up with virtually nothing—about anybody or anything, any event or any process, any feeling or any desire, that is real.

For this reason it is understandable why many men would avoid taking seriously the stories we women tell about our lives; and it is reasonable that many white people would shut down their senses to our histories as people of color. It is much easier, much less hassle, to go on our way devising theoretical schemes about what the Almighty wills or does eternally and everywhere for everyone than to find ourselves stumped by considering carefully the possibility that this is *not* the way it goes in everyone's life, and perhaps not even the way it goes in a lot of folks' lives—like lots of women, for example, or lots of Hispanics.

We women are learning how to speak the particularities of our lives and how to hear those of others. We are learning how to engage in dialogue. The details of our lives, the significance of our stories, the value of our histories cannot become clear to us except in dialogue. The learning process is never simply a monologue. Carter maintains that this has been an important lesson for her.

> Like so many white women, I've gone on the assumption that, if I'm going to relate to black women, I've got to sit there and listen to what black women tell me about their experiences, as if I have no right to speak. I've felt that, because I'm part of the dominant race, I have nothing to say that could possibly be valuable to you racial/ethnic women. So I came believing that my business in this educational situation is to learn and yours is to teach. It has begun to dawn on me that that's not what it's all about.

To this, Kate adds:

> Well, black male theologians put that model out there too: "You have to hush and listen to me." And that's problematic,

not only for white people like you, but also for us black women. Because it translates into this: I've been oppressed harder than anybody. Therefore you and everybody else are supposed to listen to me and support what I say. I guess it really is, basically, a white male device—being the "expert"—which black men have learned. And it's an effective way of blotting out black women's lives, that's for sure.

Beverly is adamant in her view that

this refusal to consider the particularities of different peoples and cultures is fundamental to the malaise of theological education. I'm serious. Most of the problems between and among us, most particularly those perpetrated against women of all colors and against black and Hispanic men, are related directly to the failure of most white men and many white women to deal with the particularities of our own lives, much less give a damn about the real life situation of anybody else.

She continues:

It's so obvious in academic culture. The white males in charge got where they are, probably starting at about age six, when they realized they weren't going to be the football players, and they started to study hard. They've accommodated their whole sense of what it means to *be*—male, white, intellectual, what it means to be, period—to a very narrow perception of reality, namely, academic culture. And they've fought their way through, competitively, aspiring all the way to make it. And it worked, at least to a degree, for them. And they live in it, generalizing this narrow reality, which makes it possible to deny there is any such thing as *particular* experience. After all, what is important except their "universal wisdom"? And who could possibly know more than they do about the world? And where else, outside their own academic circle, could they have real interaction with the wisdom of the world?

And then we come along, and say, "No, no, no." What they assume is, "The poor dears don't understand" or "They've missed the real point of the importance of all this," when, in fact, we understand all too well. We are interested in a depth and caliber of critical analysis that most of them lost interest in as soon as they dubbed themselves and each other the "experts" and the "real" knowers.

By failing to take the details of their own lives with critical seriousness as a theological resource, many white men in academia not only cut themselves off from vital wellsprings of theological competence but also shut the door on those of us who insist that we cannot know or speak of God at all outside the concrete and daily praxis of who we are and what we do.

OTHER DYNAMICS OF ALIENATION

White idealism in relation to racial/ethnic women. We use the word idealism here rather than liberalism, because none of us, either white or racial/ethnic women, is simply liberal in the classic, post-Enlightenment sense of the term. We are not merely bearers of goodwill to all people or true believers in an ethic of individual rights, responsibilities, opportunities, and "right-thinking."

But it becomes clear to us that we who are black and Hispanic tend, more consistently than our white members, to work on the assumption that conflict and struggle are intrinsic to any collegiality we are building among ourselves as women of different racial/ethnic groups. And we who are white—more often than our Hispanic and black sisters—are likely to fall back on process or on working things out, even on smoothing things over, so that we can get on with our task. Mind you, not that any of us does not intend to get on with our task, but white women, much in the style of our white academic counterparts, are able more readily than women of color to assume that the task will absorb the dynamics of our conflicts.

We black and Hispanic members of Mud Flower do not share this assumption. We believe that the best we can do—which is a great deal, as women of different racial/ethnic cultures—is to name the dynamics, speak candidly about them, acknowledge their significance as theological and educational tensions, and learn from one another, across our lines of color, more about how these dynamics affect us. This *is* our task.

94

We who are white members agree with this perspective and yet acknowledge that for many white feminists this is not the case. For many white feminists, the study of the dynamics and tensions in our life together appears to be the groundwork necessary to getting on with the task of resolving everything conceptually, if not in fact. Being able to resolve everything—that is what we mean by idealism. And all of us in Mud Flower submit that this has historically been a white, Euroamerican phenomenon, which many racial/ethnic people in our society have also internalized.

Most of us believe that this idealism is also a class-bound phenomenon that is likely to thrive in the praxis of upward educational or professional aspiration. In this respect, all of us—regardless of our racial/ethnic or economic histories—wear the imprimatur of white idealism. We have all been cultivated to various degrees in the ivy towers of the Academy in which the Idealism of White Male Culture reigns as King. Each of us is, to some extent, a daughter of this King.

What is terribly important to the work we are doing here is to show in what ways this predominantly white peace-seeking philosophy—lived and promulgated falsely as the only way to have and be a respectable educational or theological community—undermines the actual conditions of our teaching and learning.

Take Nancy, for example. Here among us is a white woman who spends a great deal of time and energy attempting to make justice a reality in her workplaces as well as in her own life. Reflecting on her coming into an awareness of racism, Nancy recalls:

> In the process of the university takeover, black students began talking about this particular university and its racism. Well, I literally didn't know what they were talking about. What I had known about racism, or what I thought I had known, had been the sort of overt bigotry I read about or saw on TV during sit-ins—overt, violent action on the part of whites toward blacks. And I didn't see it happening there in the school. I literally didn't know there was a problem. It's important for me to remember this, because the person who began to help me understand what was happening was a student whom I considered a friend and who considered me a friend. So when he talked to me about the takeover and told me I was totally

unaware, it was important. I remember that vividly, and also the YWCA, because it was through the YWCA that I first had any contact at all with people of color. There was a conference for students, a national YWCA conference, and the team of people who led it started us off by separating us by race. And the white women were asked to fill out a form that said, "For me, being white means . . . ," and "For me, being black means . . ." And then we went around and talked about being white. It was the first time I'd even thought about being white.

"And," Nancy continues, "it was the first time I began to understand that the process of thinking about being white needs to be a process of struggling with questions about power."

Similarly, Carter, Bev, and Mary began to understand the racism in their own lives—and the links between their white privilege and the structures of white power in U.S. society—as they were helped to understand by black friends, people who helped them interpret the uses and abuses of power in the world/church/seminaries.

Now, this is a salutary process, and we commend it, this way of learning and of strengthening our commitments to justice with the help of our friends. Our readers surely realize that this book has been made possible primarily by the durable bonds of friendship between and among us.

But education-through-friendship is a luxury, a possibility and a reality only under idealistic conditions—that is to say, only in those situations in which well-fed, well-clothed people agree, mutually, to participate in an exchange of ideas, stories, opinions, feelings.

These are the conditions under which this book is being written. These are the conditions under which the white women among us learned about racism. And this is well and good. But it is not the way the racial/ethnic women in Mud Flower learned about white supremacy. It is not the way Mary, Kate, or Bess learned about economic deprivation. It is not the way any of us learned about male superiority.

We offer this insight to underscore the tensions besetting us, here in our midst as well as everywhere in theological education. What happens when women, who live every day the reality of being female, come up against what feminist men have learned about sexism through their friends? We who are female are outraged by what feels to us—and is—the patronizing presumptuousness of men who have all the knowledge and none of the experience of what it means to have men's feet on your neck and men's hands fondling your bottom on the subway. When the reality of living in the oppression is met by the goodwill of the very people who represent the oppressor, what happens is that we realize our alienation. That is to say, we catch a glimpse of how fundamentally—structurally, institutionally, historically—alienated women and men are.

And here in this group, when the reality of being racial/ethnic women is met by the goodwill of white women—whose very desire for better relations between us represents to us the superficial racial harmony sought historically by white liberals—we women of color realize how truly alienated we are.

During one of our sessions, each of us brought to Mud Flower a symbol of when we first became aware of racism and classism. Bess's symbol is an old shoe, one just like her grandmother wore, with broad sturdy heels, thick black leather, and laces all the way up the ankle. This is a shoe made to be worn, a shoe built for walking, and a symbol for Bess of her lines of continuity with black women. Bess speaks soulfully of the vitality of historical consciousness, the necessity not to forget these women-past. It is always in relation to these black women that Bess articulates artfully the value of justice-making ("which is what we're here to do"), sound pedagogy ("which I've seldom experienced and hardly would recognize"), and sisterhood between women of color and white women ("which is possible, but not an easy thing").

Nancy also knows the difficulty of creating such sisterhood. She describes her experience in relation to a black feminist colleague whom we will call Carol. Alike in their commitment to racial justice, Nancy and Carol are unalike in their experiences of racial injustice. At one point in their work together, Nancy was in conflict with some white male seminary administrators about issues of sexism and racism. She assumed that Carol would support her and speak on her behalf. But Nancy did not check this out with Carol; she just assumed. It was as if Carol were simply her friend, colleague, feminist soulmate. It was as if color made no difference. White idealism is color-blind.

What Nancy failed to remember, Carol could not afford to forget:

historically, whenever white liberals have been at odds with each other, they've benefited from pulling in black folks to side with them, to bolster their positions. In this way black people have been used a great deal on behalf of white interests. In such a case the only sure loser is the black person.

It is not what Nancy would want. It is not what her friend Carol would lay at Nancy's feet personally. But it is the reality of black experience running into the naiveté of white idealism. It is best to recognize and name it; otherwise, alienation is bound to fester, and women like Nancy and Carol are bound to carry the wounds from such a misunderstanding with them into their work and relationships with women of different racial/ethnic groups.

White feminist difficulty in disagreeing with racial/ethnic women. Early in Mud Flower's work, we came up against a hard dynamic operative among us, having to do with our white members' racism. Our team was challenged by two black women to say in what ways Mud Flower is not supporting women's *separatism* from men. Are we not espousing simply the old ideology of the sixties when Black Power, for example, was "in" and white/black integration was "out"?

Mud Flower's work is radical. It is meant to send us and others digging for the roots of what theological education should be and can be. And we believe that among women this work, if it is to be excellent and worthwhile, must begin with the study of our lives, our women's lives, our lives as people who have separate histories from men, whatever our racial/ethnic heritage. Our women's stories are not separa*tist*, but they are different and they are separate, because we have been relegated historically to a separate space. Sometimes in theological education our stories need to be studied and cherished in a space separate (physically and/or mentally) from men.

The same thing is true, of course, of our lives as people of different racial/ethnic groups. There are times and places, and theological educators should recognize this, that we need to study with our own people the history of our own lives. We racial/ethnic women would like to suggest that white/Anglo/Northern European people might benefit from an honest study of their lives as the dominant racial/ethnic people in the world. And we women of different racial/ethnic groups would commend to all men a serious study of your own lives as *males* in our society.

The difficulty Mud Flower incurred in being challenged by women on this point was that the challenge was voiced by black women. In effect, this sent our white members into considerable confusion. Carter, in particular, as the convener of the team, experienced difficulty in saying to the two black women who were criticizing our project that she disagreed with their "separatist" charge, and moreover that she thought they were wrong in their analyses of the injustices of women's lives—including black women's lives. Mud Flower's racial/ethnic members were clear in our perceptions of these sisters as women without any kind of class-consciousness who were paying homage to the white men who hold the power in place.

We black and Hispanic women in Mud Flower finally had to tell the white women to quit catering to the perceptions of people simply because they were black. We racial/ethnic women had to say to Carter, our Anglo coordinator, that we perceived her hesitation to dispute black women's opinions as a racist hesitation.

By the end of our project, Carter would say that one of the most valuable learnings for her in Mud Flower was that she was beginning to be able to take racial/ethnic people seriously enough to disagree with them. One sign of this is always whether any white person can stand in opposition to a person of color whom she believes is wrong, knowing she will be perceived as racist by some people—including lots of black and white liberals. Mud Flower sensed that each of our white members grew stronger in this regard; and for that reason, that all of us—black, Hispanic, and white—wound up feeling more natural, more honest, and more at home together.

OUR STRUGGLE FOR SOLIDARITY

In our pain, diversity, and struggle, we need and want to be taken seriously. The tales of our lives bear witness to this deep need. One of the few things we are confident in speaking of as a universal is the need common to us all to be the subjects of our own lives. This is the thread that winds its way through our stories, the theme that cuts across the many lines which divide us, the core of all great stories, be they biblical narratives, or Aesop's fables, mythology, or history. If we study and share our lives, the message we hear echoed among ourselves is that all of us yearn to understand ourselves, and be understood, as valuable persons whose lives make a difference to us and to others, people able to live for self and others. Not to be so is to be dead, literally or figuratively. And we crave life.

If these are the stories upon which theological community is built, as we believe, then these stories provide the clue as to what we must be about in order to work together as a community of women in seminary, church, and society. Community grows in our acting together on behalf of our common need to be taken seriously as the subjects of our lives, to realize ourselves and be realized by others as valuable persons, seekers of life for ourselves and others. To act together on behalf of our own and others' need to be valued is to be in solidarity: advocates of justice for all women and men, including ourselves and our sisters and brothers whose cultures or life situations are different from ours.

In the biblical tradition, this solidarity is called love. As Ada notes, "It [love] is not a suggestion, but a commandment, a requirement, the sign of discipleship." (See Mark 12:28–34.) Much earlier, in the religious heritage shared by Jews and Christians, this same commandment was given to the people of Israel as the foundation of the law. The equation of love with solidarity seems to us not only appropriate but also imperative, because our use of the term solidarity makes explicit the content of the word love as distinct from a patronizing charity or affections of conciliation and goodwill. In solidarity, love means acting, putting ourselves on the line, with (not for) others, on behalf of the well-being—rights, dignity, needs—of all of us.

If we are really involved in loving, there is no question about it: we are bound to find ourselves in conflict with others and each other about whose well-being is being dismissed in order for some to believe that they are heirs to special grace. In the structures of human social relations that have historically dominated all major civilizations known to us, greed plays a mighty role. Greed is our desire to have more than others, to possess whatever we believe to be better than what others have, in order to bolster our sense of self-worth. Our willingness to love—to be in solidarity—is more often than not foiled by greed. It is in this praxis of "original sin" that we find ourselves both needing advocates and trying to be advocates for self and others. (We might add here that the assumptions structured into capitalism as an economic system serve only to exacerbate the extent to which our greed breeds injustice and holds in place every imaginable structure of evil, such as racism, sexism, and classism.)

This is our context, we who struggle to be lovers and community builders, theologians and educators. We cannot love one another— as friends and colleagues or as professional pastors, priests, counselors, teachers—if we are ignorant of, or indifferent to, our common need for dignity and rights, a common interest that does not license certain ones of us to be granted special privilege at the expense of others. When this granting of pet-status happens, as is the case when certain people are granted de facto status by "virtue" of race, gender, wealth, sexuality, religion, etc., we have no choice but to struggle against this status quo if we are committed earnestly to human well-being.

We assume that we will always be struggling for justice, in theological education as elsewhere. Our community of women—our vision, our fragments, our efforts to weave a more complete fabric— will draw its resources from our efforts to act, learn, and teach in solidarity. This is to suggest that our work together is constantly strengthened by our ability—as individuals and as representatives of different cultures and life situations—to "see through a glass dimly," and strive for that justice which is our life in the commonwealth of God.

At the end of our first weekend together, we joined in a litany written by a sister theologian, Delores S. Williams, which suggested our title.

One Woman: In my voice you will hear pebbles
All: pebbles kicked by big feet in idle pleasure
   shifting me to the roadside where
     other rocks have been booted and broken

One Woman: In my voice you will hear rock
All: rock slabbed into concrete

tarred over by heavy machines
   making broad/ways
      leading to somebody else's destination

One Woman: In my voice you will hear water
All: tears of a quiet place I've left behind
   sweat of a funky female stand they say ain't proper
      but I hold it, I hold it

One Woman: In my voice you will hear ballet slippers and
All: cotton candy and words that whirl and
   whirl like wind
      lifting my skirt exposing a beautiful nakedness
         danced on

One Woman: Rock and gravel
All: in the whimsy of God's great fancy

One Woman: My female voice
   spreads across my sisters' smile
      they love my rock and gravel and
         ballet slippers and cotton candy
            they say
All: she is
   she is
   she is

One Woman: In my voice you will hear pain
All: pain of the times I've given too much and
   a funky female stand they say ain't proper
      but I hold it, I hold it like sitting bull did custer
         strong, proud and dead-set on winning

One Woman My female voice grows stronger and stronger
   and in the whimsy of God's great fancy
All: It sings . . . and sinnnngs . . . and sinnnnngs . . .

OUR GOD-STORIES: SHARING IMAGES

I am a woman giving birth to myself
discovering the power of sisters
society alienates me from
and learning deeply from them.

I am a woman giving birth to myself
feeling excited, tired, expectant,
trusting in my own goodness,
healing old wounds,
discovering new muscles,
and unwilling, day by day,
to tie myself to the stake of oppression.

I am a woman giving birth to myself,
and the labor pains are hard,
long,
exhausting,
but this child's gonna live.

—Some affirmations
shared in a Mud Flower
ritual, February 1983

KATE AND THE COLOR PURPLE

"What I want us to do, as a way to get into this discussion about feminist theology, is to try to respond to three questions: One, when in my life did I know there was no God? Two, what resources have helped me find what God is for me? Three, what images or symbols or rituals help make God present for me? Since I've had a chance to think about this, I'll begin.

"As a black feminist, this question of what God is for me has taken me on a long journey. I grew up in a home where prayer was very powerful. We prayed every morning, every night, down on our knees by the couch. On Sunday mornings, we said at least three prayers at grace before we could eat. That was a tradition. And when relatives would come to visit from Philadelphia or some-where, we'd pray and pray. And every Sunday, we knew our food was going to get cold, because there was going to be a long, long prayer. At first my grandmother would do the praying, and then my mother, and finally, when I came home from college, my father had started leading the prayers; now he does the prayer and we join in.

"And then when I went to college and had my first heartache—I broke up with my first boyfriend—I knew God was dead. I knew God was dead because I was a Christian and I had not sinned. I hadn't slept with my boyfriend or anything. I had just lost him. For me, at age eighteen, it felt like there really was no God. The pain in my gut confirmed that God was dead. I was so broken up by the ending of the relationship that I went to the doctor for an electrocar-diogram. The doctor said that there was nothing wrong with my heart but prescribed a six-month supply of Valium for me. I lost my appetite. I lost my will to live. I lost my God. I felt devastated by the experience.

"I've moved in and out between believing there is no God and believing there is a God. But it was in 1972 that my eyes were most fastened shut to any kind of God in my life. During the summer I went to Israel on an archeological dig and was the only black person in a group of about a hundred students. It was the first time I'd ever been called 'nigger' to my face. Every weekend, we made reserva-tions at the youth hostels, and every weekend, everybody would have a room assigned to them but me. There was one woman from

England who'd walk me over to the American side of town, and I'd have to pay triple or quadruple amounts of money to stay in hotels, so I used up all my money. By the time I got back to Kennedy Airport, I had only one dime.

"The whole time I was there I received no mail. It was a very lonely, very sad experience. And while on the dig, only a few of the participants would interact with me. A lot of the archeological volunteers were Jewish kids from the United States. About 90 percent of them were Zionist. It was during this summer that I experienced Zionism as racism. There was one Christian minister who would talk to me at meals. Most of the time, I was all by myself. And I'd sit and look at the Mediterranean Sea and say, 'Why? What have I done? What is happening here?' For four weeks it was torture. There most surely was no God for me.

"I returned home, lost in the wilderness of loneliness. A death wish possessed my very being. This spiritual bankruptcy was the turning point in my life. It was at this time that I began to see that no human being could ever serve as a Higher Power in my life. I began to believe that the purpose of my life was not to be a 'people-pleaser.' I began to learn how to count on myself, how to please myself, how to be myself. In other words, for the first time I stopped being for everybody except me. And so, at just the point when I thought that there was surely no God, I came to believe more than I ever had before that there is a God—but that God is not another human being but the Creator who sustains me morning by morning, day by day.

"And the resources that have helped me claim the God that I now believe in include those prayers of my family. The whole black religious tradition has been a resource for me—that strong belief in the power of prayer. All of us in my family spent every night of the month of August going to revival meetings. And we'd go all over the county. The Baptists had it one week; the Methodists the next; the Presbyterians the next. . . . And we learned how to pray, how to shout and clap and how to get a good beat going. And so, when I began to really believe in God, I remembered that old-time black religion experience of prayer and music. I began to pick it up again. And to listen to that music again.

"I don't know all the rituals and symbols that make God present for me today. I do know that gospel music is essential, because I listen to it all the time. I also notice something when I'm playing with my nieces and nephews, because it's something about seeing my sisters' and brother's children, and having known my sisters and brother as children themselves—and I see them looking like us, and I see it is a *miracle*. I mean, I see these little children running around and I can hold them and respond to them and play Auntie Mame with them. And I experience God when I'm with them.

"The God I experience is very much what Alice Walker describes in *The Color Purple*. I mean, like Carter says, the godding—relating and holding and enjoying and empowering. Knowing God is being able to relax, slow down, live the kind of life in which I can notice the color purple. It means seeing the joy of living in common things.

"But I don't have any rituals, like in the breaking of the bread, in which I know that every time God will be present to me. It's not a given. God's not a given in rituals. But when I'm with my nieces and nephews, it's a given. God is present."

LAS PALMAS REALES DE ADA (ADA'S PALM TREES)

"I can clearly remember two experiences that led me to think there was no God. One time—the only time in my life I can remember being suicidal—was when I was not accepted for final vows in the convent. And what upset me most were the reasons, which were totally nonreasons. I mean, there was no good reason. I decided I better not kill myself because they'd be more upset about the car being wrecked—I was going to kill myself by crashing into a tree—than about the fact that I had killed myself. This experience of rejection made me think that there was no God, because in moments of rejection like that one I feel I am no good. And if I am no good, how can there be any God? Am I not made in the image and likeness of God?

"Then there was the time of coming face to face with evil. When I was seventeen, Castro came to power. And they had a couple of public trials of 'criminals of war' of the Batista regime. What was so appalling to me was the sadistic bent that became so obvious. The sadism of the 'war criminals,' the sadism of Castro and his men, the sadism of the people at large. There was no question in my mind that the 'war criminals' had done awful things. But I saw so much evil in Castro and the people who wanted vengeance, not justice.

"I remember Castro's government published pictures of these men against the wall, being shot. And I did not know who was more evil, the men who had done all the torturing during Batista's time or the men who were murdering them. The crowds were instigated to shout, '¡Paredón! ¡Paredón!'—the Spanish word for the wall against which people are executed. And the crowds would just rhythmically chant, '¡Paredón! ¡Paredon!' This was being televised . . . and I would have to leave the room because I literally would get sick. There was something so horrible about the intensity of the hatred—human life was being taken to appease the crowds, and the crowds were ecstatic over this killing. This was the first time, and one of the few times, I really experienced evil, and I knew God was not there.

"Now, what has always helped me to believe in God are those who have loved me, those who have made me feel that I'm good, worth loving. This sense of being loved has made me sense that there is God. Another experience that helps me to be in touch with the sense that there is a God has been silence. In my church, retreats are common. I'd give my right arm for an eight-day retreat every year! A time of prolonged silence—that has been a significant way in my life of being in touch with God.

"As far as symbols and images go, one thing that always makes me sense greatness, or whatever we want to call the divine, is seeing love expressed: a mother, a child, lovers—and especially expressive of the divine for me is seeing love expressed among old people. I have always found that extremely moving at the very core of my being.

"And beauty in nature, especially *palmas reales*. I grew up with palm trees all around, and I learned how to draw them when I was in the novitiate, and I still draw them all over. Every single notebook I have used has a palm tree drawn on it. I remember the first time I went to Florida, when I was coming from Peru—and I saw palm trees. And although they are not as pretty as the ones in Cuba, they are a wonderful thing to see—so strong and gentle, so tall and green. They call me to look beyond the present reality.

"For me anything that strongly appeals to the senses probably will help me sense the divine—in the Roman Catholic Church, those grandiose, well-done, mysterious liturgies, with incense. I love incense. It puts me in a transcendent state of mind. And the warmth and light from the candles . . . It's just something mystifying for me. I remember this sort of liturgy as a very pleasing, aesthetically beautiful ceremony. Maybe it has to do with associating this kind of sensual liturgy with my youth in Cuba. I remember that I learned how the ceremonies were to be done in a liturgically correct fashion. I used to rehearse with my brother when he was an altar boy, and I couldn't be because I was a girl.

"Finally, being taken seriously, that is so important for me. If I sit down with someone to talk and I feel that I'm being taken seriously, I go away with a real deep sense of experiencing the divine. I believe that in the taking of each other seriously we go beyond ourselves."

BEVERLY—THE ELECTRIC CIRCUITS

"I always feel very cheated and deprived—a good feeling of being cheated and deprived—when I hear a Presbyterian sister like you, Kate, who grew up in the black religious tradition within my denomination. And, Ada, I feel the same deprivation when I hear you, a Catholic sister, describe her religious experience. Because I've known for a long time that the interaction of my own personal family history and the staid Protestant culture I grew up in combined to make for serious religious impoverishment.

"All the religious emptiness of my culture was mitigated somewhat by the congregation my family joined when I was a baby. That particular church was rather humane compared to the dour, deeply depressed spirituality of the German Reformation tradition and culture in which I lived. I experienced God as totally beyond my experience and sensed no religious substance in my culture. But I know that my 'godlessness' always was located in my desperate search for God, in my desperate search for a religion that would make me good.

"I grew up in a desperate search to be a good little religious girl. I needed that sense, because my religious culture taught me that I was a sinner. In the first fifteen years of my life there were losses of love and loved ones in my family and environment—my father and grandmother died; my beloved older brothers went off to war. There was also a lack of emotional expressiveness in my German family, which meant that the lack of expression about these losses hurt and ran very deep. The loss of loved ones, and not being able to express feelings about them, were very wounding to a little girl whose father was dying, whose grandmother was dying, and whose brothers were going off to fight a terrible war. All this made me very religious. It was a somber, sad religion. More and more, of course, I can look back and recognize influences in my somewhat liberal Presbyterian tradition and in my community that were supporting me and calling me, somehow, to live in spite of loss. But I experienced my own expectations as shaped by the dour German tradition. My sense was that I needed God to exist as a substitute for my own life. I learned that so deeply—God would be what I was not!

"My problem, my almost lifelong spiritual problem, was that I learned to see God in what was not me and what was not in my experience, or in the people among whom I lived. Finally, of course, that's precisely where I found God—in myself/my community. I suppose I would not have had the strength to struggle so hard to be a good Christian girl so much of my life if I hadn't also been finding some message of affirmation of myself coming through the religious depression and alienation of my culture. But any message of affirmation was very indirect.

"And I also felt very guilty about affirmation. When I look back at the points in my life where I said I was not worthy to be loved by God, when my loyalty to Christianity and to the church were based on my desperate need for affirmation and community, it's clear to me that I felt worthless. Somehow affirmation was painful. I had been taught, theologically, that it was wrong.

"Ironically, though, I found—particularly as I moved out of the little town I grew up in on to college and into the wider society— that the church was the communal vehicle for pulling me into relationship with the world and into growth-producing experiences. I was not conscious that this was happening—that my experience in the church contradicted my expressed theology. I do experience much that has happened in my life as genuine grace, grace coming from sources I tended to deny it could come from—from friendship, from community, from relationship. So it came from where I was least prepared to find it. And I did not apply theological language to the concretely good things in my life. Because religion was a somber reality.

"When you talked about praying with your family, Kate, I was amazed. My family prayed only at meals. And by comparison to your experience, my experience of prayer was almost prosaic, and I felt almost embarrassed by prayer because it meant talking to God about ourselves. My siblings and I used to fight over who had to say grace at meals. It felt like public display, and *that* was embarrassing. In prayer, my family was expressing a very conventional religious need, but we simply had no mode of expression for sharing our real feelings—our pains, hurts, fears, our grief and anger. Our religiosity expressed an eroded tradition.

"In some ways, I'm grateful that the tradition was so hollow. All the things I imbibed theologically were deformed Lutheran and Calvinistic theology that I inhaled from my culture, and also from the emotional restraint of people around me. The Lutheran-Calvinistic expectation of God that we learned implied that it was in 'spiritual things'—which meant *not in our lives*—that God acted.

"Over decades that sort of religious feeling eroded in me. The first real source of this erosion that I can name were men who respected my intellectual integrity. They still articulated a version of that tradition but corrected it in a liberal direction sufficiently to encourage growth. Later I had to face that I needed more 'liberality' and more creativity than they expressed. But from my first religion professors in college onward, my affirmers were people who heard what I was saying and who were articulating some creative challenge to the most conventional Christian tradition I had been locked into.

"These mentors also respected my theological seriousness. Often their message to me was, 'Well, if we have to have women in ministry, then it should be women like you.' The other side of the message was, '. . . and not like those other, muddle-headed sort of females.' Still, the resources for growth for me have been the concrete community of Christians I experienced, and not just Christians, but the community of people who somehow were living, people who were engaged in real life, struggling for justice, and who were inviting me to live.

"Of course, increasingly in my life that empowering community has been women. When I think of the spiritual resources in my life, I think, in the first instance, of women who were hurting as much as I was hurting—and who could say so. I could not. That was my grounding experience of becoming a feminist. Many of you have heard me talk about what it was like to be assistant dean of students at Union, to sit in my office and listen to women talk about their experiences in seminary and finally realize that what they were talking about was also the source of the pain in my gut—and that I had not had any words for it.

"A second source of spiritual growth, later, was women who heard what I was saying and who thanked me for making sense of their experiences. Men have been saying that too, of course, but usually in a more abstract, less emotionally available way. I just simply never talked with men about what was deep in my gut. As a token woman, I dared not expose that—to them or to myself.

"So the connections with my experience weren't being made in my intellectual and theological framework. Increasingly in my life it has been women who were really struggling to live, women who would not let their lives be denied, who have been the deep source of the grace I've experienced. Of course, I've experienced grace in other ways and from different places, but women's community has been the place where honesty, pain, and struggle have drawn me into a sense of God.

"As to my image of God, well, I don't know if it's a symbol or an image. I don't think of it as an image, because it's pretty abstract. For me, God is wherever there is real desire, real longing, for connection. I was raised, as I said, in a Christian tradition which presumed that passion, desire, was *not* the foundation of spirituality. I was raised in a tradition where everything self-denying was the will of God. We were supposed to deny ourselves to do God's will. That tradition utterly cut me off from developing any center in myself, from appreciating the loving, desiring, longing, that *is in me.*

The whole notion of shaping my life around another's will is something I can't cope with anymore. It's pure masochism and it makes God a sadist.

"Now, finally, though, I realize that the more I long for connection, the more I begin to know what justice is, where justice is really grounded. Justice, of course, can't happen until the connections are being made, until others call you forth, connect with you, make you take yourself seriously or make you take them seriously. To me, it's a completely circular thing. God *is* in the connections. I find it embarrassing to say, because it sounds like a technological notion of God, but the image of God that makes the most sense to me is the electric circuit! God is the point where all lines of relation come together. It's a very mechanistic image, but there is power in the electric circuit.

"I also image God as gentle faces and hands, eyes that express pain and resolution. Increasingly, and happily, I experience God where there is spontaneous laughter with, not at. Most recently, I've imaged God as the color purple. Alice Walker's imagery blows me away. Celie's early God experience is so like mine. Now color has become very important to me. The thought that God is when you pass through a field and can really *see* the color purple is wonderful. It's an image that thrills me, because I was taught, somehow, that you must not equate God with anything profane, and especially not with anything in nature. God was supposed to be overwhelming experience that knocked you off your feet and, above all, delivered you from all pain and vulnerability. That is the patriarchal image of God.

"I'm learning that these partial and broken images—which are nonetheless the most empowering—are metaphors that are really there in our common life in the physical world. More and more these really bear the image of God for me.

"Because of my impoverished religious background, I realize that for me there are no consistent rituals that are indispensable to my spiritual life. I know this is, in part, because my white, Presbyterian heritage is just so awful liturgically. We did not have any sensuality in worship. It was all words. But I realize now that whenever the personal and political come together, when the experience of mutuality and the passion for justice get expressed, when they are acted

112

out in some little way, then that, for me, is authentic ritual. I'm trying to learn how to ritualize these moments.

"I don't think I'll ever have a liturgical tradition that I'm fully at home in, except the sort we've created here. But I don't want to cut my ties to my denominational tradition. I've been working with a student who analyzed her own tradition, using the music of the black civil rights movement as a point of comparison to her own. She's from the Midwest and, also like me, from a culturally impoverished, rigid, white Protestant tradition. But she loves her people. Her conclusion, in her thesis, is that she will probably never have a fully living tradition to relate to. But she's decided to struggle to bring her tradition to life. Like her, I don't want to deny my roots.

"I'm beginning to see the goal to be ritualizing more than ritual. What we've done together, we women, is that we've begun to learn how to turn our occasions of connectedness into audible, visible, sensuous movement. To keep learning how we can give expression to the holy—this is what liturgy is all about."

CARTER—¡PRESENTE!

"I have a hard time thinking about when in my life I knew there was no God. The first sixteen or seventeen years of my life, I assumed there was a God and that He was very other than me. Very much what you were describing in one sense, Bev—whatever God was, He was most unlike anything I was. He was sweet and He was far away and He was 'God' only because I had been taught that He was there—way out there. I prayed in very traditional ways—family prayer, which we had regularly; bedtime prayer; grace at meals; going to church. I could say prayers, whatever I wanted to say, and I guess I just assumed He'd hear them—not that anything would ever happen because of, or in response to, my prayers. I think maybe I was a little scared not to pray—scared of what He would do if I forgot.

"There was a sense in which God was a coping device for me. By that, I mean that I was able to project everything I thought was good onto God. He really wasn't real to me, but was some sort of an ideal. And, of course, He was old and white and male. This old white man, that's clearly what God was to me in terms of visual image. I mean, really, I saw Him in a sheet and with a long, gray beard, and a sweet face and living up above the clouds! I really thought that's where God lived. And I knew that whatever closer relationship He and I might have was going to be some other time and place than this one on this earth. I never could put together any notion of 'God-with-us,' or among us, with this image of the distant old man.

"I figured that Jesus, the Jesus we read about in Sunday school and in the Bible, also knew about this sweet old white man in the sky, and that because Jesus had been so good and had loved this old man in the sky, we were supposed to do this too. It was the way we could be good. I think that's how the God-and-Jesus-and-me connection got made for me in a fairly deep way.

"And my parents loved this old white man in the sky, and the priests in the church loved Him. They even looked like Him! I mean, all dressed in long white robes . . . But the point is that none of this had anything to do with my daily life, my real feelings and needs. All this—God, Jesus, religion—was so much *better* than anything I knew. Better, more loving, kinder than anything real— except with my very good friends and family, who certainly were the earliest mediators in my life of a positive notion of God, however unreal He seemed.

"Back several years ago, when I was speaking publicly about events and processes in my life that led up to my ordination, I frequently mentioned the strong sense of sacrament I had as a child—you know, this 'outward and visible sign of an inward and spiritual grace.' Early catechism teaching! Well, very early on, I had a sense of this. I assumed that birds and flowers and trees and dogs—and people—were holy. For some reason, the holiness of all these creatures never seemed to get translated into meaning very much in the world. It was as if somebody—God, the priests, some-body—had forgotten to tell us how holy we are. But, as for me, I figured everything was holy and that everything had something to do with that kindly old man who had made everything. And I liked that. And I think I knew, somehow, that this holiness included me— except that I never seemed to act holy enough.

"I loved silence and solitude, getting off and playing with my animals out in the yard. I was alone a lot, because I was an only child for six years. And all this while, I remember it well, I was bothered by the unjust relation between white people and 'colored' people in the South—that is, in my hometown. This is the way injustice first became known to me. I couldn't understand why white people lived over here and 'colored' people over there. And the whole segregated situation was so awful. I mean, I didn't have words for any of this, but I knew something was wrong. My parents told me racism was wrong and that it was not God's will. I guessed that the white man in the sky didn't like it, but He didn't seem to be able to do anything about it. And so my God was sweet, but impotent; kind, but not very active; and most of all for me, a coping device. I could at least talk to God about the way things ought to be in the world. And, He, I supposed, was the bringer of sweet dreams into very complex reality, a way of helping me keep going and feel good enough to function. And this went on for about sixteen or seventeen years.

"But during my late adolescence, the whole thing came crashing apart. I think I was very angry that the coping device was coming apart, as if the whole God-thing had been a hoax. Looking back, I believe the demise of my sweet dreams was rooted in an increasingly alienated sense I felt from my social world. I did not feel like I fitted anywhere—particularly around gender issues. I felt out of it, utterly out of it, as a teenage girl. I was hurt about that. I felt unattractive and unpopular with boys. Actually I was torn between whether or not I wanted to be popular, because I didn't much like the way the 'popular kids' acted. But still, not to fit in was unpleasant. And God? Religion became, for me—to the extent that it was anything at all—an academic matter.

"In college I majored in religion and did OK academically. I got into comparative religion and Christian theology and all kinds of things. And I thought this was all very interesting. But as far as I was concerned, it didn't have much to do with any real God, not for me personally. I had no particular sense of God being active in my life. Really, I was interested in philosophy. I was intrigued by the philosophical dimensions of religious thought. And that's what I pursued—all the way to seminary, which is when this more sophisticated type of coping device broke completely open.

"My first year at Union was chaotic and terrible. It was also a real turning point in my life, because all coping mechanisms were shot to hell. Clearly, there was no more old white man in the sky. But neither was there any longer the safety of the academic intrigue of thinking about the finite and the infinite. Something else was happening, and it had to do with real life: the Vietnam war, racism on campus, questions about sex and sexuality, issues I was just beginning to experience, in some ways, as *mine*.

"Vocationally I couldn't begin to sort out what I was doing in seminary, or even what I wanted to do. So I had a mini-nervous-breakdown and wound up in the hospital and then barely mucked on through my first year at Union. I think the reason I wound up in as good shape as I did at the end of that first year was because the Columbia University riots took place. And that was very exciting to me. Because, you see, it was the first real thing that had happened. In addition to the fact that Bev and some other incredibly important people and friends were in my life—which was fundamental to my turning point—the campus riots helped turn my life around.

"I began to see people witnessing for something they believed in. And it had to do with justice; I saw people putting themselves on the line. At first, it wasn't me, and then it became me. I joined in, in a way, a small way, but still a way, and for me it was a big way at the time. I can't tell you the deep, profound excitement in seeing people, for the first time, witnessing for justice. I realize now that I had been observing this all year at Union, around the war resistance, and so maybe by the end of the year I was ready to begin looking at my own values and life as a participant in resistance to injustice.

"And I could go on and on from this point of the story, much of which you know already. I can say, without any doubt, that the last fifteen years of my life have been a process of sorting out my commitments, understanding where I fit in terms of justice and injustice, and, from time to time, acting in whatever ways I can in these commitments. And the main reason the women's movement has been important to me personally is that, through it, I began actually to realize what it means to fight for justice for *yourself.* I mean, it's one thing to be always struggling on behalf of other people, and that has its good place. But once I experienced—and admitted the experience of—having my own neck stepped on, especially in the church, well, it really turned me on to what people whose life

116

situations are infinitely more oppressed than mine must experience. Not that I *know* other peoples' oppression. But feminism has helped me admit my responsibility to speak up for myself—which is what I'm doing each time I speak up for women—something my Christian heritage had always discouraged. You know, we're not supposed to be selfish. The more self-effacing a white woman, or a person— male or female—of color, is, the better Christian we are, right?

"For me, getting ordained with the other ten women, under the particular circumstances we did, was nothing less than a conversion experience. It brought into fullness this process of 'turning' I've been talking about. I mean, it brought me fully into an awareness, as you said, Katie, that I can't—and won't—live my life as a 'people-pleaser.' Which is what we are if we're forever giving over our authority to people 'above us'—or to *their* projections and images of God. Once I got ordained, there was no turning back. From that point on, I had to learn to live in the confidence of the faith and convictions I had been discovering among women and men, but mainly women, who were committed to justice-making as the primary goal of all faith, religion, and God.

"And then coming to EDS [Episcopal Divinity School], this seminary was a fortuitous move into a place that actually supports in some basic ways not only who *I* am, but who *we* are. I mean, this place has its problems, the main one being that we are so damned 'liberal' around here, which seems to go hand in hand with not getting fired up about things. But there are some white men here, including the dean, who, while they may not comprehend what in the world's actually happening among women, blacks, lesbians/gays, and others, do know that we're trying to be about God's business. And they try to be too. And that's good. And being here, of course, gave me an unusually supportive context in which to come out as a lesbian, a process and an act that I perceive to be, fundamentally, about making the connections—between sex and gender and power and justice and who's in control of whose life.

"I mean, these are the issues, all these issues that begin to sound, to me at least, so rhetorical and meaningless after a while: sexism, heterosexism, racism, classism, imperialism, atheism, capitalism, all these 'isms.' We, or I should say, I, need to learn to speak more concretely. Because these "isms" have to do with relatedness and

117

connectedness and corporateness. They have to do with what-is-me and what-is-not-me, or not-yet-me, or never-will-be-me. It's so important, I've come to believe, to make the connections between what I know to be real and what others have experienced; to find out what overlaps, and what doesn't, and why, and how these experiences become the contexts in which any of us speaks of 'God.' More and more, I realize that it's in relation to people with whom I *cannot* identify, in the immediacy of firsthand experience, that I need to seek the images and meaning of what is happening in the world.

"I really do believe there's something in common about us—maybe what Tillich would call our destiny—as well as our freedom. I think that God has to do with that common ground and with that seeking among us for the connections and with the resources we find to work together. The women's movement has really given me this sense, which continues to be radicalized by engagement with other people. It's become so important for me to own who I am—and who I am not; otherwise I'm bound to live not only without any clear sense of myself as a person, but also in a very arrogant way, always assuming that, because I've experienced something, it's everybody's reality.

"Those women [Sweet Honey in the Rock] sang last night about when we've had a good meal we need to remember that one child is hungry. 'Be aware,' they sang. That's powerful to me, because I know that my life—my destiny—is bound up with that child; and my freedom too. And it's that relation—between that child and me, and me and that child—that is God to me. And that's why a term like godding is powerful to me—because we're involved, either doing it or not.

"Either God is with us, among us, carrying us on and pushing us into life *together*, or there is no God. And symbols of God? Yes, like others of you, the color purple—literally, physically, a color. And physicality itself—like jogging. This is important to me because it's movement and has to do with body. And the most powerful religious image I've experienced liturgically—and not even firsthand—is that amazing affirmation, *¡Presente!* Any of you who saw the Oscar Romero funeral on TV, or who have seen what goes on often in Latin American *comunidades de base,* may recall when the sisters and brothers who've been killed are called forth. And they come! They are present! I mean, the fists go up and the voices are raised, *¡Presente!*—and you're aware that these people *live!*

"That's resurrection! And that's presence and power—and we don't have to be dead to be present and powerful! And I believe that fully—that the dead and the living are brought together. The concert last night was so wonderful. I still remember the pregnant woman up on the steps talking about her freedom and her bondage and the freedom and bondage of her sisters and brothers. And I realized she was talking about us *all*. And that all of us are *¡Presente!*

"Anything that is bold and decisive and has to do with justice and freedom and solidarity among people is powerfully religious to me. It doesn't have to carry the name Christian at all. Its power just *is*. And it is *good*.

"And so, that's about it. God didn't mean anything to me—except as a coping device—until I began to realize that justice-making and love-making and making-the-connections are where God lives and moves and has God's being.

"And one of these days we'll talk about how all of this relates to the liturgy and to the church and ecclesiastical matters, and I don't know that it does. I don't know that it does at all. But that's another discussion."

BESS—MOVING THE STRUGGLE

"I want to start first with God and then, maybe, touch a little bit on being a Presbyterian, because I'm a Presbyterian too, but there's a black religious ethos and foundation that wears well when the Presbyterian stuff grows thin.

"Now, this is my black feminist notion, and I don't know what black philosophers of religion might have to say about it. But there's something I want to say about *the validity of contradiction for the life of logic,* because that's what our life in America is. That's what my life, and everybody's I know who's black, has been about.

"When I was a little girl, we were very poor, no doubt about it. My father had left, and we were too proud to go on relief. In the South, where I grew up, it was all segregated. And my mother was a very beautiful woman. And if you went out to the welfare agency, you had to plead with the black man who was giving out the money. Or else your father could give the black folk who worked there a case of whiskey or whatever and be bought off. So we decided—my grandmother and mother, who was reared in a house of women primarily—not to take welfare. Not that. We took food stamps, but we would not take any welfare that meant you had to go through these men.

"Now my grandmother talked about God. And, for me, all of this touches a little bit on the coping mechanism Carter talked about. God was ever-present, I guessed. But the contradiction for me, as a little child, was that I could never get together with all God was supposed to be about. Like when I was sick with a stomachache and Grandma was putting on these hot and cold applications and feeding me bunches of herbs. And in the middle of the night (I was still awake, because we had a light that went all the way down the hall into the bedrooms), I heard Grandma asking, 'Well, she's gonna be alright, God?'

"But then I couldn't put together the notion of this God, when, throughout the black community, there were these white pictures of Jesus. They were all over. And, to me, it was total contradiction.

"I don't think I realized it much then as contradiction, because the whole black lifestyle and black politics and the way we lived in America was contradiction. I mean, you know, we have a Constitution; we got all these rights—blah, blah, blah, blah. But we still have this contradiction of racism and we still have to fight. Contradiction was a very important principle in my life, to my understanding anything.

"But I couldn't get that together—who this white man on the wall was and what he did. And he was in no way like the God the folks talked about, even the minister. No way did this God make sense to me. The only way I could bring the God my grandmother and mother talked about into any sense of reality was in music in the black church. And I couldn't even do it in the sermons of the black church, because a lot of them were like the picture on the wall of the white Jesus in terms of what they were saying theologically.

"Yet, in some way, all this talk about God did not yield total unbelief in me. Like my grandmother believed in God; and, remember, there was a lot of contradiction there. I'm not a very orthodox person. And all the contradictions did not yield total unbelief because, when I would get in those situations, real tight spots, like civil rights and battles of the sixties, God would come through—not to deliver us from this, but certainly to *move the struggle* and to *clear the lines*. It was like, you know, God's going to come down and move these mountains. The spirituals and music made more godlike sense to me. God was going to move the struggle, and somehow, we knew, something would happen.

"So I guess it was more a God of hope and faith than any God who would come in and make it all right. And I think, for me, this has to do with the whole underpinning of the religious tradition in my house. We had the Baptists, one aunt; we had my grandfather, who was a Presbyterian; we had my grandmother, who was going to be a Seventh-Day Adventist. So we had religion of an eclectic character, all having to do with coping and struggling and hope. So I think that's basically how I understood God.

"I'm a child of the sixties, no doubt about it. And I came of age in the civil rights movement, in those demonstrations—in Mississippi, North Carolina, some parts of Alabama. We had white policemen coming at us and we had our spirituals, our songs. That's all we had. And it was there—in those freedom marches and in our spirituals, there in our black religion—that God was for me. Not God in any trinitarian sense. Not God in any embodied sense of Jesus. Jesus was not part of my God-image. It was a holistic spirituality. These songs called up a whole spirituality among us, in our community They called us into the movement—black, white, blue, pink, brown. And that calling up became God to me.

"But I had never entirely disbelieved in God. I'd gone on my way through the years remembering those prayer petitions my grandmother and my mother had been into. But it's like it was the toughest thing I can remember—trying to put together in my consciousness exactly what Bill Jones asked (although I didn't know about it until later): You know, 'Is God a white racist?' At any rate, I think I had always believed, in a way, that God was there somewhere, but not human. And who was in charge of the action? God? God was there? God moved in, maybe, but not in ways I could really see.

"And as I got older, the faith that I had as a little girl and the way I believed in God had no consistency. I had learned more fully to live in contradictions, and these included contradictions in my belief and unbelief. And today I think about God very metaphorically. It's the only logic that does any justice to my experience. And these metaphors, these metaphorical ways of speaking about God, are resources I have now for understanding who God is in my life. And I do shy away from symbols, because it seems to me that the real formation of symbols (and I'm not going to tell you that people today don't have them, because they do) is the road to orthodoxy. It seems to me that symbols support systems, and systems support those who have political power. And if we get into that, well, it's just going to be more of the same.

"And the resources I have now are certainly my work with women, really going back exploring what these women's religions were all about, and how they affected my life, and my experience of the contradictions in my life. And I often say to myself—I love to say this to myself over and over—'In the beginning was chaos, and then the Word. . . .' It makes me respect the chaos so much as a part of creation. I realize now that what's been happening is that I got more and more educated and pushed more and more *against* the chaos; and this has meant that I've been afraid of the chaos. I mean, that's what we've been taught in education—to be afraid of chaos! But it's been with women, certainly this comes from my working with women, that I've begun to really understand that creation can only come out of chaos and that chaos is the mother of creation and the source of our validity. This has been a great learning for me, and it's one of the resources I use.

"Now in the middle of the civil rights movement, when Stokely Carmichael made his famous statement about the position of women being prone, I began to need to define myself in other ways—besides being black. And I had to go back to the condition of these women—my mother and my grandmother. And this took me right smack back to their God, because there was no way of understanding them, and there's still no way of understanding them, without understanding their God. And I think, in a sense, this led me into the theological seminary.

"And from the very beginning of theological education, the theology marketed in the seminary seemed ridiculous to me. I typed papers for some of the men and I said to myself, 'I don't know anybody who believes this. This is crazy!' And the only theologian I thought was even halfway sensible was Schleiermacher. But I had gone into seminary, remember, out of an experience of total disillusionment with the civil rights movement because we women were getting ourselves trampled under the feet of men. And I needed and intended to grapple with what *women* had experienced and what their religion was and what their faith was all about.

"Certainly another resource for me has been the liberation movements, which tend to reinforce my faith that God is. The civil rights movement is, of course, part of this; and certainly black religion. And certainly the rituals that women do. And scripture.

"I want to talk about scripture. I have just discovered that my faith is a very scriptural faith. And I didn't say biblical. A very *scriptural* faith. I find myself turning to scripture at will. You know, I turn and say, 'Now, this should be scripture,' and it really *is* scripture. So my faith is very scripturally informed. And I find this wherever people talk, and especially women, wherever people talk about God building in them and for them a greater capacity for connection. That's scripture.

"And, you know, we should have a sense of these connections in the black community. We should know our history, our historical connections to each other and others, and with nature, with the wind, with the flowers, with the birds. I mean, it's where we've been. And, of course, I've read all my life (and, I have to say, some bad literature), and reading has been very much a resource, a part of informing who I am. Like reading Alice Walker. Reading Alice Walker about nature and the prayer tradition. I mean, getting informed about, and connected to our prayer tradition as black women is very important to me. Getting connected to this prayer tradition we've inherited from a place and an existence beyond the present and that has affected our lives. Alice Walker picks right up on this and expands it so that prayer can be seen and made visible among us. Prayer is not just 'talking to God,' but now, through our connectedness and through nature, God is talking to us. This has informed my faith.

"And images I use to reinforce and express this faith are often sound biblical images. Images of connectedness, like the olive branch. That makes such good sense to me, that olive branch. I mean, the Lord tells us that where the rainbow is, a bird went out with an olive branch. This is, to me, a fantastic image of connectedness not just between God and the Jews or the children of Abraham, but among all creation.

"As for specifically Christian tradition, I consider myself a Christian, but much more in a sense, I think, like Carter. It can't be a matter of lending our complicity to exclusivity or superiority or the pretensions of a higher wisdom. For me, it's a faith that reaches back into the tradition in which the whole earth is blessed. And then I can move up into early Christian churches, and lots of contradictions are apparent to me, about who's in and who's out, and women, and property, about who owns whom and who's in charge of whom and what. This is full of contradictions in Christianity. And these contradictions are not foreign to my experience as a black woman. The problem with Christians is that they try so hard to deny contradictions. Just look at how constraining and how restrained and how controlled our language about God has been through the centuries.

"And now, I'm trying to understand connections between black women and white women and how we make these. And there'll be gains and losses and faults. But if there is God, moving the struggle, carrying the olive branch, not smoothing over the contradictions . . . well, I'll be exploring all these things and probably be dealing with metaphors for the rest of my days."

NANCY'S RELIGIOUS LEGACY

"I guess I've never thought that there was no God. And I think part of it is that, at the time in my life in which that might have occurred to me, I was either too out of touch with God for it even to be enough of a reality to think about; or I was too afraid of God to even allow the idea to enter my mind. I'm not sure which.

"I also was raised in a family that was very religious. I was raised as a Southern Baptist. So I was raised in a very expressive kind of religious context in which prayer was a very important thing for me also. We prayed together as a family every day. As far back as I can remember, that was very important. And when Carter said the thing about the coping mechanism, a lot of stuff clicked for me, because I was raised to be very religious and to pray and go to church regularly. And by regularly, I mean four times on Sunday and on Wednesday for prayer meeting and on Thursday for choir rehearsal and for the missionary society, which met on Wednesday also.

"And prayer was really important to my family, especially in times of crisis. That tradition of praying was really central. One of the crises I remember vividly was that I had a relative who was arrested and imprisoned when I was, I think, about ten years old. My family was, of course, in a state of distress, and there was a lot of praying going on.

"The other time I remember vividly was during the Korean war. We lived near the airport, and I would hear on the radio about the war, or would hear the news on TV. I wouldn't actually watch it because it was too scary. But we lived about four miles from the airport, and that meant that the flight patterns were right over the house. I was just old enough during World War II to remember blackouts—when people would come around and say you had to turn out all your lights and pull your shades down in preparation for a possible bombing. I remembered that, and then, during the Korean war, I would get very scared when I was in bed at night because the airplanes would come in and I was sure we were going to be bombed. And I remember praying a lot that we wouldn't be bombed. And that was really a very intense experience of God as a coping mechanism to get me through my fear.

"And, well, you can imagine the church had to be the center of one's life, because there was not that much of life left! I grew up next to the church, too. It provided my social life as well as my religious life, pretty much my whole life. Day to day, people would come to our house to get the key to the church.

"But also for me growing up, some of my most important role models, interestingly enough, were never the pastors in the church, but always were the women directors of religious education and the Sunday school teachers. So that from an early time on, some of my most powerful role models were women. And I think that was because they provided some other ways for me to think about what I was going to do. (I was supposed to be a majorette—I failed!) Anyhow, there were these other models for me besides teaching school and being a nurse, both of which seemed to me to be at best unpleasant. (And eventually I did teach.)

"So the church gave me some emotional connection. I would hang out at the church and help the woman who was director of religious education paste and cut and make posters, and I thought that was a very good job. I mean, it was not at all an unpleasant kind of experience.

"And the Bible was an important part of that youth experience. One of the big events in my youth was taking a trip all the way to Richmond to hear Billy Graham. It was a Big Event. So the idea of there being no God never entered my consciousness. It was not even a possibility to contemplate.

"When I was in college, I lost a lot of intensity about religion. It wasn't so much a rejection of it as doing other things. And during my college years I began to see connections, since the people I met were often involved in some kind of justice work. Connections between religious commitment and social and political commitments. I was in college from 1958 to 1962, in the midst of the civil rights movement. It was absolutely boggling to my mind to have people on that college campus putting racial justice commitments together with the safe religious tradition I had been raised in. In fact, in my religious culture (though not in my immediate family), this sort of politics—sit-ins, demonstrations, etc.—was seen as the work of evil, being carried on by outside agitators. I mean, people talked about it in that kind of language. And so, it was incredibly important to me to begin to see a connection between social justice and faith, and it got me back to connecting at some gut level with parts of my religious tradition.

"The thing I remember most vividly about these connections has to do with the Vietnam war. I mean, in the meantime a whole lot had happened, in the civil rights movement and with Martin Luther King, and my political consciousness had been moving right along. A whole lot had been going on in society, and in my college and seminary years, helping me in some way make some connections. And then, in the Vietnam war, the religious tradition in which I'd been raised got challenged to its roots.

126

"It was incredible, this business of fighting a war in order to 'win the hearts and minds' of people we were killing! And so demonstrations against this war were important to me. One was scheduled for Washington, one of the big ones, and everybody was saying there was going to be violence, that it was going to be a real mess. And the people I was with were saying, 'Well, I don't believe in violence. People who want violence are going, so people who don't want violence had better be there.' So a bunch of us were going from Duke. And I decided not to let my parents know. I knew it would worry them, especially because of all the publicity about violence. They'd known about other demonstrations I'd been involved in, and it hadn't been a problem. But I wanted to spare them.

"And I remember that my parents called me on weekends very often, so I decided: I'll call them on Wednesday, because it will be close enough to the weekend that they won't call me while I'm gone. And it'll be far enough away from the weekend that they won't think to ask if I'm going. Well, of course, they asked me if I was going, so I told them that I was. And they were quite upset. My father accused the march of being communist and Benjamin Spock and Bill Coffin of being communists. A huge tirade. Well, we fought and fought and fought over the phone. And this was the only time I ever really screamed and fought with my father.

"So I wrote them this huge, long letter, and I sent them pictures of the Marines setting fire to Vietnamese huts, and I sent them all these articles about the war. And I wrote them, 'You taught me this is wrong. You have to see. If what we're doing is burning huts in Vietnam to save them from communism, that's not what I was taught is right.' So I sent them this long letter. And my letter crossed with a letter from my father. He wrote me twice in his life, and that was one letter. (The other was to ask me about a Christmas present for my mother!) But in this letter he enclosed a check to pay for my telephone bill, which had been considerably higher than I anticipated when I placed the call!

"I tell the story because I think it's an example of why I've never been able to separate myself entirely from my religious tradition. As much as I've been embattled with it, I've never been able, or really wanted, to leave. And that story says something to me about the depth of my religious roots, which have always been there, growing, even when people who have nurtured me, like my parents, haven't had a concrete social analysis to bring to their faith, or to mine.

"I guess I grew up believing that the Christian faith really teaches justice, that we're all children of God and that therefore we all will inherit the earth. And even without a political analysis of what that meant or any clue about how to act it out, except in a one-to-one understanding of fairness, that basic teaching was there. The biblical tradition which teaches that remains important to me. And that's partly because it provided the tools for me to remind my parents what they taught me, and to let them know that what I was doing was connected with them. So that I will work to change people like my parents politically—because they taught me, somehow, that I must."

MARY'S WEAVING

"Well, goodness me. We ought to be singing these wonderful words. I've gotten so involved listening to the wonderful array of differences and commonnesses that I've almost forgotten my own story. There's so much to honor and so much to weave together in this array.

"That weaving image helps me when I think about my own story. A lot of my religious stirring has been disentangling the messy ball of yarn that is other people's notions of God—which have been given to me as though they were supposed to be mine—from the one that's really mine, and then seeing so many different threads in the skein that I have a hard time weaving my own religious experience together. (I would actually rather do this with literal yarn!)

"The question about our experience of when there was no God helps me weave together some of those strands for the first time in a way that I had not seen before. So I want to start there. I was sitting in my office one day in the middle of writing my dissertation and having my contract reviewed and all the rest of that nonsense, writing some article, when I looked up and said I didn't think that God existed.

128

"I spent most of that summer walking around thinking, Well, God doesn't exist, and what difference does it make? The world was just exactly the same as it was before that. I felt somewhat relieved about this. Some of you have spoken about God as a coping mechanism; that's also helpful to me, because my experience that summer was the last vestige of my letting go of the coping-God I had latched onto while I was growing up.

"I've been fascinated by many of you talking about prayer in your homes and your getting your sense of religiousness there. My family never prayed together, never mentioned religion. My grandmother read the Bible. For a while my mother was involved with the Jehovah's Witnesses and God only knows what else. But they sent us children to the Lutheran church. The adults never set foot in church. But they sent the children because that is what you did. Everything that happened in church was interesting to me; I enjoyed it and went gladly. I did all the things you were supposed to do—Sunday school, confirmation.

"Meanwhile, in my family, there was this ugliness, this completely demonic stuff going on, compounded by poverty and by my father's abusing my mother and abusing us children. As a teenager I started having nightmares about monsters and vampires and werewolves after me. I got so that I could not stand to be alone or sleep at night because of vampire nightmares.

"Somewhere along in this period, a conservative Baptist family were wonderful friends to me. They took me in and were a model of family life and love and religiousness all mixed together in ways that were very salving to my wounds. So at sixteen I went forward at a conservative Baptist revival and found Jesus.

"What I found in Jesus were two things: first was an amulet that I could wear around my neck when the monsters were after me. I would clutch it and I would say the magic incantations that would keep the monsters away—praying, in other words. Jesus protected me from the vampires. At the same time there was a second odd thing going on—the disenchantment of the world. My world had fewer and fewer monsters, demons, or other holy things in it. Like my grandmother believed that when you got warts, you should wrap a string around them and then bury it in the full of the moon in the backyard. All that enchanted stuff, full moons and the monsters, began to disappear.

"To make a very long story short, my Lutheran pastor didn't really appreciate my running around with conservative Baptists and started trying to win me for Lutheranism. That was a relief, because the only thing you could do with your mind among my conservative Baptist friends was to memorize Bible verses and recite them to each other. I didn't find that very satisfying. By the grace of God, I guess, I ended up not going to a conservative nonaccredited Baptist Bible college to memorize more Bible verses.

"Instead, I went off to a four-year college and arrived there in 1964 to find the civil rights movement, the peace movement, the student movement, the antipoverty movement, all in very short order. That was the religious turning point of my life; from these I discovered that there were people struggling for justice, many of them Christians who felt and believed that it was essential to their faith to be struggling for justice. The antipoverty part of this work was especially important to me because that was the first time I learned that it was not my own family's fault that we were poor. It was not God who had done this. It was people, social structures, and we could not undo it.

"As a teenager I also started covering my birthmark with cosmetics, and I lived in this great personal closet, afraid I would never have love or intimacy because I was a freak. I add that here because I went to work on the west side of Chicago in the summer of 1966. Two things came together for me that summer: one was marching with thousands of black people to confront Mayor Daley. The other was that I took off my makeup that summer. They were part of the same dynamic of living in this religious community of social activists. The two things came together somehow: the combination of personal healing with community work for justice, both embedded in a theological matrix. I didn't really understand how these dynamics interacted.

"But I knew that I was in religious turmoil, and I started thinking about religious social ethics. Eventually I went to graduate school in social ethics, the first year I was married. In that first year I had vampire nightmares in a very serious way. So I started therapy. It was a wonderful moment in my life when the therapist said it was

130

perfectly understandable, because my parents had turned into werewolves and vampires every day. That ended the disenchantment phase. And it was wonderful, salutary, demystifying.

"All confused together in here were my experiencing of demons, the personal pains of my birthmark, and the struggle for justice. I had no idea of how to make sense of it or even if I should try. It was a personal/social/intellectual/religious mess.

"The women's movement started opening that up for me and putting the strands back together and making sense of my life. Especially helpful was my realization that the personal is political, and other integrative insights from early feminist theology. I was finding some sort of God that I could live with and not be in rebellion against or bored by. I began seeing a God who spoke to my experience in the same power and resonance and depth which, presumably, in earlier strands of the tradition, had spoken to people.

"Now I'm not exactly sure what else goes into that story. The experience I'd had marching in '66 grew. I began to have mystical experiences on the L-train in Chicago, or later in the subway in New York City or at historical sites in Algeria. For instance, once in Germany someone casually said that these cobblestones under my feet were eight hundred years old; I was suddenly gripped by this astonishing vision of eight hundred years' worth of human feet, polishing those cobblestones, wearing them down, grasped in an immediate unity of vision. If there is an image or a phrase that sort of sums up where I am today, it's June Jordan's phrase, fluid holiness. So I've learned to call myself a social mystic. That has been very interesting also, since Lutherans are not supposed to be mystics. I once sat in my office, struggling with Lutheranism and feminist theology, and I had a vision of a female Titan, an immense Earth Spirit, standing out in the Hudson River, looking in to make sure I was all right.

"In the last several years, since my summer experience of saying that God did not exist and that it didn't really matter, I've been in a process of progressively re-enchanting the world in terms that are hospitable to me and mine, rather than in terms that are alien and destructive like the terms that I learned growing up.

"Today I'm very excited about non-Christian images and symbols

131

as well as about the social mysticism, about which I really do not know how to speak. For example, "Changing Woman" from Navaho religion is very important to me, for she expresses that fluid holiness. I appreciate and cherish all that is healing and all that is justice-making and all that is beauty-making in a fluid and hospitable way. I don't find that very much in church.

"The dimension of church that still has some sense or experiential resonance to me is the eucharist, with its earthy, fluid symbols. I learned that when I went to the first eucharist celebrated by a clergywoman in the early seventies. I looked at this woman pouring red fluid into a cup and offering it to people and calling it the Blood of Christ. It was as though, in that moment, something about her body fluids and my body fluids, which had been despised for so long as deadly and ugly in the tradition, had been healed for me. I'm still trying to figure out what all of that is about.

"I go to church these days and behave like a perfect liberal. I omit the parts I don't like (especially the male language), and I do the parts that I do like. But I don't take public responsibility for that. I go there as much to be in the same place with people whose lives are in transition like mine as I do for the worship. That gives me great pain, because reclaiming my Lutheran heritage is important to me.

"Unlike the Calvinism that Beverly grew up with, the Lutheranism I grew up with was very earthy. Drinking and being celebrative was a very important part of that. Although I am more and more suspicious daily that patriarchy is essential to Christianity, still I want to claim those parts of the tradition that do not support the inertia of the status quo and do not passively accept all the social evil in the world as what God wants. Which is what, I am afraid, much implicit Christian social ethics teaches: the passivity of the status quo.

"But the work for justice that comes out of joy and grace (something I occasionally read in Luther) somehow manages still to have a hold on me. It's in the joy that I experience among those who are acting for social justice that I most deeply feel religiously alive. My anger and pain at all that's wrong in the world comes from the same place in me that my joy comes from, because life is meant to be joyous and hospitable and healthy and beautiful. For that reason this system we're living in must really be fought.

"Bess talked about poets and theologians, and I share her yearning there. I often wish that theologians were poets and artists rather than the constructors of algebraic and geometric formulae. I want churches to be places that genuinely open their arms to the pain of our lives and our movement. If they're not, and if they will never be, well then, I *will* leave. I stay mostly on the wager that my fighting to make them so can help to make them so, and because I deeply believe that is a wager worth living. I'm not sure at what point in my life I would decide that wager is no longer worth making.

"In the meantime I have a very deep sense that there is nothing more beautiful than listening to people tell their stories about faith and God. They express, as nothing else can, who we really are, and what we really believe in, and the meaning in our lives. It pains me that ministers and teachers seldom ask for stories like those we have been telling today, and they do not learn to honor and cherish these stories as central to their work. If there's anything worth calling theology, it is listening to people's stories—listening to them and honoring and cherishing them, and weaving them together, and asking them to become even more brightly beautiful than they already are."

Chapter Five

THE SHAPE AND SIGNIFICANCE OF FEMINIST THEOLOGY: A CHRISTIAN PERSPECTIVE

If there's anything worth calling theology, it is listening to people's stories—listening to them and honoring and cherishing them, and asking them to become even more brightly beautiful than they already are.

—Mary Pellauer

• FEMINIST THEOLOGY: A FRESH WAY OF LIVING AND BREATHING •

During a consultation we had with women teachers and ministers in Rochester, New York, Toinette Eugene, PBVM, who teaches at Colgate-Rochester Divinity School-Bexley Hall, insisted that we

> say clearly that feminist theology isn't simply a matter of moving the images from "masculine to feminine" or of women doing theology for the benefit of women, but rather that we're talking about a whole new way of thinking, a fresh way of living and breathing.

We concur wholeheartedly. "We're talking about a whole new way of thinking, a fresh way of living and breathing," a way of doing/teaching/learning theology that springs fresh from a new experience and understanding of what we are doing in the world—and of what God is doing among us.

We have been doing feminist theology in every conversation we have had and on every page of this book. For that reason, we were uneasy about separating our God-stories from this chapter and did so for editorial rather than substantive reasons. The stories stand, alone and together, in the order they were told, as witness to the ferment and power experienced by women in feminist theological circles. Being present when they were told, calling forth one another's voices, hearing one another into speech, listening with profound respect, was to experience a deepening of our relationships in Mud Flower. The God-stories were as important to our collective life as our stories about racism and classism. Perhaps they were possible only *because* we had told our stories of race and class first. The God-stories chapter may be an icon of the experiences we have had in women's groups around the country and in classrooms where feminist method is practiced. We are all diminished because story-telling is not a regular part of our work together in classrooms and churches.

Human stories are rich with lived experience, laden with passion and struggle for meaning. Our own God-stories are filled with theological implications that might be developed at length, perhaps in seven disparate directions. Those who read the stories carefully may have noticed that we have theological differences among ourselves. These distinctions need not be resolved. They are not necessarily contradictions and, indeed, provide the substance for learning, growth, change. While we generated spontaneous images whose full working-out may lead in diverse theological directions, we were conscious of responding to one another's words, of recognizing our common places and our separate places, and of deepening the full range of our connectedness with one another as each story was added to the flow. All the while, amid our differences, we have been moving, at times immersed, in a single, broadening, deepening stream of recent theological work: feminist theology.

Feminist theology may be thought of as a terrain that we have been exploring. Sometimes individuals or groups follow different pathways on its maps or investigate differing features of its landscape. We owe our readers some indication of how we situate ourselves in this terrain—some idea of where we have found its hazards and its vistas, its potholes and its watering places.

Thus, in this chapter, we first situate ourselves and our work within this larger territory. Then we proceed to emphasize, as we have done all along, the crucial importance of the inclusive character of this feminist theological enterprise. Next, we explore issues related to language, both sexist language and new imaging, and issues arising in the spirituality of feminist theological politics. We end with some suggestions about the critical role of ritual, both in the larger movement of feminist theology and in our own process.

WAYS INTO FEMINIST THEOLOGY

When used in seminaries the term feminist theology often signals the work of a growing body of church-, synagogue-, or academy-based women whose well-worn books dot the shelves of women's centers in theological schools throughout the United States: Mary Daly, Rosemary Ruether, Elisabeth Schüssler Fiorenza, Letty Russell, Carol Christ, Judith Plaskow, Virginia Mollenkott, Phyllis Trible, to name a few. Mostly Christians, nearly always white, these feminist theologians have labored publicly for over fifteen years to draw attention to women's lives as fundamental to the theological enterprise.

From our perspective, however, such printed works are only one manifestation of feminist theology. Feminist theology happens in grassroots situations wherever women name and confront our lives. It is happening everywhere, and it will continue to happen. How this folk-generated feminist theology can influence and challenge academic feminist theology is something very important to all of us. We realize that we need to reimage feminist theological contributions so as not to limit them to the book-centered, academic-discourse contributions that can be easily filed, catalogued, and packaged.

Undergirding the feminist theological movement is the struggle for the liberation of women in the United States, a fight that began in the early nineteenth century and was revivified in the middle of the twentieth. Because in the late nineteenth and early twentieth centuries, the women's movement became publicly a white women's effort, few white or black women remember that, initially, the abolitionist movement and the woman suffrage movement incorporated a lively indictment of racism and patriarchy within Christianity. These nineteenth-century justice-workers struggled to disentangle Christianity's potentially liberating message. We also too often fail to remember the important work of such contemporary theologians as Nelle Morton and Pauli Murray, who have been building for decades on the experiences and insights of those early traditions embodied in such feminist abolitionists as Sojourner Truth and Sarah and Angelina Grimke.

While we cannot name all the forerunners of our present work, we will cite a few without which we would not be doing what we are today. The public appearance of Mary Daly's *The Church and the Second Sex* (1968) crystallized a diagnosis of radical misogyny in the Christian tradition and mobilized a search for alternatives. By the mid-1970s a growing chorus of Christian women had begun singing the stories of our lives as the arena of accountability in which the legitimacy of all theology is to be tested.

The significance of this theological movement among Christian women of our generation cannot be underestimated. It is to this day the spark of much provocative and excellent Christian theological

137

work being done in this country. There is, among women scholars and ministers, growing clarity that the methodological assumptions of feminist theology are transforming the epistemological underpinnings of theology itself. And there is growing excitement that the fruit of feminist theology is less bitter, more sensual, and more spiritually edifying than nonfeminist (masculinist) theological approaches.

Giving a few examples of feminist theological work may help flesh out our excitement, as well as illustrate different—and not necessarily mutually exclusive—approaches to the terrain of Christian feminist theology. There is a postchristian way being explored by many Christian women. Mary Daly's own later work, *Beyond God the Father* (1973), proposed that the women's movement itself was an intrinsically religious phenomenon (an ontological revolution, as she put it). It was not *made* religious because of its association with other religious things, such as the Bible, churches, or clergy. To spell out the meaning of that insight, her subsequent *Gyn/Ecology* (1978) generated a new level of critique (the cross as subverted symbol of the old women's-religion) and a new language, one in which women's capacities for spinning and sparking were the central locus of meaning. Daly's postchristian work is required reading for Christians who are attempting to understand feminist theology.

A second route into the terrain of feminist theology is to insist that Christian doctrines, symbols, and practices be reinterpreted on the basis of women's lives and women's history. This approach, which seeks to bring a feminist hermeneutic into mainline/malestream Christian theology, was opened up by Valerie Saiving's essay, originally written in 1960, "The Human Situation: A Feminine View." This work addressed concepts central to twentieth-century theology: sin as pride and salvation as self-giving, agapic love. That both concepts corresponded to the dominant male's existential and sociocultural situation—rather than to women's experience— provoked many women to rethink theological categories taken for granted. Saiving's important contribution has been extended by other scholars (Plaskow, Farley, Andolsen) but has made little impact on local congregations where Euroamerican male-defined notions of sin and salvation are pervasive.

A third avenue into feminist theology is exemplified by Ruether's early collection of essays, *Liberation Theology* (1972), conjoined with the work of Collins (1974), Russell (1974), and Hageman (1974). Ruether's book was only one expression among U.S. feminists of growing interest in liberation theology. It illustrates the emergence, in a white feminist theological context, of a critique of many interactive forms of oppression: cultural chauvinism, anti-Semitism, male gender superiority, white racism, economic exploitation, and U.S. imperialism in relation to the Third World. While liberation theology has often been perceived academically as a legitimate theological challenge growing primarily out of Latin American base communities or the black power movement in the United States, feminist liberation theologians ask that we perceive the indigenous roots of this theology in all liberation struggles, wherever people are working for justice and taking themselves seriously as redemptive agents.

A fourth and vital way into Christian feminist theological space is through the stories, both fiction and nonfiction, of women's lives as presented by such artists as Alice Walker, Ntozake Shange, Judy Chicago, Audre Lorde, and Adrienne Rich. Such women have helped us see that theology need not be dispassionate, nor need it be done only by those who think of themselves as "theologians." Anyone with a story to tell, an image to paint, or a poem in her heart is able to contribute to the movement of feminist theology.

During the past decade, new insights have emerged in the context of feminist historical investigations. In tracing sexism back through the Western tradition, feminist historians began to learn that "great" periods of history were ambiguous for women. Historical theologians have begun to note that heretical movements were often more congenial than orthodoxy to women's lives. Feminist scholars have begun to realize that alternatives to orthodoxy are not confined to the past and that they are alive and well—if underground—in a West dominated by Christianity. Thus, witchcraft and wicca have become attractive to many as the ancient religion of the goddess. These options are growing rapidly around the country, signaled by increasing numbers of workshops and conferences, magazines and writings, such as those collected by Charlene Spretnak in *The Politics of Women's Spirituality: Essays on the Rise of Spiritual Power Within the Feminist Movement* (1982).

Jewish women have been active and visible in the contemporary women's movement from its earliest days. Studying critically patriarchal assumptions in contemporary ritual life and in commentaries on the Hebrew Bible, Jewish women have restored the bat mitzvah and created new liturgies and prayers, networks and magazines. Like other U.S. feminists of nondominant racial/ethnic/religious groups, Jewish feminists have also been spurred to a critique of their own continuing oppression within the women's movement.

Christian feminists have to take responsibility for anti-Semitism in our lives and work. For instance, some Christian feminists have interpreted "Jesus was a feminist" to mean that he was unlike, and superior to, others of his Jewish contemporaries. Furthermore, there have been obvious scholarly errors made by Christian feminists who compare antiwoman rabbinical statements from one era with prowoman Christian statements from another age.

In the earliest days of the women's movement within the church, women like Peggy Ann Way made process theology an attractive option for feminists. While the process theology emphasis on the centrality of relationship is shared by many feminists, the texts of process theology tend to be difficult reading and are often inaccessible except at the graduate level. Moreover, Christian feminists disagree about the value of process *ontology* in our theologizing. The influence of process theology has been to this point mostly on academically based women.

Because evangelical Christianity has often allied itself unapologetically with sexism, nonevangelical feminists often fail either to acknowledge or to appreciate fully the theological contributions of such women as Nancy Hardesty, Letha Scanzoni, and Virginia Ramey Mollenkott, whose work reflects strong feminist commitment. What these women write or say places them in ongoing professional jeopardy within the evangelical community.

We have learned that to consume passively theologies produced by others is not to do theology. Breaking dramatically with women's social role as economic, emotional, and religious consumers, we have been discovering theology as a *creative act* that incorporates our present experience and is resourced by our roots—the traditions from which we have come.

For Mud Flower, the most important features of this creativity are

140

that it is foundationally oriented toward justice and that it is relational in character. To do theology ourselves we must begin with our experience of ourselves in relation. To comprehend anyone else's theology, we also must understand both how it reflects the theologian's praxis and in what ways this particular theology affects others, including ourselves.

Many feminist theologians share the conviction that feminist theology is intrinsically relational and justice oriented—or steeped in a commitment to right relation. Several years ago in the Boston Theological Institute, a group of women faculty fantasized publishing a course guide for incoming students in which each course would have been listed as either "feminist" or "masculinist." What was envisioned was not whether course contents related to female gender issues but whether awareness of the relationality of the learner to the subject matter was incorporated into a course. These women were suggesting that it is possible to teach any subject matter—the theology of Karl Rahner, José Miguez Bonino, or James Cone—in such a way that all women and men students are encouraged to study the material in relation to their own lives and values; and, moreover, in such a way that students are taught to be on the lookout for, and to notice, the connections (or disconnections) between what theologians write and the actual life situations, or praxis, in which they work.

In a feminist course on Augustine, for example, no one's questions or opinions about Augustine's social location or his views on women or sexuality would be dismissed as irrelevant. They would be taken seriously as questions yielding insights. It *is* possible to teach Augustine, Thomist philosophy, Reformation history, canon law, the history and theology of the black church, and certainly the Bible, on the basis of feminist method. Doing so often involves unlearning old assumptions or relearning well-known materials from a new point of view. We suggest that much resistance to feminist method in theological teaching comes from resistance to entertaining this fresh look at materials long held to have been "mastered."

Our assumption, then, is that theology is shaped in dialogue between and among ourselves—who we are, what we are doing, together or separately, in concert or at odds with one another. The study of theology takes place in this dialogue, between and among ourselves, as well as between ourselves and the authors of the texts as we engage them in our disparate life situations and our common educational praxis.

To insist that *how* we do theology is as important as what kind of theology we do is to challenge the split between content and method so often implicit in approaches that ignore, or trivialize, students of theology. Doing theology involves both the process and the insights we bring to our work as teachers and students, writers and artists, speakers and preachers. No less than others do we struggle with the pervasiveness of the content/method split. We discovered in our discussions that we could hardly identify or address the problem without falling into it.

Although this dialogical, relational epistemology is widely shared, feminist theologians are hardly a monolithic bunch. We have diverged, over the past fifteen or so years, into various theological movements. Our bond as feminist theologians is marked by the complexity of our tensions and dissonance. Although, as we have noted, there is no *necessary* animosity, or mutual exclusivity, between, for example, Christians and postchristians, there is often tension between and among us at just these points. The fact is, in evaluating others' perspectives and choices, we are also evaluating our own. Thus, we have strained relations in feminist theological circles. Many feminist theologians, once Christian, have left the church; some refer to themselves as postchristian. Many formerly Christian and formerly and/or nominally Jewish women have become practitioners and theorists of wicca and other female-affirming religions.

Among Christian/postchristian women like ourselves, some have moved in the direction of understanding women's experience in primary relation to the organic constitution and movement of our cosmic context. Others of us, including most members of this collective, are concerned primarily in finding theological relation through the ethical, sociohistorical contexts where issues of gender-justice are shaped by prevailing economic and racial, national, and international structures of power. For many of us in this latter group, our work requires interdisciplinary approaches, while still other feminist theologians focus their work more centrally in existing disciplinary discussions. Among all of us are varieties of religious experience that take ecclesial and/or ritual forms of both "higher" sacramental traditions and "lower" evangelical traditions, and of both more traditionally conservative biblical witness and more customarily liberal testimonies to the power of human reason.

There are broad and sometimes subtle differences among us. They do not always result in clean and tidily differing theological camps or in conflicts and theological arguments. Although we have named our collective as oriented more toward history and society than toward nature and cosmos, many of our stories emphasize nature. Kate, Beverly, Carter, and Bess all speak of Alice Walker's color purple. Carter refers explicitly to physicality, sexuality, jogging. For Bess the olive branch is an image of God's blessing among all creatures and the whole earth. Ada speaks of palm trees touching her deeply and of being moved by the Roman Catholic liturgy's appeal to the senses of smell and sight. Similarly, the power of prayer is highlighted in the narratives of Kate, Bess, and Nancy. The sacraments are emphasized by Ada and Carter. Mary speaks of herself as a social mystic. Carter and Beverly speak of liberalism as important in certain ways to them even while they struggle with it. Others of us, even those for whom our other conversations indicate struggles of various sorts with political and/or theological liberalism, do not find this theological movement or any other important enough to be mentioned in our religious stories.

Regardless of our theological/philosophical differences, many Christian feminists continue to learn and to teach in lively relation to the experiences and spirituality of Jewish women, postchristian women, wicca, and sisters with different cultural and religious commitments and symbols from our own. Our relations to women who are not Christian have helped to sharpen our intellectual inquisitiveness and our intellectual honesty. Our relationships with Jewish women, for instance, have forced several of us to acknowledge and struggle with Christian anti-Semitism and therefore to be suspicious of dominant christologies and other Christian concepts, such as the relation of law and gospel, and of the Hebrew Bible to the Christian Bible.

Alongside the now vast array of books and essays by Christian women (and occasionally men as well) who write unapologetically as feminists, are many resources upon which we draw that are not written or marked as specifically theological material. We have mentioned Alice Walker's *The Color Purple* (1982), which has become for most of us a basic theological text. We have mentioned also the poetry, stories, and other contributions of women artists like Lorde and Rich. We have learned a great deal about our work as feminist theologians from critical feminist collections such as Cherríe Moraga and Gloria Anzaldúa's *This Bridge Called My Back: Writings by Radical Women of Color* (1981) and Evelyn Torton Beck's *Nice Jewish Girls: A Lesbian Anthology* (1982). Such books as these, together with contributions by Starhawk, Angela Davis, Michelle Russell, and other women whose politics and spirituality are profound and most decidedly *not* Christian, are expanding the ever-deepening wellsprings of feminist theological resources available to women, including Christian women.

So it is that Christian feminists have come struggling all the way into a theological place marked by our differences. We hold in common a relentless interest in the liberation of women. We are learning to ask how these differences matter and especially how they matter in each particular praxis. More and more, conventional religious differences—those of denominations and doctrine—have paled in importance to us as we have listened attentively to our own and other women's stories, and as we engage in common struggles for justice.

When Carter attended a meeting of about twenty male theologians (all but two of them white) who were discussing our project with her, one of the seminary deans asked, "But where are the women in your group in relation to the sacrament of baptism?" In other words, "Is this—from a masculinist perspective—a Christian project? And if so, how?"

We hear this question as getting right to the heart of what our work is all about. Yes, indeed, we are Christians. But we do not *begin* our work on the basis of any formal creed, confession, rite, or sacrament. To be faithful, we must respect the objections of many women, including some of us in Mud Flower, that baptism—a Christian ritual we own in various ways—is a patriarchal institution that sets women apart from one another for the sake of male bonding in the name of a Father, Son, and Holy Ghost.

144

We *begin* with a commitment to justice for all women and men. We *begin* with the study of our lives, taking seriously as theological data the truth and illusion, the small places and macrostructures, of who we are, where we have been, what we yearn for, and how we act in relation. Yet we also assume a connection between our lives and work and the life and work of Jesus and his friends, both past and present. As our stories show, we maintain a variety of relationships to our denominational heritages, although we reject traditional dogmatic, ecclesiastical interpretations of what makes a true believer. Nor can we ignore the deep and devastating critiques of Christian sexism that have been so fundamental a part of the experience of the women's movement in the church during the last fifteen years.

While we are Christians, our religious journeying has helped us affirm also that we are postchristian-Christians: postchristian-Calvinist/postchristian-Lutheran/postchristian-Baptist/postchristian-Anglican/postchristian-Roman Catholic. We are able, at least for the proximate present, to tolerate the ambiguity in these formulations, as long as we continue to struggle for the transformation of these traditions. Strengthened by the lines of continuity, jarred into struggle by the lines of conflict, we are proud and we are confident to refer to ourselves and our theologizing as *Christian.*

INCLUSIVITY IN FEMINIST THEOLOGY

Early in our work, we held an afternoon consultation with about thirty feminist theologians, including seminary professors, writers and authors, parish and campus ministers, pastoral counselors, and graduate students in theological studies. Our twofold purpose was:

1. To share the gist of our project: that we had received a grant for research on "implications of feminism for theological education"; that we had decided to build our work around the study of our lives; and that we had agreed, from the beginning, that Christian seminaries are in serious trouble, having failed, by and large, to appropriate either the meaning and value of women's lives or the intellectual/professional offerings of women and men who bring a feminist commitment to theological education.

2. To get responses to our work: Did these other feminists think we were on the right track? Were we being naive on one hand, cynical on the other? Were there any glaring oversights in our work? What did we need to emphasize, elaborate, clarify?

The consultation was too large and too short to carry us into the intricacies of in-depth conversation we had hoped for. There was resounding concurrence that Christian seminaries throughout the United States are in pedagogical, curricular, and theological shambles, in no small part because the well-being of women and racial/ethnic people is regarded as unessential to the enterprise.

Several specific questions our group raised with the consultants were acknowledged as important, but we had little time to discuss them during the consultation. Although Mud Flower has worked with these concerns in mind, we have had neither the time nor the resources to pursue these questions in detail:

Questions about the relationship between the denominations and the seminaries: Who sets the agenda for whom? In what ways do the churches express feminist concerns? What ought the relation to be between church and seminary? How can this relation be built and/or enhanced?

And questions about the experiences, commitments, and interests of feminist graduate students: How can women or men with a feminist perspective work creatively within the constraints of Ph.D. programs, which harbor such fierce resistance to curricular and pedagogical change and such serious contempt for feminist methods and women's perspectives?

Not surprisingly, a high level of interest in the issue of graduate studies was expressed among those women in our collective, as well as in the larger group, who are themselves current or recent graduate students or who teach at the graduate level. Special concern about the relation of church to seminary was shared by women who are involved primarily in the church as parish pastors, campus ministers, or educators for ministry.

The larger group broke along these lines into smaller discussion groups—several on church, one on graduate studies—which were asked to report back to the consultation as a whole. What Mud Flower learned after the fact has helped us realize how true it is that working inclusively of one another's life experiences is critical to the theological task—and how hard it is to be inclusive, in our theological work, of different perspectives.

At the time of the consultation, we were aware that certain women in each of the groups, and in the larger meeting, were more outspoken than others. Most of us in Mud Flower, however, did not think much about who the more vocal and less vocal participants were, and what patterns this participation created; and in what ways our roles as conveners of the consultation were contributing to the dynamics. We were to learn later from some of the participants—in particular, from several black women—that they had felt shut out by what they experienced as a white and racist agenda. For instance, when one black consultant asked a question about the theological basis of the project, she sensed that her input was dismissed out of a stereotypic assumption that because she was black she was pushing for a stronger emphasis on the Bible. Another black woman had felt her contributions on the issues of graduate study squelched by white professors, who, she perceived, assumed that they were experts on the subject.

Retrospectively, as we attempted to analyze our responsibility for the alienation several women experienced at the consultation, we had to acknowledge that we had indeed had a part in generating such an in-group dynamic. We recognized that the bonding that had developed among us, and also between some white members of Mud Flower and other well-known white feminist sisters, made others feel like outsiders.

The perceptions of the women alienated by our actions raised another dimension of that same critical issue we have emphasized in chapters two and three: How can we work together—again, with women whose life experiences or social locations are different from our own—without disregarding the interests and insights of others?

Racism, class dynamics, and homophobia may be more visible and prevalent sources of division among women than are the more recent marks of professional stature (faculty positions, numbers of well-known publications, age, professional rank). For that reason, we may not see the extent to which dynamics of professional stature operate among us. Several factors work to make us oblivious to these new, professional divisions: First, women who are often sensitive to our powerlessness in most institutions and gatherings do not realize that such power may be attributed to us. Second, since we believe in mutuality and sisterhood, we may be reluctant actually to see another hierarchical pattern that blemishes our vision (remember the white idealism we mentioned in chapter three). Third, we have longstanding experiences in educational settings of not being heard by those in authority. In a setting that aims to be feminist, we do not know how to relate creatively to female authority figures: If they take us seriously, can we trust them? Can we respect them? And if they do not take us seriously, can we destroy them? (For they sometimes seem to us more reprehensible than men in authority.)

We have much to learn about how we, any of us, can recognize, accept, and live graciously into the power of our own theological authority in such a way as to invite ongoing dialogue. We who aim to be teachers or ministers have much to learn about structuring situations and behavior in which we are clear that we seek to learn as well as to teach. We also have much to learn about how often, and why, we give our authority to people who we assume expect it, deserve it, or know what is best for us. Finally, we have a long way to go in being able to live unapologetically into our power/authority as creative theologians and teachers. We ought not to be ashamed of our power. Nor should we abdicate it, flaunt it, pretend it is nothing, or project it onto other women—and then either worship them, destroy them, or both.

Our consultation suggests that these dynamics of alienation may be especially acute between women of different racial/ethnic cultures. These are situations in which white supremacy and/or ethnic arrogance predictably may fester. The racism in any given situation may be an active force generated by contemporary white feminist theologians, or it may be a ghost of the scarred historical relation between white women and women of color. In either case, our sense is strong, as women of color, that we are, yet again, excluded from the possibility of being taken seriously by white women. And our feelings, our insights, and our lives demand engagement, if we, as racial/ethnic women, are actually going to do theology with white women that includes the lives of black, brown, and other women of color.

What, then, of doing theology that is genuinely inclusive, theology that seeks out the stories, insights, and analyses of those people usually excluded from theological discourse? Can feminist theologians be so broadly inclusive in our work that we simply accommodate all opinions, values, and interests? Will we, like many of our white male liberal colleagues, stand for so much that we actually stand for nothing? How do we draw the line between becoming exclusive and dogmatic cliques, on one hand, and a sort of theological sponge, playing let's-keep-everybody-happy, on the other?

The stakes of such questions are raised when we add the dimensions of serious engagement with persons who are not Christians. What if our words, the truths we speak, we who are white, Hispanic, black, Christian women, serve also to avoid any serious engagement with the lives of Jewish women, Muslim women, women of other religions? How do we, how can we, hold both to the truths of our experience and also participate in giving birth to new truths that can be claimed as ours only in reciprocal relation to those whose religious commitments are remarkably different from our own?

These are hard questions, and it would be foolish of us in Mud Flower to pretend we can answer them. We insist, however, on their significance among women in Christian theological circles. Our clue to the answers of how we stand open to one another is the quality of the dialogue we involve ourselves in and expect from other women and from those men who express interest in feminist theology. We say this, understanding that we are calling for long-term dialogue that must reflect our conflict and provoke our pain before any creative cooperative unity can emerge among us. Only in the context of relationship between concrete persons and groups can any answers to our questions be found.

We believe that we can do feminist theologies of liberation as black, Hispanic, and white Christian women in relation to one another as well as in relation to Asian women, postchristian women, Jewish women, and others. We are just beginning to trust that the complex, dialogical, and cooperative character of authentically reciprocal relation holds the key to any worthwhile, liberating theology—that is to say also, to a deeper experience of God. In this sense we believe that there *is* room for everybody in feminist theology.

Thus we underscore again that, in our God-stories, there are some genuine theological differences among us. Struggles for justice are central to each of our theological positions: civil rights, the movement against the war in Vietnam, the Columbia University riots, the Cuban revolution, the women's movement, the antipoverty movement, the gay/lesbian movement, the movement against U.S. imperialism in Central America. These concrete movements for social justice are located in different moments of our lives and religious experiences. They shape our theologies in different ways.

Such social/political movements opened the eyes of several of the white women in Mud Flower to the transforming lesson of "a connection between social justice and faith," in Nancy's words. For Bess, however, the music and songs of the black church went hand in hand with the civil rights movement.

> We had white policemen coming at us and we had our spirituals, our songs. That's all we had. And it was there, in those freedom marches and our commitment spiritually sung, there in that black tradition, that God was for me.

For Bess, those songs of the black church "called us into movement." This theology of justice is shaped very differently from, for example, Mary's sense that she had learned in church "the passivity of the status quo." When Bess adds that the "calling-up into movement" was God for her, it was a very different god from the sweet but distant and impotent god that Carter names as the god of her earlier years.

Today, many of us, perhaps all of us, might affirm Bess's sense that being called up into movement is one of the primary ways we experience God. But if white feminists are not sensitive to how critically important Bess's experience in the black church is to her theology, then white women may perpetuate racism by an assumption that the patriarchy of the black church tradition is identical to what white women have experienced in the white church.

Similarly, Carter's speaking of her earlier god as a coping device was a helpful concept for several of us who followed her in the telling of our narratives. But once again it is important to notice the nuances in the way we use this theological concept. Carter, Nancy, and Mary all seem to contrast their needs for a god who helped

150

them cope with events or social forces with which they were help-
less, with their later discoveries of a god who enables them to
struggle for justice. In different ways, their association of god with a
coping device is pejorative. Bess, in contrast, mentions coping in
direct continuity with struggle and hope. Alive to the real, lived
contradictions for her mother and grandmother, Bess affirms completely that "God would come through—not to deliver us from this,
but to move the struggle and clear the lines." This point is explicitly
connected to Bess's black feminist theology, to exploring the religion of her foremothers. She intertwines the doctrine of creation
and ongoing human creativity with a critique of theological education: "It's been with women, certainly this comes from my working
with women, that I've begun to really understand that creation can
only come out of chaos and that chaos is the mother of creation and
the source of our validity." This affirmation of women-and-chaos is in
direct opposition to Bess's experience of education, which, she
adds, makes us "afraid of chaos."

Bess's artistic skill may combine with her life as a black woman
and mother of five to produce this powerful and complex nuanced
set of judgments. Her insights, however, resonated in all our lives as
we recalled the high premium on order in many of our educational
experiences and in many theological perspectives. It is also true to
all our transformations in the women's movement, and to our experiences of genuine dialogue: They are not orderly. Our dialogue
does not proceed along lines that, "logically," we would expect it to
go. Our education cannot have its results programmed. Our lives do
not always make sense in the obvious or ready-made ways that many
linear, logical arguments make sense. (Perhaps our Boston consultation was not planned with enough room for chaos—trying to control
results often happens when planners are conscious that time is
short.)

We do believe, then, that there is room for expansive diversity
among women's lives within feminist theology. Our primary commitment as feminist theologians must be to the inclusion of voices of
heretofore excluded and marginated women. We must stand back,
get out of the way if need be, and make room for women whose lives
have passed unnoticed in the realm of theological education. Our
ultimate vision and commitment is that there is room for us all, in

our wisdom and our foolishness, our candor and our hiddenness, our public lives and our secret places. There is room for our mistakes, our imperfections, our stupidities; room for our alienation, our rage, and even for our prejudices and bigotries—provided we want to unlearn them. There is room for everybody's story and dreams, faith and doubt, history and present/future, as we come to know ourselves in relation to others. Only more experience, and more experience in dialogue with those who differ from us, can help us sort out more carefully which insights, which intellectual/political directions, will prove to be most illuminating and perceptive in our common theological/educational work.

Can we be exclusive, then, of any one, any attitude, any behavior? Yes. There is no room in theological education for refusals to engage in dialogue, for closed minds, or for shut-down hearts. There is no room for indifference to human well-being. We can and we will exclude the trivialization of women, of lesbians/gays, of people of color, of people from different ethnic groups, or of religions or cultures different from our own.

We do not judge harshly anyone's naiveté or ignorance about oppression, their own or that which they perpetuate against others. We know, from our own painful experiences, that these are steeped in real social forces which, generation upon generation, hold injustice in place. We cannot be cruel in our impatience that sexual, racial, class, or religious bigotry will not be tolerated. And yet, we must stand clear and firm that, *regardless of attitudes*, certain *actions* are unacceptable—period. Changing attitudes alone will not undo the sources of suspicion and division among us. Praying for openness or sermonizing about openness and dialogue may be helpful resources in their times and places, but neither of them substitutes for actual acts of reciprocity, dialogue, learning, change.

As theological educators, we must assume an openness to learning as indispensable to education, and we must draw a sharp line between those who are open to learning and those who refuse to learn. Of course, men and women who refuse to learn can enroll in classes in feminist theology, although such persons tend to avoid feminist studies—if they are able to, as they usually are.

No one can be open to feminist theology if it is not offered, or if there are no faculty members in seminaries to teach it. No one who is white can be open to dialogue regarding racism in the abstract, without either black persons concretely present with whom to speak or other white persons willing to take the responsibility to address white racism. No theological seminary in our time can make claims to concern for inclusiveness if it does not have, in its faculty and student body, increasing numbers of women of different racial/ ethnic groups as well as racial/ethnic men. Without such inclusive personnel, theological seminaries are cutting themselves off from the most challenging development in the contemporary realm of theological education.

The exclusive nature of most theological faculties and academic curricula, however, is no reason for feminist theology to be as exclusive as are the institutions in which we must perforce live and learn and work. We are not interested in replicating patriarchy but in undoing it, transforming it. The excluding patterns of our theological institutions are the strongest reasons for feminist theology to place its commitments to justice for *all* oppressed persons front and center. As our experience at the Boston consultation demonstrates, even persons whose central focus is inclusivity are able to structure situations that function to set up new hierarchies of ins-and-outs and to perpetuate racism. Feminist theologians must be vigilant to the unseen ways our commitments are belied by our practice and be ready to change yet again in directions productive of greater justice. As our feminist foresisters put it, echoing the once lively tradition of U.S. revolutionary struggle, "eternal vigilance is the price of freedom." As economic distress grows and various political backlash groups wax and wane, no one searching for justice can afford to rest on her laurels.

THE LANGUAGE OF FEMINIST THEOLOGY: INCLUSIVE OF WOMEN'S EXPERIENCES

Both confusion and excitement beset us today in theological education, due in no small part to issues stemming from theological and educational language. Many of our colleagues in theology have studied the problem of religious language. Some of us share the fascination with such questions, which have been virtually the central issue of twentieth-century European and North American theology and philosophy. As feminists, however, our concerns do not stem from the familiar statements of such problems (such as how religious language is used and to what it refers; its similarities or differences from scientific language or other language games). Rather, what is of importance to us as feminist theologians is twofold: First, the political and ethical dimensions of our language structures and language use, which often go unnoticed by those inquiring into linguistic questions; and second, the dimensions of creativity in language that are so essential to bringing women's experience into speech and thus fully into our symbolic universe(s).

Sexist and racist language, such as speaking of "the doctrine of man" or using black as a synonym for evil have been commented upon at length, especially in terms of the way the English language itself functions. While we cannot provide an in-depth treatment of these issues here (we refer the reader to the bibliography), we do believe that in any discussion of theology the issue of how power and language intertwine is critical. We believe this is why all of us in seminaries are witnessing such unrest and frequently virulent debate around inclusive language, nonsexist liturgies, and the place of feminist theology and women's studies in theological curricula. Language is ordinarily recognized as a valid, even critical, focus for theological reflection and analysis. In fact, in Christian traditions no metaphor for divine revelation is as central as the Word. But when feminists draw attention to exclusive language or urge worship committees and faculty members to speak and think more inclusively, our concerns for language are treated with contempt, as distractions from *serious* theological scholarship and worship, as trivial, or as antiintellectual. We and many other women find this situation ironic, painful, and brutalizing.

Such pain and conflict are only one side of what we are experiencing in the engagement between gender justice and theological language. We perceive a radical, terrifying disjuncture between the prevailing symbolic universe of Christian theology and our well-grounded senses of identity as women in struggles for justice. Yet we have also found in that very disjuncture opportunity for creative response and discovery.

Women have struggled to bring our experiences and insights into

154

the realm of common discourse, as we have "heard each other into speech," trying new approaches: Daly's method of "wrenching the semantic field" has challenged us, and investigations into forgotten traditions have transformed our sense of ourselves. We have developed metaphors and images or poetic creations for our own time that are fraught with insight. All this is exciting.

The basic language issue for us as Christian women in theological education today has to do with the creative effort of bringing our female lives into the ongoing work of constructive theology. It has to do with exploring the differences and similarities that would result were all our lives—the full panoply of our concrete variations as poor and rich women in our cultural, racial, and ethnic diversity—taken with full seriousness and sensitivity in the theological enterprise. The constructive project of inclusive language has justice as its center and its aim—reshaping theology so that our lives and work themselves are an ongoing praxis of transforming the Christian symbolic universe toward justice for all women and racial/ethnic men. Our work in this book shares this aim and central concern.

If it is true that the patriarchal disease of our theology is deep, our need for new language also runs deep. The social and relational perspective of the Mud Flower collective leads us to presume that such far-reaching transformation will not occur quickly. We see a dialectical relationship between the languages we use and the social institutions that are part of the same symbolic universe. Social and symbolic changes go together, and must both be addressed. The cultural and collective organizing function of language means that language is an individual's tool only within a specific social and institutional context. Linguistic change will never be sustained if its institutionalization does not occur.

To acknowledge that the required changes are massive and that they will take time is not a counsel of pessimism, however. The all-pervading nature of situations and dynamics of injustice is itself the reason feminists emphasize the necessity of beginning with the study of our lives. To take our lives seriously is to establish a beach-head against injustice, enabling us to begin to work the small changes in our lives that release new power and energy. Patriarchal yardsticks are not appropriate for measuring feminist transformations; at this stage of our struggle, big changes—as in taller skyscrapers or GNP growth—are misleading. To begin with the bits and pieces of our daily lives, striving for honesty and authentic speech, is to start with the power we have at hand.

There are particular emphases in women's stories that have far-reaching implications for the ways we do theology. The feminist phrase, "the personal is political," characterizes the nuances of our narratives. Anyone paying careful attention to our stories, the way they are phrased, the terms in which they are told, the order in which anecdotes are related, will notice the way this conviction shapes our theologies. Kate, for instance, brackets her story of injustice while abroad—"the first time I'd ever been called nigger to my face"—with two stories about personal love and intimacy; all three of those stories dramatically make the same point: "There was no God." Carter experienced simultaneously a "mini-nervous-breakdown" and the Columbia University riots, much as Mary found the freedom to change in a uniquely personal way regarding her birthmark during her work with the civil rights struggle in Chicago. Bess parallels "remembering these prayer petitions my grandmother and mother had been into" with the question, "Is God a white racist?" Beverly's statement of her experience summarizes this feminist sense that public issues and personal experience must be seen and understood together.

> The more I long for connection, the more I begin to know what justice is, where justice is really grounded. Justice, of course, can't happen until the connections are really being made, until others call you forth, connect with you, make you take yourself seriously.

This insight, that social injustice and personal pain, or seeking social justice and personal healing, go together is a deeply needed corrective to much contemporary theology that wrongly denies this connection.

In the constructive task, the theologian, learner or teacher, cannot operate as though she is distanced from the truths she speaks. Something new cannot be discovered, revealed, or offered unless the discoverer owns up to what difference this discovery or insight makes in her or his life. In coming to new theological learning and linguistic transformation, each person must strive to speak words that adequately convey the significance of what she is attempting to describe. For us, this may mean speaking with passion, always with integrity, sometimes in ringing phrases, sometimes in quiet but firm tones. It does not mean toeing an ideological or ecclesiastical or intellectual line, nor does it involve mechanical displays of emotion; but there needs to be a dimension of expressiveness in our theological work now too frequently missing in theological education.

Since constructive theology cannot be routinized, there are no ready-made formulas for doing feminist theology. However, the experience gained through the last fifteen years of groping search for critiques and alternatives to dominant methods has taught us something. To begin, as we did, seriously telling our stories enabled us to stay close to our particular experiences. In this process, we also found that it was critical to attend carefully to the images we used and to the process of imaging itself. Recall that Kate initiated our session by asking us to name the "images, symbols, or rituals" that made God present to us. Her instruction to the group, based on a hermeneutic of no-God/God, was central to the stories some of us told, although not to others. Still, her call for our images made for such lively, vivid, and memorable communication that we named and remembered each person's story by its most striking image.

IMAGING: THE PRIMARY LANGUAGE OF FEMINIST THEOLOGY

Consider the contrast between this conception of theological language and much of the theology taught within theological schools across the country. There the subdisciplines of systematic theology, philosophical theology, historical theology, or dogmatic/confessional theology focus on concepts. Theological work is presumed to proceed in deductive or analytical modes of thought; the primary value of theological reflection to the reader or student appears to be clarity, coherence, precision, universalizability of abstraction, and order. Theological adequacy is measured by these characteristics and also by conformity to one's theological tradition. These theological criteria have their place, but when enabling people to do theology

157

in a constructive fashion is a genuine concern, such criteria must be understood as, at best, provisional, and as subsidiary to other values.

Feminist theologians, aiming to create theologies shaped by female experiences previously unacknowledged and unattended to in Christian tradition, need quite different criteria for adequacy. Feminist theology must be inductive, synthetic, and imaginative. Its primary values include perceptiveness, insight, depth and breadth of critical illumination, and respect for the diversity of experiences of persons in different social locations.

A feminist critique of patriarchal theology is not exhausted when we have identified the exclusion of women and racial/ethnic men and those of nondominant cultures from the explicit conceptual frameworks built over generations to articulate and shape the religious experience of Christian believers. As numerous feminist theologians, including Nelle Morton and Mary Daly, have pointed out, patriarchy reaches to the nonverbal, nonconceptual level, stultifying the imagination itself. It is precisely our recognition of this tenacious hold of patriarchal images, functioning at prerational levels, that convince us of the long-term nature of the feminist struggle. Many can give verbal assent to the equality of women and men but simultaneously insist that we must continue to affirm the image of the church as the bride of Christ, or of the Godhead as male. Clearly, surface acknowledgments of women's claims to equality do not yet touch the heart of the problem. Even women who profess to be feminist have internalized these theological images of female inferiority. The transformation required of all of us, female and male, involves precisely the deepest levels of ourselves and our social order. Imagination is as political as language is.

Thus, images, rather than conceptual discourse or linear logic, are the roots of feminist theology, our primary language. Images are not simply the first mode of our expression, the one we employ before we get down to serious business, but the most basic—and usually the most substantive—language of feminist theology. To image is to portray what is experienced in word pictures, stories and narrative, sound, movement, art. It is a nonexpository form of communication that mobilizes our imaginative faculties.

During our discussions of what feminism is, we found ourselves frustrated at the inadequacy of our linear, analytical statements. It was not that what we were saying was wrong, or without substantive merit. Rather, in our process of defining feminism, our work seemed to beg for a more animated spirit than our language was reflecting.

Bess helped bring our conversation to life by sharing two stories.

> When I was a child, the boys in the neighborhood had this game, with rope; you know, they'd get a rope and then pull and tug, tug o' war, till finally some side would jerk the rope away from the others, who'd fall down. And the girls, we weren't allowed to play with them in this tug o' war; so we figured out how to make our own rope—out of those little flowers, dandelions. You just keep adding them, one to the other, and you can go on and on; anybody, even the boys, could join us; and the whole purpose of our game was to create this dandelion chain—that was it. And we'd keep going, creating, till our mamas called us home.

> In one of my first theology classes, we were supposed to do skits—a women's skit and a men's skit, about creation. And the women, we got in a circle and sat on each other's knees and just swayed back and forth. And, you know, those men—they went out of the room and came running in and flashed the lights off and on, boom! atomic explosion! crash! boom! and then, in the skit, one of the men would shout, "Don't let her be born! Don't let the sibyl be born!"

Images of tug o' war and dandelion chains; of circles/touching/swaying, and of flashes/noises/atomic explosion. Images of creation, of men's lives and women's lives in relation to creative process. And the sibyl? An image, we suppose, of women's mythological power to undo what man has done. Bess's images sparked new energy and refreshed communication among us; a continuation of the discussion's themes was charged with new interest and passion.

Imaging is basic to appropriating our experience. To image is to recall experience, although not necessarily in a literal way. The experience out of which the image rises may be distilled into its essential meaning, often represented by a sign or symbol, and connected synthetically to other dimensions of experience. Images are intensely participatory, calling for connections with the experience of others if they are to be received meaningfully and powerfully, as Bess's were, by our collective.

Images call for interpretation, but they lead us into that interpretation without short-circuiting the circle of response, which happens often when we attempt to explain, elaborate, define, or systematize insights before we have lived into them. Furthermore, people interpret an image in different ways, and these varying interpretations elicit collaborative reflection and theorizing. There is no single, univocal, or correct interpretation of an image. While an image may speak more readily to some groups than to others, the character of images protects experience from reductionist manipulation. There is, after all, no uniform or "best" way to comprehend or conceptualize a human experience, which is why collectivity and accountability are critical in the doing of good theology.

Images are usually more complex than concepts precisely because they distill and synthesize, condense, displace, and expand meaning as experienced. They may be ambiguous and untidy, luring us toward hitherto unexplored horizons of meaning. They can accomplish tasks of suggestibility that discursive concepts, bounded by their definitions and made for precision tooling, do not typically achieve.

Imaging enables a process of holistic expression and communication that informs and nourishes our emotional depths, resisting fragmentation. Images initiate movement in our life processes, and in our conceptual processes as well. They follow a "transformational logic" rather than a static, linear connection. The value of imaging, as a mode of theological teaching and learning, is that it creates relationship—concrete bonds—among those engaged in the process.

In our stories, identifying images that are most alive to us, certain features of our religious experience stand out as potentially rich material for theological elaboration. Some are those we typically associate with women, others not. Kate's sense of experiencing a miracle when she plays with her nieces and nephews expresses the singular importance many women attribute to our relationship with children—not a theme much reflected on theologically in much malestream theology. Beverly's electric circuit image stands out because, as a technological image, it is not what sex-role stereotyping would lead us to expect from a woman. The rich resonances of the biblical and natural sources of religious insight appear in Bess's olive branch, and here it is an image of peace-making that does not participate in "smoothing over the contradictions." It is posed as a compassionate, if demanding, invitation to dialogue between black and white women. Carter's "*¡Presente!*" image is a powerful contemporary restatement of resurrection, energetically inclusive of women and men who have given their lives for justice. Nor can the meaning of any of these images be exhausted by this list of associations.

A theological process grounded in imaging invites us to draw from our own lived-experience, to present ourselves, our sense of reality, and to make sense of the stories, words, pictures, or sounds that others share. Imaging makes us aware that we are bringing our own lives and perceptions to theology. Activating our imaginative resources makes clear that the concrete truths of our lives, memories, and values are foundational to our conceptual work. The sharing of images—of what we remember, what we value, what we fear or long for—involves vulnerability and ability to touch and be touched. This means that the theological context must be one in which certain procedures about trust-keeping and nonjudgmental listening operate. Imaging is a gift we share in doing feminist theology, and like all gifts, it must be respectfully received if the power of shared existence is to emerge.

It is not accidental that concern to recover the imaginal dimension entices feminists to take seriously postchristian spirituality, wicca, or other of the world's religions. Many of these alternative traditions are rich, complex, and deep in the images they provide to women, as Mary's mention of "Changing Woman" from Navaho religion in her story illustrates. Each of us has learned from such alternative sources how deprived we have been by Western Christianity, how thoroughly we need a transformation of images, how much more there is to learn about ourselves and our global sisters from a fuller appropriation of imagery—and we expect to continue to be transformed by appropriating new traditions.

As crucial as the ongoing transformation of images is, however, we agree that it is but one critical dimension of needed social change. In fact, from our perspective, changing images are as much a sign of other ongoing social change as a source of change. Our point here is that images are a source of spiritual transformation in ways that concepts are not; they replenish our spirits, nurture us, sustain us as we learn to abide in the pursuit of justice, which is our politics.

• THE SPIRITUALITY OF FEMINIST THEOLOGICAL POLITICS: A CHALLENGE TO DOMINANT SPIRITUALITY •

We are troubled by the emergence on seminary campuses of a deep fixation with "true" spirituality. This seems especially the case among white/Anglo seminarians. A decade ago many theological students had therapists. Today many seek spiritual directors. We are troubled by what passes for concern for spirituality not because we reject the expressed need and desire to know God, but rather because so many seem to accept the nonreflective, nondialogic, nonrelational interiority of the experience of God. We believe this equation of spirituality with privatized self/God relationships is thoroughly ideological (Euroamerican), a sacralization of the view of the world that makes members of dominant cultures, classes, and races unaccountable to others in their daily lives and religion.

In theological education today, "spirituality" sounds to us like a code word for:

- getting myself together
- feeling good about myself
- not getting carried away by such transitory things of this world as political movements
- what to do since there is no sense of community among us
- attempting to be holy, a *serious* believer in God
- attempting to imitate the mystics and the contemplatives
- and especially a way out of *conflict*

FEMINIST SPIRITUALITY

A number of our colleagues who are spiritual directors have claimed that the preoccupation among many students today with their interior lives is merely a corrective to the excesses of the 1960s and early 1970s, a suggestion laden with assumptions that we do not share—especially the charge that the student activism of a generation past was excessively other-oriented. Our colleagues who advocate spiritual direction also claim that the new spirituality will lead to a more radical love of neighbor as self. We are skeptical of this claim, if only because this spirituality has become popular at precisely that point in contemporary history at which many Christians have lost interest in social justice. Nor do we buy the dubious theory that human dispositions swing back and forth, like pendulums, between self and others, spirituality and politics, or pastoral and prophetic work. To the extent that our lives lend credence to this theory by such dualistic shifts, or through separating private concerns and public participation, we are leading unintegrated, unfocused lives. By contrast, we believe that when community is strong and growing, when justice is a constant and common concern, when women and men are as "caught up" in the lives of others as in their own lives, only then can we rightfully celebrate our spirituality—the movement of God's Spirit among us.

Insofar as persons who seek God by way of spirituality share a pressing, burning desire to realize more fully the power of God moving among and between and within and beyond us, we welcome their contributions as those who share a common pilgrimage. All of us become arrogant pretenders if we assume sure knowledge of The Way to God, to goodness, to peace, or to justice. Among the seven of us, there is now some confidence—as well as some mixture of grief and relief—that there is *no* such way to God to be found by any one, or two, or even seven of us, if we are looking only at ourselves, our own interiors, as the locus of spiritual movement. We have insisted that we must begin by examining our lives; but we have also come to affirm without qualification that no one of us, nor all of us together, can find, or be found by, God except in the movement that carries us beyond the boundaries of our skins (or our group), and in so doing helps us realize more fully who we are, where we stand, what we can or must do, as persons in relation to other persons, groups, and living things.

Serious efforts in seminary to teach, learn, and practice spirituality as a profoundly social and historical discipline would, we believe, contribute to the struggle for justice. As Ntozake Shange demonstrates, "to find god in myself and to love her fiercely" is a formidable, anguishing task, and a high calling. Dorothee Sölle, Thomas Merton, and scores of earlier Christian mystics have insisted that the quest for God, and the concomitant desire to stand open to the power of Spirit, are not, in either the first or final place, a private enterprise. Spirituality is fundamentally a communal commitment, a bonding between and among us, a relational pilgrimage—with God precisely as God is engaged and accepted in our love of neighbor as self.

All of us who are theological educators should be doing all within our power and resources to help teach a spirituality—or a spiritual politic—in which standing with our neighbor means standing with that neighbor in struggles for her/his rights, well-being, and dignity. If we are consumed by that spirituality which is of God, there is no way to get ourselves off the hook of being justice-makers. What this also means concretely for us as women is that our spirituality is real and dynamic when we are doing any or many of the activities involved in standing for justice, such as:

- attempting to take our lives seriously
- refusing to compromise the well-being of a sister in order to keep the peace
- colliding and joining in conflict with each other, and with men, on behalf of any woman whose life is being ignored, trivialized, or put down by women or by men
- refusing to relinquish the women's issue—what affects our own and our sisters' lives—for the sake of some presumed "greater cause"
- refusing to ignore and be silent about the effects of racism, classism, sexism, homophobia, and other structures of injustice—such as discrimination against the handicapped or the elderly—that inhibit the movement of the Spirit among us
- standing open to new learnings; to confession, repentance, and conversion; to naming and growing on the basis of our mistakes.

That spirituality is inextricable from political and social responsibility is no new notion. Remember the prophets and Jesus, the histories of many women and men whom the church today regards as saints—Martin Luther King Jr.; Simone Weil; the late Archbishop of San Salvador, Oscar Romero. What *is* new in the spirituality we propose is that it has to do centrally with the liberation of women of all racial/ethnic heritages. When the God who calls us to speak the truth of our daily lives is the same God who solaces us at her bosom and calls us into movement, we cannot separate spirituality and politics. The wellspring of the effective, creative power we call God is the experience of right relation—just, reciprocal, mutually empowering relation. This is the bond by which all are empowered, a connectedness to others in which there is no assumption that any*one* should be in control of relation, or that any*one* should be on top of any other, either dominant or subordinate to others.

Whether those in relation are races or classes of people or individual people—spouses, friends, lovers, educators, learners—right relation consists in giving *and* receiving, teaching *and* learning, speaking *and* listening. Put simply from this perspective, classism, racism, sexism, and heterosexism are structures founded and perpetuated upon the lack of right relation—between those with access to wealth and those without; between people of color and white people; between men and women; and between those of whatever color or class who support (or are perceived to support) the insistence that the genital relation between male and female is normative and necessary and those whose lives do not conform to this demand. Wherever there is a lack of right relation, those who hold the power do not experience any need to receive from, or learn from, those who are without power in relation.

Without a vision of justice we readily forget that the rich literally live off the work of the poor. We fail to remember that since they "founded" this nation, white people have been dependent on and enriched by the work of indigenous and black people. We do not see, much less acknowledge, that the dominant culture consumes the fruitful labors of Hispanic migrant workers; or that men "make it" professionally because women keep their lives in order, tend "their" homes, nurture "their" children; or that married and straight people in this nation feed themselves fat on the intellectual, cultural, and economic contributions of single people and homosexuals.

Those who possess power in our world/church often fail to realize the value of what others give to their lives. Worse yet, when they do become aware of what others have done for them, many holders of power make gestures of appreciation—a tip, a raise, a present—without acknowledging the ways in which their possession of power continues to exploit others. To confess wrongdoing? To admit complicity in injustice? No, there is too little confession—and much denial and rationalizing—among Christian people. To be actually sorry for oppression is to be converted, to turn around, "to go sin no more," to make every effort to change the way we live our lives. By contrast, when the possessors of power in our society are faced with the pain and anger of those who suffer economic, sexual, or racial injustice, they most often denounce these complaints as irrational and mobilize their massive political and economic resources in order to keep the powerless "in their place"—to keep the poor, people of color, all women, and all gay men/lesbians under the thumb of The Man.

Right relation is born of, and breeds, ongoing desire for and efforts toward the empowerment of all persons, to the end that no one is left without food and shelter, tenderness and respect, appreciation and self-worth, work and play, leisure and responsibility for the common good. No one is without power to participate in naming what is real for us, and in shaping the patterns of our lives and faith as a community—whether of women, of Christians, of blacks, or of Hispanic peoples.

Working toward right relation is the heart of feminist spirituality. Like all good things, it has a utopic ring to it: it is a call toward a way of being as yet unrealized; it is a vision of how we might better experience and understand the possibilities of our lives together. But it is not simply "future" or as yet "no-where." Our creative potential is actualized even now, as it has been all along, whenever we are reciprocally engaged. Our creative power is source and resource for our struggle, because through it we experience ourselves and others as loving and loved, bearing life and brought to live, givers and receivers of blessing. Therein God lives *in* the roots of our spirituality and politics.

At the close of our first session together, we celebrated a wicca ritual. We stood quietly in a circle and recalled other women who have empowered us and whom we have empowered. Some of us

166

named particular women, calling them into the circle to be with us in our work. We prayed for these women, named and unnamed; and also for those we had forgotten or have not known; we prayed for one another. Finally, in witness to the power of naming and touching, each of us in turn addressed the woman on her left, named herself, and extended a hand in friendship. "Kate, my name is Ada-Maria, and I give you my hand." Then each of us spoke again, addressing by name the woman beside her. "Your name is Nancy. May it be well with you." Finally, each of us named herself again, turned to the sister beside her, and affirmed "My name is . . . and it *is* well with me."

This ritual reflected our faith in our collective power to bless and be blessed, our experience of mutuality as enabling. Those of us who are systematic theologians by training might be able to explicate a theology of mutuality—at least one of us has done exactly that—but in no way can the power of right relation be experienced simply by writing, reading, or talking about mutuality. As Bess said, "You have to live the reality to know it." Nothing is clearer to us than our responsibility, and the responsibility of all learners/teachers, not merely to talk about spirituality, creation, liberation, or human and divine well-being, but rather to enable one another actually to participate in creating and liberating relationships and in communities and institutions that foster human well-being in the commonwealth of God.

THE LIMITS OF OUR WORK: FEMINIST POLITICS AMONG WOMEN IN SEMINARY

In choosing to study our lives in relation to one another, we are aware that we excluded other possibilities. Beginning with our lives has enabled us to perceive our deep differences, but we are aware that our lack of inclusivity renders the particularity of many other women in theological education invisible. Our decision to emphasize, in this project, the relation between white, black, Hispanic Christian feminists, was, de facto, a decision *not* to attempt a more inclusive study of groups of women in seminaries. We do not and cannot represent the particular experience of women whose diversity is not represented among us. Yet not to acknowledge the significance of our experience of relations with them would be a critical omission. Women of every cultural and racial/ethnic group are moving into theological education today. Asian women, indigenous women, women from Eurasia come as pioneers, seeking a praxis of ministry that empowers their communities. Often the only women of their culture in a seminary, these sisters' lives are sometimes rendered invisible not only by dominant male glibness about universality, but by the cultural insensitivity of white women like ourselves as well. Here we can only acknowledge this reality, and emphasize that the alienations among women that we have named here do not begin to exhaust the needed confrontations among Christian women. Nor does our responsibility for right or just relationship end with the alienations that separate us from Christian sisters.

Relationships Between Christian Feminists and Those of Other Traditions of Western Monotheism: Judaism and Islam

Judaism. As we have noted already, we see relationships between Christian and Jewish feminists to be both exciting and promising and fraught with difficulty. With Jewish feminists, we have an opportunity to re-gather threads once woven into a common religious heritage but destroyed by competition and Christian anti-Semitism. Still, we have a vast and fertile terrain on which to work together in theology, especially when Christian feminists join Jewish sisters in a shared insistence that right relation, or justice-making, is the arena in which God moves and acts.

We must recognize the often subtle, and always violating, character of Christian feminist anti-Semitism that extends an oppressive constant in Christian life and theory. Whenever Christian feminists blithely caricature Judaism as the source of patriarchy from which Christ delivers or portrays "law" as transcended by the Christian gospel of liberation, we demonstrate our insensitivity to Christian anti-Semitism. Our historical knowledge is superficial, if we operate in the "faith" that, somehow, Christology provides an answer to Jewish expectations, or the salvific solution to Jewish spiritual questions. We must rather learn to acknowledge a strong relationship between Christian anti-Semitism and Christian theological forgetfulness of justice in history. In feminist Christian-Jewish relations, we must learn our own tradition's history of oppression, come down to earth in our theologizing, and learn from those we have oppressed.

Islam. In our predominantly white educational situations, few Christian feminists have had the opportunity to engage feminists from the tradition of Islam. This has resulted in a gap in our theological education, especially in view of the political and religious turmoil in the Middle East, a conflict rooted in the historical tensions among Jews, Muslims, and Christians.

While members of Mud Flower are disturbed by the blatantly racist treatment of Palestinians by significant sectors of Israeli society, we are distressed by the ongoing role of important segments of the Christian world in producing, maintaining, and benefitting from such imperialistic practices against poor, darker, and often Islamic, people throughout the Third World, including the Middle East.

Christian and Muslim feminists might benefit mutually from working together on ways in which theological arrogance, national chauvinism, and the oppression of women go hand in hand, however disparate their various cultural manifestations. But such dialogue and cooperation between Muslim feminists and *white* Christian feminists is unlikely to be fruitful unless white Christians understand that, in relation to Muslims, our *religious* imperialism has been frequently steeped in our sense of *racial* superiority.

Relationships Between Christian and Postchristian Feminists

Within and beyond the seminaries, relationships between Christian and postchristian feminists are especially poignant, and often heated. The relations are poignant, we believe, because so many women are postchristian even as we remain Christian—and perhaps

169

vice-versa as well. The radicality of our faith claims must now encompass and celebrate lines of theological continuity between our own lives and the lives of many who have been cast out of the churches as heretics or who have never been, or desired to be, Christian. We cannot disavow our relation to sisters who challenge Christianity.

We believe that as feminists, Christian and postchristian women have more in common than not. All of us are outraged at what Christian men have done to women in the name of the Christian God. All of us struggle against the domination and all-controlling omnipotence of the Great White GodFather, who reigns over the lives of all women and men in this society; it is to his demise that we are all committed. Furthermore, our lives are in fundamental relationship with the lives of these other sisters. We have the same needs for paychecks and child care, for opportunities to worship and participate in spiritual community in ways that do not damage but enhance our well-being, for being taken seriously emotionally and intellectually and vocationally. We struggle with the same social forces.

We acknowledge, however, that Christian (or Christian/postchristian) women and explicitly postchristian feminists have chosen different strategies of struggle, which have their own integrity. We concede that our choices have often been made pragmatically. We Christian feminists often remain within the churches because of historical circumstances related to our most concrete responsibilities. Because we owe accountability to the communities that gave us birth, because of our desires to transform the sexism and racism and classism of our own communities and traditions, because of our loyalties to the future prospects of girl children and woman baptized in the churches to which we belong, we stand our ground and continue to claim our relationships to Christianity. Similarly, postchristian feminists often leave Christianity because of the specific conditions of our/their historical situations, because of their accountability to the communities that gave them birth, because of desires to expose the sexism and racism and classism of the Christian tradition, because of loyalty to the future prospects of women. Christian feminists must be able to tolerate existentially the messy mixture of conflict and nurturance and of truth and evasion we find

170

in churches, but postchristian feminists also have to tolerate the ambiguous mixture of evasion and courage in the new religious ethos. What separates us is not our basic commitments, but our differing analyses of how transformations toward justice may be best achieved. Postchristian feminists believe that alternative communities offer women options that they do not have within Christianity, and that the existence of alternative communities of faith may render obsolete the deifications of God the Father or make the spirituality of male supremacy obsolete. Christian feminists believe that working from within religious institutions offers women options we do not otherwise have for embodying female spiritual power in a public, and therefore transformative way, and see this expression of female power as the best route to the transformation of male-oriented systems of deity. No more than postchristian women can Christian feminists give uncritical obeisance to the existing structures of the patriarchal church. Our loyalties among Christians are centered and enfolded within the community of faith that makes justice happen. Where justice is being done, the people of God are taking shape among us.

Leaving the churches is often a more viable option for white women than for racial/ethnic women. We who are feminists of racial/ethnic backgrounds and communities cannot always make moving beyond God the Father our only, or even our most pressing, concern. In the day-to-day lives of feminists of color, there is a struggle to get beyond God the White Sister, who, for all we can see, patterns her life on the same racist and classist presuppositions as the Great White GodFather. We have less to fear in the black male Christ than in the Goddess if her face is white.

In spite of this, all of us recognize that struggling to learn to do theology in predominantly Christian theological schools often is an agonizing business for postchristian feminists, whose questions are ignored, whose presence is felt to be threatening to Christian orthodoxy, whose intellectual integrity is challenged or trivialized, who are stereotyped and systematically caricatured by administrators, faculty members, or other students. In the absence of women-centered and women-directed theological schools, such religious feminists seeking theological degrees have little choice except to attend the patriarchal Christian institutions that provide

171

needed degrees. Like us, postchristian women have to winnow out the intellectually and spiritually useless chaff, seeking diligently for the few resources that are genuinely helpful to the theological reconstruction they seek.

We Christian feminists often depend on these postchristian feminist sisters to keep us honest, to push us beyond our own constricting provincialisms, or to point us toward new relational/theological/ritual possibilities. We also must hold ourselves accountable, however, so that our gratitude to these no-nonsense, woman-loving postchristian friends and colleagues acts itself out in clear and unqualified solidarity and respect. We must be clear that we need our postchristian sisters and that we are asking them not to throw us out of their lives along with the church. We want them to give us the benefit of doubt, not to read our motives for staying in the churches merely as a lingering need for male approval or male identification. The seriousness of misogyny means that we need each other. In our collective creativity we believe we can find new ways to be in solidarity, to open new lines of dialogue and honest discussion.

Relationships Between Christian Feminists and Those of Other Religious/Spiritual Traditions

Insofar as a good many feminists are practitioners of wicca or of various Eastern rites, such as Zen, the concrete ecumenical issues among feminists pose new and exciting challenges. In our pluralistic world, persons who are neither Christian nor monotheistic must be taken seriously by any of us who profess justice.

Among us Christians in the United States, ignorance of other religious traditions is often a major problem. Popular Christianized stereotypes of other religions abound, especially in the form of fear of paganism. Courses that clarify the religious pluralism of the world should be available to all Christian seminarians, including the study of that old religion, wicca. Such courses must focus on the practices of popular religion, not only on the rationalized religious systems of dominant elites. This is especially important in feminist theology, because "official" religious systems are articulated by men, whereas women's spiritual impact is great in people's religion, in spiritual practice "from below."

Our religious ignorance as Christians correlates with our fear of getting too close to the practices of other religions. Is it really the unknown that we fear? It is more likely that we may really fear learning about ourselves, that we carry various emotional and traditional taboos. Our fear is of being tainted by unchristian, pagan practices, of being seen as heretical. We have insisted already that whenever Christian women historically have been interested in the empowerment of women, we have been branded as pagan. We believe, especially in the case of wicca, that we may have learned to be afraid of our own womanpower. Wicca has much to teach Christians about the value and beauty of female species being; and about our relation as women and men to the earth and sky, the cycles and seasons. These lessons, which also are harbored in other traditional religions—those of Native American, African, and Asian traditions—bring sorely needed correctives to dualistic Christian historicalism, which invites us to perceive ourselves as set over against "nature," and our own human "nature" as set over against God.

Relationships Between Feminists and Other Women in Theological Education

The most troublesome relation among women in seminaries at this juncture is between those of us who embrace feminism and women who believe feminism is a negative and dangerous force. This is often the line between "good" girls and "bad" girls, and the side on which we are characterized depends on who wishes to render a divisive judgment. Our relationships to women who do not identify with feminism take different forms depending on the mercurial quality of institutional politics.

At the moment there are many women in seminary who think of themselves as sympathetic to feminism but who wish to avoid conflictual situations or fear being too clearly labeled as feminist. Some women construct theological positions that put the highest possible premium on reconciliation, goodwill, and the need for individuals to change their attitudes. Such women are often concerned about alienating men. Inclusiveness and harmony may become such preoccupations that processes of social change are seen through rose-tinted glasses. When our most pressing desire is for conflict avoidance, for peace with men rather than for justice and respect among women, we punish sisters who are not so fearful of conflict. Often white middle-class women are reluctant to see that gender alienation and male supremacy are massive political realities, structural problems in the world/church, matters for which anger, conflict, outrage, and impatience are appropriate, healthy responses.

To the extent that we try to avoid conflict with men, our feminism really means that we are interested, primarily, in making it in a man's world. Invariably such women, who may rise occasionally on the professional ladders of success, will usually be *white* women who, like their male counterparts, have had access to *economic privilege.* This sort of tepid fear of conflict lends credibility to the charge that feminism is a white women's affair. The problem with the sort of feminism women who fear conflict espouse is that it masks a failure to take seriously the concrete life experiences of most women in this world, most of whom are not white and do not have access to money or to conditions that support easy access to power.

Even so, we must remember that some of the white authors of this book began our feminist journey with this sort of liberal misconception of what feminism involves. We acknowledge this starting place very much as part of our story and pilgrimage. None of us intended to be indifferent to the lives of other women, but we failed earlier in our lives to make the connections between our own lives and those of racial/ethnic or poor women—the vast majority of women. We have had to work at acquiring the tools for analyzing the power dynamics of sexism—why, for example, once women can be ordained, only certain women make it through the screening processes; or why ordaining women as ministers and priests does not change automatically the structures of ecclesiastical power or church life.

Then too, all seven of us have at times muted our conflicts or swallowed our anger in order to survive in the system. A strong message of women's socialization is that we should be cooperative. The "good" Christian woman, we have all learned, is a people-pleaser. As Kate's and Carter's very different stories indicate, these habits are difficult to overcome. Only direct engagement in the struggle for our own and others' well-being can move us into deeply centered convictions of justice, and a feminism deep enough to ground that struggle involves trying on new behaviors in supportive environments.

Still, no woman can dictate the particular pathway of change for another woman. Feminism that becomes a conformist ideology is not worthy of our loyalty. We are insistent, though, that a feminist perspective needs to move toward systemic inclusiveness. As we have pursued the connections in patterns of injustice, our personal styles have changed and our awareness of the pervasiveness of sexism has deepened. While none of us has been rewarded for these deepening insights, such changes have become sources of our survival wisdom and our creativity. The stakes involved in any woman's appropriation of feminism will become more apparent as she leaves seminary to enter the job market. Whether she enters parish ministry or academic teaching, pursues specialized ministries, or elects other vocational options, a feminist analysis strengthens her capacity to cope. Feminist analysis and feminist theology enable women continuously to understand what is going on and provide resources for strategizing new options. Active participation in the methods of feminist theology—studying our lives—helps us maintain a level of theological reflection that supports our struggle to live creatively as justice-makers.

Our agenda as Christian feminists is to live more and more into our commitment to justice, especially in terms of women's well-being. Our woman-to-woman relations are the ongoing test of our theological integrity. Can we be honest about our faith and doubts, our values, our vision? Can we be candid enough with one another to name manipulation; compassionate enough to demonstrate that our passion for justice extends to sisters different from ourselves?

RITUALIZING FEMINIST THEOLOGY

No summary of the meaning of feminist theology in theological education today is complete without underlining the centrality of ritual to feminist spirituality. As a particular form of action, ritual embodies who we are together. It is a visible, audible, sensual testimony to the ongoing process of theologizing. It enables us to see, touch, taste, hear, and be filled with a sense of our power in relation, to enter our common vocation sensuously. Ritual, like story telling, is imagistic theologizing—which is why it is also the vernacular of the feminist theological task.

The ecstasy of songs written and sung by Susan Savell, Carole Etzler, Stacey Cusulos, Sweet Honey in the Rock, Izquierda, Holly Near calls us forth in community. Lynn Gottlieb's chants, rising from among the throng in the cathedral, invoking the Spirit to bear with us as we bear up our broken efforts toward peace, express feminist faith. Sarah Bentley's call to five hundred churchwomen to reach out and touch one another, leading us to leap together, mobilizes our delight and proffers pleasure never before experienced. Delores Williams' quiet singing of the question "Who do you say God is?" and her antiphonal collage of answers from the black religious tradition breaks open a whole new sense of the richness of imagistic tradition. Through all this women connect with the heartbeats of other women, are united through common rhythms, are changed by new visions, touched more deeply by one another's lives.

Our rituals are our mangers. We and God-with-us are birthed anew in them and empowered to new efforts to make right relation. Rituals ground our solidarity, and without solidarity, there can be no community. In the absence of community, feminist theology is stillborn. Rituals are our way of witnessing to our work as advocates, theologians, and sisters.

Our ears desire sound, so we sing. Our bodies yearn for movement and we dance. We experience ourselves and our God/ess alive and interactive; women and the Sacred, moving, mingling, touching, tickling our fancy. Ritual is the license we give one another and God to don bright colors and move in circles and claim this moment as a *kairos*. Only where there is death does ritual cease. Without it we literally die.

For feminists, images and rituals that perpetuate racist, sexist, or classist power relations in common worship are not merely offensive, they are evil—reproducing patterns of oppression within the people of God. Through our rituals and stories we are reenacting who we are before God, telling and retelling who we are, where we have come from, where we are going. They are celebrations of the deepest truth of our lives with one another and with God/ess who struggles with us for our redemption and bears us anew into life. When our worship in churches or in seminary chapels repeats or reinforces unjust relations as sanctioned by God, it is a travesty. And when our worship is lifeless and remote, out of touch with our daily life experience, imported from the experience of persons far away, expressly in an ancient vernacular, we must either perform feats of simultaneous translation or settle for disengaged boredom and meaninglessness. In feminist celebration, vivid and joyous involvement is called for. Authentic celebration requires creativity, loving care, wisdom, and hard work. We believe the mediocrity of much that passes for Christian worship in the seminaries and churches is the result of laziness, lack of theological integrity, and failure of imagination. What we have experienced together in our ritualizing is what many women have come to expect—deep sharing and power. More and more feminists are turning to alternative rituals. Many of these are created concretely in relation to whatever collective activity its participants are engaged in. Ada, whose love of ritual enriched our work, constantly reminded us that rituals "insist on being born out of a process" and are not just imported into it. All of us learned to value her criteria for good feminist ritual: a ritual must have intrinsic relation to the activities in which it is embedded; leadership for feminist ritual must be shared and rotated; and ritual thrives on brevity.

Rituals guided by these criteria were a regular and central part of our process of collective theologizing. Regularly, at day beginning and end, one of us was designated to plan and lead a ritual. Some, like Bess's litany ending chapter three, were written beforehand and brought to be celebrated. Others, like the wicca ritual mentioned above, were borrowed from ritual contexts in which we had participated earlier. Sometimes we meditated on a poem or used focusing exercises for "centering." Always, our aim was to be in touch with spiritual power—with and among us, and beyond us as well, through all our connections.

Feminist theologizing requires rituals as tongues require words to

177

speak, ears require sound to hear, or hands require movement to sign. Theology requires embodiment—stories, litanies, songs, movement. We image our world speaking out of our experience, enriching our experience as bonds we forged. Feminist theology aims to enable our shared authority to name our world. It requires us to draw deeply from our cultures and our traditions but also to respect our full creativity in reshaping responses and transforming traditions.

Just as we embrace books not conventionally religious as sources for theological inspiration, so feminists celebrate cultural occasions not formally religious as part of our canonical ritual—women's concerts, women's art, sometimes even women's space in classrooms. (Some of us begin our feminist courses with brief rituals.) At one of our meetings we gave priority to attending together a concert by the remarkable black women's musical group, Sweet Honey in the Rock. Their music, their performance, their presence, their politics, all radiantly exemplify, strengthen, and extend the visions we hold dear. We also scheduled time for play or meals with other friends in the cities in which we met. We attempted to be aware of the rhythm that makes for productive work. We believe we must respect the principle of living humanely even as we struggle for more humane lives. We prepared meals together and cleaned up together, partly out of our commitment to feminist principle that no one person should get stuck with most of the routine tasks, but also because this is a natural way for women to relate to one another, sharing work we all know needs to be done. We sometimes suspect that one reason men do not work more cooperatively together is because men do not cook and wash dishes together. Thinking reflects the praxis of which it is part and intellectual competition fosters fragmented intellectual work. The cooperative efforts natural to women's culture are not "natural" dimensions of ongoing theological work. Even if we have been socialized in women's culture, we sometimes had to establish certain rules of thumb to make our process work and avoid falling into male-dominant patterns. (If Ada Maria helped to prepare this meal, she need not help to clean it up. If Mary wants coffee, she should make it herself, familiarizing herself ahead of time with how to do it so she needn't bother Beverly, our hostess, who happens to be talking right now.)

Just as dominant theologians neglect the power and beauty of black culture, so malestream theologians ignore the power of women's culture and women's rituals. The theology of culture needed in theological education is not one focused on elite male preoccupations, or the "high" culture of elitist aestheticism. Our focus needs to be on cultures that are either invisible or perceived as unworthy of serious and central theological reflection. Repeatedly, Ada reminded us that among Anglos, Hispanic culture is related to only as a source of entertainment, not as a challenge to the values of Anglo culture. The time has long passed when anyone can ignore or trivialize our ways of naming the world and imaging human existence.

Chapter Six

TRASHING THE TERRIBLE, TITILLATING LESBIAN: DIALOGUING ON SEXUALITY

Who the hell wants her epitaph to read, "She was a good, obedient girl who did what she was supposed to do"?

—Carter Heyward

Mud Flower is undivided in our perception that, as much as any other single phenomenon, lesbianism is shaking the foundation of the Christian theological enterprise. And why? Because the lesbian represents the woman who is not doing what she's supposed to do. She is not male-dependent in her life nor male-identified in her attitudes and ideas. Whether or not the individual lesbian knows

180

this is the case, intends it to be, or wants it to be, she bears the image of the woman who rejects fundamentals upon which the church is built: assumptions about "natural" and "moral" orders; creation, procreation, and recreation; gender roles; family structure; the valuing of the spiritual as opposed to physical realities; and the concomitant disvaluing of women, bodies, relationality, and emotions, and the strength of human bonding and commitment. To take the lesbian seriously on her own terms would mean a radical reformation of the church.

What follows is a glimpse of where we are "on sexuality" and of why we understand this to be a critical force in theological education. We have spun out analytically and woven together into one conversation bits and pieces from our actual discussions. The proximate correspondence between each of us and a particular character in the dialogue is meant not to shield our identities but rather to honor the imaginative work of this reconstruction. Most of all, we employ this style to emphasize our *common* voice as our *dominant* voice on the subject of sexuality. May we greet you as One Body, reflecting a prism of the passionate theological possibility we so earnestly desire.

Sister Lavender: When I get going on sexuality, there's no ending. It's such a morass, and so complicated. It's never been so clear to me that our tensions around sexuality have to do with where each of us is in relation to white male expectations of what we're supposed to be about. And lesbians aren't exempt from this at all, believe me. We too inhabit this great patriarchal space. And none of us should fool ourselves about that. Even now, I feel like men are looking over our shoulders. *White men*—even if they happen to be represented by men of color, or by women.

Sister Gold: I agree with that. Most of my problems have been brought on by heterosexual women, white and black, who're living out of the expectations of those men, black or white. And I agree, it all goes back, in every situation, to those white men who sit at the top of every pyramid.

Sister Green: You don't mean heterosexual, do you? Don't you mean hetero*sexist*—women who've bought into looking at the world, including their own best interests (so they think), through

181

the eyes of men? Look, unaware lesbians can be as heterosexist as anybody else. Surely we don't want to perpetuate the white-male-constructed notion that sexuality is primarily about who sleeps with whom.

Sister Gold: I guess you're right about that. I'm talking about women who're so attached to some man, people you think are your friends; but then, when push comes to shove, it's always the man. That's what I mean by heterosexual, but you're right, I'm sure it's not just heterosexual women. I guess what scares me about these heterosexual women, what really gets me and worries me, is that I am one. And sometimes, you know, it's just not clear what the cost of this is.

Sister Silver: Well, nothing, and I say that quite literally, *nothing* in my experience has been as divisive among women in seminaries as this very thing. Every time anyone has a problem or any group is angry at another group, "the lesbians" get the blame. The real issue may be racism or sexism, but suddenly everyone's talking about how "separatist the lesbians are," or how "there's no place in the black community for lesbians."

Sister Gold: And this also means that in the seminary, the women's center, and the women's caucus, anything that is lifted up especially for women is a place to which black women had better not go. And everybody says it's because of white women's racism, and a lot of it is, but a hell of a lot of it is that men—in this case, black men—are scared of losing their hold over "their" women's lives.

Sister Red: It's very common among Hispanics too, using lesbianism as a controlling device. And what I've found, and this is an extremely big problem among us now, is that many Hispanic males, who would lose "respectability" if they faced their own homosexuality, manifest a serious hatred of feminists and lesbians. They cannot stand the fact that feminists and lesbians are willing to talk about their sexuality openly. This threatens these men so much! Among some of the clergy now, it's not even a subdued misogyny. They're out there just putting us down. Sexuality may be the number one issue dividing Hispanics in the church right now, and the worst of it is that it is not an issue that is discussed openly. And the men in charge of the church communities, many of them closeted homosexuals, are obsessed with sexuality because they are so scared of it.

182

Sister Lavender: Well, it's the damned truth in all the churches I know anything about, at least in the predominantly white churches in this country. All these closeted male clergy, out to kill off women and gays. These church fathers are *obsessed* with sexuality themselves. Many of them, the closeted ones, are preoccupied with finding ways of keeping their cover. All the while, they complain that we lesbians and gay men and feminist women in general (because everyone knows a feminist is a lesbian, right?) are obsessed with sexuality. *We* are the one-issue people!

Sister Red: I know, it's so true. Wherever we go in the church, and I mean the "liberation" church—where all these men like everyone to think they would die for justice—they try to put us down by calling us lesbians. They want us to think they are above it all, that they don't have time for such small matters as sexuality. A well-known public speaker on justice matters told us that all these woman-questions (sexuality seems to have bypassed *him!*) belonged to the "microcosm"—and that he deals with issues of the "macrocosm."

Sister Yellow: It gets back to their failure to deal with the small places of their lives, their own particularities—like the way these men treat their own wives, or lovers, or members of their congregations, or students.

Sister Lavender: I continue to be startled by how deep this issue is—not only as it's used as a weapon by men against women, but also how terrified *women*—including feminist women—are of actually dealing with "the lesbian menace." So many women are terrified by everything represented by lesbianism, even by being associated with lesbians. I keep learning this, and it is very painful for me—how shameful a thing most women believe lesbianism is. Some of my most active feminist white sisters do not, if they can help it, own who I am in any public way. It's very clear to me, in church circles, that many of my sisters would prefer to look the other way when I come around. I mean, I've had folks ask me to speak—but please, not to talk about "that." And, most recently, I had the experience of finding myself quoted several times—in a major, church-related, feminist publication—and, unlike everybody else who was quoted by name, after my quotes were such phrases as "a woman faculty member" or "a woman priest."

Sister Yellow: Damn.

Sister Purple: It makes you realize how much power you have, or I hope it makes you see this. I think it's as critical an issue as what Martin Luther King had to do in getting blacks to realize that going to jail was not going to destroy them. As long as black people in the South could be terrified of going to jail, no justice was going to come. And when people went to jail singing and coming out alive, it meant that as black people we had faced the fear of incarceration and therefore we could stand and fight against any oppression. Facing the fear of lesbianism has that same kind of power.

Sister Green: And women trash lesbians because we've been taught that by being "good girls," we will be accepted. It's the illusion of believing ourselves to be isolated individuals, never basically involved with other women, and able to rise above the commonness of female being.

Sister Silver: This may be the most basic lesson women learn, or have confirmed, in seminaries: Don't get involved with other women! Rise above it! Be exceptional! And this means it's the basic lesson women must *unlearn.*

Sister Gold: I agree; homophobia is the deadliest form this lesson takes in seminary. It's like cancer; I see clearly in my experience how it kills. When I was teaching, I was shocked. I didn't even recognize it, but some lesbians in class started coming to me and saying that there was definitely some homophobia in the class. And I didn't know from nothing what the hell they were talking about. And I said, "Well, you know, I just don't see it. I don't see it." And then, I got some papers back after we had read Rita Mae Brown's book [*Rubyfruit Jungle*], papers from heterosexual women, and you would have been astonished. After the word "lesbianism" in these papers, these women had scribbled up their papers with dots, dashes, crosses, hostile, crazy signs and marks. And I said to myself, this is like Nazism, and it's going to kill these lesbians. And I'm not talking simply about the scribbled marks. It was the anger against lesbians that I felt and saw with my own eyes when I read these papers. Nothing mild—plain hatred and vehement rage. And I began saying to myself, "Oh, God, we've got to find some way to do something about this in theological education."

Sister Silver: You're right, something has to be done, purposely, to call people on these attitudes. In fact, some real, honest-to-God/honest-to-woman theological education has to be done.

Sister Gold: Take a course in liberation theology, for instance, and you have white men and black men and white women and black women and maybe some Hispanics and some Asians, and here they come, to deal with liberation, right? And everybody deals OK, maybe not really at profound depths, but OK, with racism and sexism and imperialism and maybe even classism, and then some gay man or some lesbian says, "Hey, there's another issue here"—and suddenly nobody except a few gays wants to deal with it. And the "open pedagogy" everybody's been excited about? Well, suddenly you have "closed pedagogy"—because these folks don't want to deal with sexuality. Well, I say, "OK, we're going to have some directed, 'closed' pedagogy. We're going to deal with this, and this is the professor's prerogative at this point."

Sister Red: I'm happy your "closed" pedagogy makes them deal with sexuality, because I think the problem goes beyond homophobia. It's really about sexuality. I can't tell you how many friends I have who are powerful, vocal advocates of liberation who tell me I should not accept invitations to speak to gay groups or work with gay or lesbian groups—because "It will lessen your credibility." But what these same people are really saying, and this is borne out in their actions, is that they really are scared of *sexuality,* their own and everybody else's.

Sister Lavender: You are right, of course. It *is* about sexuality, period, and we must not lose sight of that. And yet, I'm adamant about calling attention to gay and lesbian oppression in particular. Because it's awfully easy for us, and certainly for church people elsewhere, to forget that sexuality is a political reality and that lesbians and gays are victims of particularly transparent institutional political discrimination and cruelty.

Sister Red: I'm not denying the need to stress the discrimination suffered by lesbians and gays, but I think we have to keep in mind that the root of the discrimination is the lack of acceptance of the importance, and intrinsic goodness, of sexuality in all human beings.

Sister Green: Yes, and also the fear and hatred of women—misogyny, which in the Christian tradition is inseparable from homophobia, heterosexism, and sexism itself.

Sister Lavender: Sisters, we need to say that the major corpus of Christian doctrine is built on this fear and this hatred. And we have to deal with this. We have to deal with it every day in our Christian seminaries. It means making a profession out of our commitment to overcome heterosexist practice and doctrine.

Sister Gold: It means dealing with heterosexual obsession as a problem, because of which homosexuals suffer.

Sister Green: It means dealing with our passions for one another on the basis of our actual embodied (that's such an imprecise word!)—actual physical—responses, which don't compartmentalize neatly into "hetero" or "homo."

Sister Purple: It also means knowing that the people who are most resistant to these learnings are the ones whose own sexualities are least clear to them.

Sister Green: And it really does mean dealing with sexuality as a political issue; I couldn't agree more. Our eroticism is political. And by that I mean it has to do with power, the ways it's used and abused in society, the ways that power is exercised as control by men over women and between and among all of us. And *nobody* is exempt from that, gay or straight. We know that there are connections between power, as we encounter it around us every day in the world, and how we ever *experience* our eroticism or fail to experience it.

Sister Lavender: Absolutely. Eroticism has to do with our creative flow and energies, our basic relationality to one another and to everything.

Sister Purple: It's what this whole project we're working on is about—calling the lies of our culture into question. And it's deep, and it's systematized institutionally. It's evident from the way some people act that some of the biggest names in print, I mean the theologians before whom we are supposed to bow, are some of the most sexually frustrated. You just know by the way they relate to each other and the way they relate to women, these men love to have women, and maybe men too, falling all over them, making them feel so big and orgasmic. And then, what happens if some of

186

these women are lesbians, women who don't need to have sexual intercourse with men in order to feel like real women? Well, these men can't stand it—and they can't stand for anybody else to stand it. Even God.

Sister Gold: That's right. They can't stand even for God to stand for it.

Sister Yellow: That's the bottom line.

Sister Purple: I can remember Ruby P. Jones in my school, an all-black school. "Don't go into the bathroom with Ruby P. Jones or you'll get raped," we heard. I was a Christian, so I could go into the bathroom because good Christians weren't supposed to discriminate against or ostracize people who were different. So I went in, and I came out, and everybody said, "What happened, what happened?" She was supposed to be deformed, a freak of some kind, a half-woman. And men had all kinds of things to say about Ruby P. Jones. It was all right for them to rape you, but not all right for this woman to be attracted to you. And yet, everybody was intrigued by Ruby P. Jones. Here she was—a strong, able-bodied woman—and people were mesmerized by her. But it was like the fear of going to jail. The fear of being associated with Ruby P. Jones was so real.

Sister Green: I think it is critical for us to say again that this issue is fundamentally related to everything else we're talking about. I teach a course called Sexuality and Social Order, and I insist that the first learning for everybody is a greater awareness of who *they* are, because I'm convinced that unless we're reasonably comfortable with ourselves, our own sexuality, we are unable to be comfortable with anyone else's experience.

But at the same time, I'm becoming more and more aware that, for a lot of men and some white women, this experience of our own sexuality contains the final lie and secret that we are not going to have exposed. The fact is that people live split lives, split between private desire and public role or between experience and fantasy or between what we have and what we want. Living split lives, therefore, people do not want to take any responsibility for the choices they make.

Then right in the middle of this flight from responsibility, we have some folks in the gay movement working to reinforce the notion that all sexuality is divided into two parts, heterosexuality and homosexuality, and we can't help being one or the other. Some gay men actually ask straight people to accept them because they can't help being what they are!

My own experience and teaching and sharing issues of human eroticism leads me to affirm that we are all born "polymorphous perverse," exactly as Freud said! We all learn patterns, and some of us learn strong patterns of homo- or hetero-eroticism. If people are aware at an early age that they are different, they reinforce the pattern in a homosexual direction; if not, they just assume they are heterosexual. But all of us start out capable of deep, sensuous responses to the touch of others. And most of us do not lose a capacity for that. We are freaked by our *own* homosexual feelings, not by others' feelings. So we project. We all differ in our sexual histories.

Sister Lavender: Right, we differ not necessarily in terms of what titillates us at all, but in terms of how we relate to general pressures for social conformity, especially in terms of gender expectations and deep emotional attachments. And the self-awareness of deviance, especially if it comes very early, gives direction to the ways we learn to *experience* our eroticism. As a result some gays and most straights feel as if they were "born this way." Some of us experience pressures for gender-role conformity more easily than others. And then, for many of us, our experiences and our patterns—including our patterns of feeling—are not rigid.

Basically, our eroticism is part of our history, and it's no more biologically determined than anything else about us. A great deal going on in our culture supports this—the fact that biological determinism is basically false and that, therefore, *all of us* have to accept some responsibility for what we feel and how we act on these feelings and for the choices we make. And one of the things we're up against is that lots of people will go screaming and kicking to their graves about sexuality, that "this is just the way it is"—which is to say, we have no choice. We must conform.

Sister Silver: Gay and straight alike.

Sister Gold: And especially lots of these theological types who like to talk about "the way God made it"—because that way everything has its place, and nothing changes. Everything conforms.

Sister Green: Yes, and also some of the psychological types who agree that everything has its place.

Sister Lavender: Things like the anima and animus that are there potentially to be "developed." Like we're supposed to "individuate" and achieve "balance" and come out looking approximately the same.

Sister Green: We need to teach and say everywhere we can that our sexuality, our eroticism, is as much of our history as is anything else about human beings. And then be able to say, Yes, that's fine, who I am is good as long as I take responsibility for myself. I need to be able to say, I'm going to live this way and express this and be a loving person through the relations I enter. Sexuality is the one part of life that many still think is somehow out of their control. We simply have to fight that false notion. We have to refuse to sanction that lie. We have to make it harder for people to go on justifying not getting in touch with where they are. People have learned to be morally irresponsible—living split lives; living lies; living fear-ridden/anger-driven/emotionally repressed lives—utterly irresponsible. We must make folks stop projecting their fears on others.

Sister Red: Don't you think this has particularly strong confirmation in Christian history, this business about everything having its "natural, God-given" place?

Sister Green: Well, I always start my course by saying that Christianity teaches genital fixation by teaching that sexuality is only something you do when you get married, when the penis gets shoved into the vagina. All our thinking about sexuality and all our experiencing sexuality has been conditioned by this false notion that sexuality means one thing: intercourse between a man and a woman who are married—

Sister Yellow:—for the purpose of procreation.

Sister Gold: Oh, come on!

Sister Lavender: You laugh, but that's exactly what a liberal bishop said publicly to a bunch of us gay men and lesbians several years ago.

Sister Purple: Will somebody tell me I'm dreaming?!

Sister Yellow: It's all-pervasive, that's right, leaving out women's perspectives on our own sexuality. For instance, nobody mentions the clitoris in seminary discussions of so-called human sexuality in print or in person. Vaginas are basic to human reproduction, not necessarily to women's sexuality. Men are naturally confused about the difference between reproductive and sexual capacity, since their bodies combine the two functions in one organ. But women's biology makes it starkly clear to sexually alive women that sexual pleasure and reproduction can be different experiences. We've got to start saying "clitoris" out loud and insistently so that we don't ignore and trivialize women's pleasures in sexuality. Taking women's bodies seriously makes it obvious that discussion about sexuality in the Christian tradition has been framed by men.

Sister Red: Another thing that happens when we take our bodies and our female experience seriously is that we free ourselves from the male understanding/projection that sensuousness and sexuality are totally controlled and mainly expressed by genital organs. In my culture, where emotions are much more freely expressed than in this culture (and perhaps this means that, in this one area, we Hispanics might have less of a split between the private and the public), bodily expressed affection between friends is not uncommon. There is nothing uncommon about two women walking hand in hand down the street. And men kiss each other as a sign of greeting and affection without that being a sign they are gay. It is important that we claim aloud and repeatedly that the expression of our sexuality is not exclusively genital and that all affection carries with it a sexual expression, a bodily expression, a sensual expression.

Sister Green: Indeed! Is it any wonder that so many men—especially white, upper- and middle-strata men—in the U.S. walk around repressed, running around in circles—both away from and toward this monster, this passion—which they're terrified will gobble them up?

Sister Lavender: If they only knew how sweet she is!

Sister Red: And don't you know how berserk everything would be, in the churches and seminaries and everywhere else, if gays were really accepted publicly! I mean, *so many people* . . .

Sister Silver: A lot of gayness! And also straight people who'd be happier, because all of us could just *be.* We'd quit bothering each other, and trying to hide, and being defensive and pent-up and hostile and afraid. People are *so afraid.*

Sister Lavender: You know, I'd been back on campus this semester about three days when a woman student came to me upset because she'd decided the "whole class," my theology class, was gay. And this woman knows I'm a lesbian, right? And I pointed this out to her when she began making some pretty tactless comments about gays. And her eyes widened and she said, "Well, I'm talking to you because you're the only lesbian I know who has any integrity." And I said, "I beg your pardon!" And she told me how the gay men and lesbians on the campus didn't have any integrity. And I, of course, differed with her and said that seemed to me a distorted perception. And one thing led to another and she wound up saying that she was really upset because it turned out my theology class—in Anglican theology, mind you—was actually going to be a course on sexuality! And I said, "Now, how have you reached that conclusion?" And she said, "Everybody's going to want to be in the sexuality working group." (There are fourteen working groups, *one* of which is on "sex roles, gender, and sexuality in the Anglican Communion.") And she said, "Everybody wants to be in that group on sexuality." And I said, "Well, that is not, in fact, the case. In fact, very few, three or four, have chosen that group."

She was so puzzled. She said, "Well, I thought everybody was going to be in it." Then she fell silent, and so did I. And after a few moments, I thanked her for her voicing this frustration so early in the semester. I said that, although I was not clear just what was upsetting her, I was glad she felt she could come see me. And then we discussed homophobia for a long time, And I tried to explain, drawing on some partial parallels like racism and sexism and other social diseases, how this fear of homosexuality is, in fact, a deep-seated social illness that besets us all. I didn't want her to feel like she'd just won the prize for homophobe of the year. But I did want her to begin to see that she is, in fact, suffering from an illness. And that she's not alone.

Sister Yellow: Well, this is all enormously helpful to me, because I have the feeling that it's female sexuality in general people are afraid of. And I also know that, during the last ten years or so of my life, I've learned practically everything I know about my female sexuality from lesbian women. It's been both liberating for me personally, to begin to "hear" my own body passions; and anxiety-producing, at the same time, to realize that this has not been something I could learn from my husband. Because my husband does not know these things. I've learned about myself, as woman, as sexual being, from watching lesbian women relate, and from being related to by lesbian women, and from listening to lesbian women; and what I've learned is something about the powerfully social and intimate nature of my sexuality. I mean, I owe my lesbian sisters enormous appreciation and gratitude for teaching me to experience my sexuality as a woman rather than to experience my body and my passions through men's eyes.

Sister Green: Yes. And this is also, I think, why lots of women are so afraid of lesbianism. Somehow, for the reasons you've just articulated, Sister Yellow, lesbianism both invites women to break the chains of male dependency in their lives and threatens them terribly if they cannot do this. You know, one of the recurrent accounts voiced in my class by white women who are lesbians is how, in their first lesbian experiences, they had to cope with feelings of being dirty: women's bodies touching, women feeling sexual pleasure with each other. These are the things we've learned are wrong, bad, nasty. And we've learned that our sexual feelings are somehow redeemed and our sexual selves somehow completed in our sexual transactions with men. The stunning recognition that this is not the case can be almost too much for a woman to bear. And the lesbian becomes the image of this autonomous, non-male-dependent woman. Coming to a place where you affirm woman's sexuality as strong and good and complete is hard!

I remember this woman student, an adamant feminist who'd been fighting feminist battles, who was in my class. And about the third week of school, she threw a fit and said, "I get the feeling that everyone in this room thinks the Christian ethic of sexuality should change, and I think that's appalling!" And she gave us this long speech about women needing these protections, the traditional sexual ethic, and the affirmations of marriage. In this context she sounded like a fundamentalist. And she played that role in the class until the day we got to the discussion on sexual violence. On that particular occasion, I had the class divide into a women's group and a men's group (the men, it turned out, couldn't even talk to one another when they got together). But the woman who'd been reading us the riot act about how much we needed a traditional Christian sexual ethic had a lot to say when we were in an all-women's space.

As soon as the men left the room, the woman began to pound the table and shouted, "That son of a bitch!" And she told us that her loving husband sometimes raped her when he got fed up with her needing space or room to breathe. And this was the woman who'd been talking about the virtues and protections of traditional marriage!

Sister Gold: And what she was really asking for was some sense of how to survive and live a good life. You know, we women have been educated that this kind of "protection" can only be given by men when, in point of fact, whenever women need protection, it's usually *from* men's expectations, demands, and even violence that we need to be released!

Sister Green: Well, this taught me a lot about where lots of women are today. And why some are trashing lesbians. It's out of feelings—misdirected and dangerous and real—about needing security and protection, which most women have never had anyhow. They think that, if it exists, it's going to come from men. At another level they know better, but they can't go public with this knowledge or they'll lose their man and everything, all that security that goes with having a man.

So they publicly denounce lesbians, women who aren't male-dependent. But when they get into all-women's space, well, then they sometimes feel free to state their case, strip off their masks, and speak freely. But they can't let this happen in the "real" world, the men's world.

Sister Purple: Some of these same dynamics are present in relationships between white women and black men. Especially this business of women learning to feel that their bodies and their relationships with other women are somehow tainted. The same thing is true, in this racist society, of white women who have sex with black men. It's like black men make white women unclean. Then white men, and this happens a lot, will tell the white woman, "It's OK, you're still OK, even though you've slept with this unclean man. We still love you, even though . . ." This is also what gets said by men to lesbians: "Even though you're dirty, and weird, and doing things that aren't good for you, it's OK, we'll condescend to have a theological dialogue with you."

Sister Red: That reminds me of the time a black man came and did a liturgical dance in a service being attended by mainly white women. The reaction was so agitated and negative that we couldn't even talk about it. I think white people project their eroticism on black men, almost as if these white folks have to put their own feelings of impurity off onto somebody else.

Sister Gold: And all the while those white men, straight or pretending to be straight, walk around being "spiritual" and "academic," or so they think.

Sister Yellow: And "excellent" and "competent"—

Sister Silver: And scared stiff—

Sister Purple: You mean, scared limp—

Sister Silver:—right, scared limp that some insatiable sexual creature's going to come around and taint their pure theology.

Sister Lavender: And here we are, doing just that. What strikes me as both poignant and outrageous is that this God-awful fear of sexuality, women, gayness, bodies, feelings, and loss of control is, in fact, *a fear of creativity*—even a fear of genius, of feeling something, thinking something, conceiving something terribly real and fine and constructive. A fear of doing something that would make a critical difference to a lot of people.

Sister Yellow: You know, when I first heard you say that I was puzzled. But then I got to thinking about it and now I'd say the same thing in a slightly different way. Sexual pleasure, or orgasm, is really about *ecstasy*—at least that's what it is for me. And ecstasy is a central religious theme, even a mark of revelation. It's led me to suspect that controlling women's sexuality is also about controlling alternative sources of religious knowledge.

Sister Lavender: Well, the reason I teach in the area of sexuality is that I know of no more profound theological issue. I am convinced that, to the extent that we are afraid of our sexual being, we're afraid of God, because what is God if not the wellspring of our creativity, our relationality, our ecstasy, our capacity to touch and be touched at the core of our being?

Sister Gold: You're right there. These men, and a lot of women too, demonstrate by the ways they live their lives, and certainly by the ways they write theology, that they are terrified of God—if what they mean by God has anything to do with love or justice or relationship or creation or passion or ecstasy. But you know, some of them don't mean any of these real-life dynamics when they use the word God.

Sister Lavender: Nope, all they mean is something to speculate about. Something to keep themselves busy wondering about.

Sister Silver: Sure, theology becomes, for them, a way of avoiding taking human life seriously.

Sister Yellow: And when we say we're going to deal with sexuality as a theological issue, whatever else we may mean by this, we mean that we intend to take human life seriously.

Chapter Seven

THE MUD AND THE FLOWER

The best way we can say anything worthwhile in this book is to *demonstrate* the very process of feminist theological education.

—Nancy Richardson

As we bring our work to a close, we are edging into a confidence to speak boldly—to believe in our vision—because we are on the verge of understanding the hard and splendid truth that haunts Christian seminaries: Only insofar as our strongest loves and fears, hatreds and hopes are known to us and shared with others can we actually learn/teach anything worth knowing about God. If theological education does not enhance the knowledge and love of God, we might as well go home. For what then is the point? If, however, Christian seminaries are to be arenas in which we spend our time well, then they will be contexts in which God is met, recognized, and named

196

in our daily, commonplace struggles for dignity, meaning, and justice.

CONFESSION/CELEBRATION: THE LIMITS OF WHAT WE LEARN

Too seldom in theological education are we expected to state and own the limits of what we have learned, the gaps in our knowledge, the contradictions in our education, the ambiguities and rough places in our theologies. Without such candid assessment of what we have been able to teach and learn, the quality—and constructive significance—of our education is diminished. And our capacities to *continue* to learn and teach give way to the facades of intellectual/ theological pretension. Thus, we confess particular limits and gaps in what we have done. And we celebrate the educational value and theological power of this confession.

The effects of racism. We confess the extent to which women of different colors and cultures can go only so far together. Despite our goodwill, which was massive and real, we have produced a predominantly white book in which there has been room for black and Hispanic women to have some voice. We black and Hispanic women celebrate the room that has been made for us (it's hardly ever happened before in all our many years in seminaries). But we do not delude ourselves into thinking for a moment that this is truly a "rainbow book." A white woman initiated it, calling together women she knew, and, from beginning to end, worked as primary author and editor of all our words. That's called *white power;* hence, we confess the whiteness of "our" voice. At the same time, we hear the power of our southern black and Spanish brown witnessing coming through in these pages. And we celebrate Carter's call and the coalition of resources that made *God's Fierce Whimsy* possible.

In Ada's words:

> It's painful to read through this book from the perspective of Hispanic culture and see the marginality and tokenism of my

197

presence. But I also feel that you other six have taken me seriously, struggling with me, listening to me, helping create a place in theological education in which I have been able for the first time, in relation to either white or black women, to struggle with what it means to be Hispanic and female and Roman Catholic and a liberation theologist and still not go crazy. Mud Flower has given me a ray of hope. And I thank you.

More effects of racism, sexism, and . . . We are having a hard time conveying to you exactly how difficult it has been for black, Hispanic, and white women to work together—not only *across* racial/ethnic lines but also *among ourselves as black women* and *among ourselves as white women.* Our difficulties with one another have been all too frequently because each of us suffers from the effects of racism, sexism, heterosexism, classism—the various "isms," which we ourselves have ingested and have taken on as our own. And having ingested the sexism of the culture, we find that we too can reflect its misogyny in our distrust of ourselves and our questioning of the adequacy of women's work. And black and Hispanic women living in this culture cannot but internalize its racism, taking on themselves and projecting onto racial/ethnic men their sense of inadequacy and the hatred that is the cornerstone of white supremacy.

Ada, our Hispanic member, has at times been alone, aware that she is neither white nor black. Alone—that is to say, ignored and silenced by the rest of us. Kate confesses, "The problem that I have with Hispanics is that, as a black, I never know where I am with you." To this, Ada responds, "I feel exactly the same way in relation to black people."

And there has been the difficulty, which we name in chapter three, of our white members' reluctance to challenge our racial/ethnic members' perceptions, as if we black and Hispanic members do not deserve to be taken as seriously by white women as they take one another.

And a problem has arisen among our black members of how their participation in Mud Flower is being perceived by other black women and men. Have we black women sold out? "Are we handkerchief heads?" asks Bess. "Mammies?" asks Kate.

198

Carter has already been told by several white male theological educators that this project would be taken more seriously if it were a "real" research project rather than "an attempt by white women to relate to black women"—a transparently racist statement. Which brings us to a racist dynamic none of us can simply crawl out of and get away from: in the theological education enterprise in the United States and Canada, white/Anglo/Northern European women *are* the custodians of white Anglo/Northern European men's assumptions about what is or is not "theological" or "educational." Carter, Bev, Nancy, and Mary cannot simply quit being custodians. They, and we black and Hispanic women, have had to work consciously at their letting go of some of these long-standing assumptions—about what is theological, what is educational, what is excellent, what is what. We celebrate that Mud Flower has worked extremely hard at this and that each has worked from her own integrity.

Homophobia. We confess that we never dealt candidly with our own homophobia, despite our dialogue about what a problem it is in theological education (chapter six). In our final session together, Carter noted emphatically her disappointment that even Mud Flower could not seem to crack through "the fear about our own women's strength"—which was Carter's way of describing the homophobia she experienced among us. When she said this, we were silent, so real is our fear. At the same time, we celebrate what we were trying to convey in chapter six: There is no more fundamental moral, intellectual, pastoral, or political problem in today's seminaries than homophobia. Until we confess this and name its place in our own work and relationships, our creative/liberative capacities will remain clogged with the residue of self-denial, sexual repression, and a fear of women—which is a fear of our own power. Frightened as we are, we celebrate this womanpower sparking among us.

Classism. We confess that we did not deal, explicitly and insistently enough, with the class issues among us. The wounds of economic elitism, and the mystification of class as a constant issue in our daily lives, confounded us from meeting to meeting. The exchange between Katie and Mary (chapter three) was as close as Mud

Flower came to laying bare the places in which any of us—white, black, Hispanic—has been educated by the economic realities in which she has lived, worked, and related. We are mindful, more now than ever before, that class has shaped our perceptions of human and divine life. We celebrate our having brought some class analysis into this realm of theological discourse and our intention to keep the fires of class-consciousness burning in our theological work.

Motherhood. We confess that Mud Flower did not lift up and look hard at the institution of motherhood, especially in relation to several of us being mothers, all of us having mothers, and a couple of us being in the process of deciding whether to be mothers. We did not say much in our work together about how our having children or not affects our senses of ourselves as feminists, theologians, black women, white women, Hispanic women, lesbian women, straight women, spouses, lovers, celibate women. What does it involve and what does it mean for us to be parents? How does this experience set us apart from (or does it?) women who have not made this choice? And have we experienced having children, or not, as *our choice?* How have our feelings about having children, or not, affected our relationships with one another in Mud Flower? Is there a connection between our experiences of motherhood and of sisterhood? How shall we draw honestly from our experiences of having been mothered, and of mothering, in our work together as theologians and educators? We confess that there have been a few rough places in our work that might have been less rough had we studied seriously what it may mean that several of us are mothers and several of us are not. We celebrate our recognition of how significant motherhood is to our work and relationships as women. We celebrate also our right to choose whether, and under what circumstances, we will be mothers. We confess that this is very recent, very liberal, and—like most rights—very class-bound. We confess, furthermore, that within the antisexual/antifemale constraints of traditional Christianity, our right to choose motherhood is severely sanctioned by whether we live our public lives as married, heterosexual women.

We celebrate our children. We celebrate (although sometimes it is hard to celebrate) the choices we have made to be, or not to be, mothers. We celebrate also the possibility for which we struggle: that someday *all* of us—and our sisters, daughters, granddaughters, god-daughters, namesakes, and nieces—will inhabit a world in which motherhood is fully and freely a gift and an option, available to all who desire it, whether married or single, lesbian or straight; black or brown, red, yellow, white, or some brilliant combination thereof. We celebrate the realm of our God/ess in which motherhood is a gift forced upon no one, and an option that all who desire it can afford. We celebrate the utopic day in which there will be no hungry children and no women desperate for children or for senses of themselves as valuable, sane, creative people.

Our failure to talk about writing and language. We confess that we did not discuss enough the process of our writing. Several of us, including Carter, are writers, and we enjoy writing. For others of us, writing is neither particularly enjoyable nor easy. For theologians—and especially academic theologians—this is a serious pedagogical issue: What is involved in writing and reading theology? What, especially, is involved in writing theology together, in a collaborative mode? What happens when one person does not like another's style? Or when one of us cannot understand another's particular usages of language or grammar? What happens when we are *mis*-communicating among ourselves because we are employing and understanding language differently? Such questions were present in Mud Flower's work, and they are never far away in theological education. They may be especially acute in cross-cultural situations in which, frequently, language—even the same language—cannot be assumed to mean the same thing to different racial/ethnic groups. We celebrate the power of language; our skills as writers; and, in our misunderstandings, our desires to understand and be understood.

Tension in collaboration. We confess that, toward the end of our work, we were overwhelmed with difficult dynamics among us—so much so, that finally we gave up paying much attention to our process in order to draw the project to its close. Because we had begun to believe deeply in what we had been learning together, all of us agreed that it was more important at this time to get our book published than to work on our relationships in Mud Flower. As we brought this work to a close, we were aware of how critically in need of attention some of our relational dynamics are.

We celebrate the publication of *God's Fierce Whimsy* as an honest, analytical feminist reflection on what is really involved in theological education. Yet we confess that we are puzzled, even as our "product" goes to press, about what the concrete implications of Mud Flower's relational difficulties may be for theological education.

We have noted repeatedly our belief that good education depends on a critical study of our lives in relation to one another and to the subject matter. At the same time, studying our lives is likely to move us into anxiety, collectively and separately. When we experience the threat levels, the fears, or the anger as if we are alone— moving in separate spaces/cut off from one another—our capacity for collaboration is put to the test. It is a test Mud Flower has barely passed.

Like the Beatles, the longer we worked together, the better we became: the stronger our perceptions, the clearer our voices, the more interesting our contributions, the sharper our insights—and the more complicated our lives in and outside of Mud Flower. The "mature" Beatles—by the time they produced their last album— could not work together in the same studio. They sang/played separately and let the engineer mix their parts for commercial purposes, Happily, our difficulties were not this extreme, but we did incur some troubles in Mud Flower. And we had to decide either to work with one another toward resolving these relational/vocational problems, or to finish this book.

We confess that we chose the latter. We celebrate that we chose the latter. We confess—and celebrate—our suspicion that this very dilemma is inherent in all creative theological education. To give up entirely on either process or product is to cut ourselves off from the relational source/god of our theological commitments to a justice, which, in our case for example, is served both by our relational dynamics (including our difficulties) and by the completion/ publication of *God's Fierce Whimsy*.

Only a starting point. We confess that we have offered here only a starting point, a springboard into further discussion as to what *God's Fierce Whimsy* may mean for a theological curriculum; theological pedagogy; the rise in the numbers of women in seminaries; most mainline churches' refusals to wrestle honestly or constructively with issues of misogyny or homophobia; racism, ethnic chauvinism, and class elitism that continue to haunt the enterprise of theological education; and so forth.

We celebrate our realization that the most we could do, with limited time and resources, was to offer a starting point. More importantly, we celebrate our recognition that our starting point had to be the study of our lives. Most of all, we celebrate this study of our lives as a serious contribution to feminist theology, to social theory, and to the history and the future of theological education in the United States.

RECAPITULATION

We are persuaded that the liveliness of that future depends on putting the methodology we have used here at the center of what is meant by "theological education." Still, as we have stressed, studying our lives can be genuinely revelational—the occasion for authentic transcendence—only as our theological schools become genuinely inclusive. Real education and spiritual growth occur only where it is impossible to avoid the conflicts and tensions that rend our world and the lives of each of us. The difficulties we have encountered in probing our brokenness, even in spite of existing bonds of trust, should stand as a sobering reminder of the meaning of what we propose. Nor can we pretend to have more than a provisional sense of what it will mean for seminaries and theological schools to shape their work with enough inclusiveness and cultural diversity to make for genuine intellectual depth. Currently, we see no evidence that any sector of theological education in North America has even begun to scratch the surface of the changes needed to bring excellence to theological education. Here we can only reiterate the most obvious implications of our learning for its ongoing work.

Justice. The fundamental goal of theological education must be the doing of justice. This means:

1. Education is never neutral. It is either for justice, which requires the liberation of all people from structures of oppression, or against it.
2. The scholar who is indifferent to justice in his or her scholarly work is not an excellent scholar.
3. Dealing with issues of justice entails an understanding of the interstructuring of injustice. That is, sexism cannot be understood apart from an understanding of racism and "compulsory heterosexism," and all three are maintained through the class structure of economic injustice.

Curriculum. The assumptions about what constitutes the core of theological curriculum that have dominated theological education for the last one hundred years can no longer be considered adequate. This means:

1. Cultural pluralism is critical in the attempt to examine the value of what is taught and what is learned as well as in the persons involved in the teaching/learning process.
2. That which constitutes excellence or competence can no longer rest on knowledge about white male culture, or on an assumption of knowledge as detached from the life experience of the knower.

Pedagogical method. What one learns and how one learns it are integrally related; the process *is* content. This means:

1. Theory is formulated in the course of action. Our definitions cannot be brought to our work a priori. Education is, therefore, a process—action *and* reflection, mental *and* manual work.
2. Education is a collective process in which dialogue is essential.

3. A dialogical process assumes a mutuality between teachers and students: educators learn and learners educate.
4. Learning from our mistakes must be explicit, which means that our mistakes must never be hidden in the educational process.
5. An adequate pedagogy entails accountability, collaboration, beginning with our lives, diversity of culture, and concrete active commitment to the work of justice.

BLESSING

Kate: Like a stumbling runner Mud Flower didn't give up. For that reason, it became my church.

All: Blessed be the people's church, which doesn't give up.

Bev: It's been an experience I would not have missed. We have seriously *done* theology. And this is rare.

All: Blessed be *women doing* theology.

Ada: It excites and scares me to realize that the future belongs to those who see that, without justice, nothing matters.

All: Blessed be the justice-makers, without whom nothing matters.

Mary: What a mingling of pain and excitement, loving and learning! Somehow, in Mud Flower, the pain has been bearable. And the learning has never been more intense.

All: Blessed be the intensity of good learning.

Bess: You know, most of the people in seminaries will not have the foggiest notion what this project is about or what its significance is. But I've enjoyed knowing that we and those other women will be sharing a treasure, a secret, from which we can draw our strength and our pride.

All: Blessed be the secret from which we draw strength and pride.

Nancy: Mud Flower has been an energizing, creative, difficult adventure. Best of all for me has been learning how the study of our lives, far from being privatistic and narcissistic, has pulled us all into more radical places of engagement with the whole created earth. I have enjoyed this, our work, the delight of being with you, the laughter we found. . .

All: Blessed be this pleasure.

Bev: My life has been touched, turned, transformed, and I've seen it happen to each of you in our work. For each of you—and for myself—I am enormously grateful.

All: Blessed be.

Kate: I embrace you all as my sisters, because "we ain't what we gonna be, but we ain't what we was." We have moved.

All: Blessed be our moving on.

Carter: We've created together a texture nappy and thick, strong and wildly complex in our differences and on the basis of some common vision. And "mud flower" is an apt image, because our work has been very hard—and really very good.

All: Blessed be God's fierce whimsy, and our part in the sacred dance.

MUD FLOWER
Delores S. Williams*

How will I walk this rope?
My foot size ten
    broad, careening
Woman I am
    black,
I have held her in my gaze
    white woman
Smile slashed across her face
    like the great pumpkin
    friendly
Asking to know me and
    I her
Should we together
    probe our-
    selves mythed
In the strength of

*This poem was written for Beverly W. Harrison's fiftieth birthday, August 4, 1982. We are grateful to Delores S. Williams for having provided thereby a name for our collective.

Men we've forgotten
    Should I say
Fuck the guilt
    Should she say
Fuck accusing
    Should we say to each other
Your people will be my people
Where you go I will go
    Shall we together
    admit alone
    We
Are the people . . . ?

Notes

Chapter One: In Search of Commonground

1. Our work has been commissioned by the Association of Theological Schools (ATS), the organization that accredits seminaries and schools of theology in the United States and Canada. All accredited seminaries are members of ATS and can participate in the setting of standards by which members must be continually recertified as providing the resources for good education. The substance of our book is meant to challenge some basic theological and educational assumptions that for the most part ATS has not seriously questioned. There are, of course, exceptions to this. We are not the only people in the world of theological education concerned that prevailing curricular and pedagogical winds are weak and ineffective. Nor are we the first to suggest that the study of theology must begin with the study of our lives. But we are attempting to show the relation between poor theology, dull education, exhausted resources, and structures of injustice such as sexism and racism. We certainly do not claim that to explore the relation between sexism and theology or between racism and education is novel. We are grateful to many who have paved the way for us here. But we do imagine that this may be among the first public statements in which women of different racial/ethnic and religious backgrounds have given corporate voice to a contention that theological education is, in some fundamental ways, a bad experience for women and men of all colors and cultures

who seek primarily to know and love a God of justice. In this book, we hope to be laying groundwork for dialogue with others in theological education.

In the spring of 1982, Leon Pacala, executive director of ATS, spoke with Carter Heyward, who teaches theology at the Episcopal Divinity School in Cambridge, about doing a research project on feminism and theological education. Carter agreed to coordinate a collaborative project in which other feminists would join in exploring implications of feminism for theological education. Carter and Leon agreed that the project would be conceptual and analytical (rather than, for example, a data-gathering task), in which feminist dynamics, perspectives, and goals would be assessed as they pertain to theological education. Having submitted a proposal and received a grant, Carter recruited a team of collaborators to work with her.

Mud Flower met over five weekends (September 1982 to February 1984) to discuss feminism and theological education. During our first meeting we decided to make the study of our own lives the basis of our work, in relation to which we would seek testimonies, confirmations, contradictions, and challenges from others. Carter would be the coordinator and principal editor of the project, since she alone had the time, via sabbatical, to make our work a central focus of her own. The rest of us would contribute written reflections to the project and would assume a constructive role of critiquing what Carter wrote or compiled from among our contributions. All of us would talk to others, especially other women interested in theological education, soliciting their input and responses to our work.

In 1980 The Pilgrim Press published *Your Daughters Shall Prophesy,* a book remarkable in its revelation of emergent womanpower in theological education and in its implicit, devastating critique of the structures of theological education that continue to squeeze women's lives to the margins of institutional life and presuppositions. The authors of the book called themselves the Cornwall Collective, after the site of their first meeting. Their work was significant in signaling another way of authoring besides "soloing," whether literally or seriatum (as in collections of pieces written by different people). We would like to imagine that our project stands in continuity with the Cornwall Collective's, both in method and content, although we are a different group with another, related task.

With the exception of Nancy Richardson, who coordinated the Cornwall volume, none of us worked directly on it. Whereas their focus was women's programs and feminist resources in theological education (they studied extracurricular resources that had been developed by women), our concern is the seminaries themselves and what is done or not done on behalf of the best interests and well-being of women. In both the Cornwall Collective and the Mud Flower Collective, the groups have attempted to work collaboratively, such that each participant is able to own the project as both *hers* and *ours*. For us, like the Cornwall group, at the heart of our interest is a basic and shared commitment to the well-being—the rights, dignity, welfare, and uncompromised value—of all women.

2. As this book unfolds the reader will notice that Hispanic feminists are struggling to gain visibility within both the feminist and the Hispanic communities by naming themselves and not just being included under such terms as women of color, racism, etc. Hispanics are black and white and every tone in between. The oppression they suffer has a specificity within racist oppression that we will call attention to in this book by frequently using the term racial/ethnic.

3. Carter Heyward, *The Redemption of God: A Theology of Mutual Relation* (University Press of America, 1982), p. 134.

4. Jackson W. Carroll, Barbara Hargrove, and Adair T. Loomis, *Women of the Cloth: A New Opportunity for the Churches* (San Francisco: Harper & Row, 1983).

Chapter Two: Can We Be Different but Not Alienated?

1. Alice Walker, *The Color Purple* (New York: Harcourt Brace Jovanovich, 1982).

2. Zora Neale Hurston, *Mules and Men* (Philadelphia: Lippincott, 1935; reprint ed., New York: Collier Books, 1970), pp. 18–19.

3. George Frederickson, *White Supremacy: A Comparative Study in American and South African History* (New York: Oxford University Press, 1981).

4. See Carter Heyward, *The Redemption of God*, especially pages 25–59 and 149–72, for the source of my use of the term "godding."—KGC

5. Cherríe Moraga, and Gloria Anzaldúa, eds., *This Bridge Called My Back: Writings by Radical Women of Color* (Watertown, Mass.: Persephone Press, 1981), pp. 27–34, 71–75, 94, 101.

6. See Amari Baraka, "Philistinism and the Negro Writer," in *Anger and Beyond: The Negro Writer in the United States*, ed. by Herbert Hill (New York: Harper & Row, 1966).

7. Langston Hughes, *The Ways of White Folks* (New York: Knopf, 1934).

8. See Richard Sennett and Jonathan Cobb, *The Hidden Injuries of Class* (New York: Vintage Books, 1972).

9. Carter Godwin Woodson, *The Mis-Education of the Negro* (New York: The Associated Publishers, 1933).

10. Cynthia Neverdon-Morton, "The Black Woman's Struggle for Equality in the South, 1895–1925," in *The Afro-American Woman: Struggles and Images*, ed. by Sharon Harley and Rosalyn Terborg-Penn (Port Washington, N.Y.: Kennikat Press, 1978), p. 43.

11. Ibid., p. 44.

12. George Jackson, *Soledad Brother: The Prison Letters of George Jackson* (New York: Bantam Books, 1970).

13. Alice Walker, *Revolutionary Petunias and Other Poems* (New York: Harcourt Brace Jovanovich, 1973), p. 5.

14. Gloria Hull, Patricia Scott, and Barbara Smith, *All the Women Are White, All the Blacks Are Men, But Some of Us Are Brave* (Old Westbury, N.Y.: Feminist Press, 1982).

15. Gloria Naylor, *The Women of Brewster Place* (New York: Viking Press, 1982), pp. 129–73.

16. Lillian Eugenia Smith, *Killers of the Dream*, rev. ed. (New York: W.W. Norton & Co., 1961).

17. RSAC is a network of professional women in New York City, mostly denominational executives, who have been meeting for the past ten years to discuss, analyze, and strategize around issues related to the intersection of race, sex, and class.

18. Smith, *Killers of the Dream*, p. 27.

19. This reference is to an incident in Carter's childhood when she was molested by the black yardman who was employed by her family. As Carter recalls, "I was five or six and I liked Jeff. I knew he wouldn't hurt me and his fondling of me in the garage never bothered me. What did bother me was the reaction of the police captain, and all the other white men when my parents called them. I couldn't understand why all the fuss. What had Jeff done that was so wrong? And I felt guilty because I had told on him."

Chapter Three: In My Voice You Will Hear Pain

1. The title of this chapter is taken from Delores S. Williams' "A Woman's Litany," which Mud Flower shared as a ritual in September 1982. This poem appears on pages 206–7.

2. "We don't have a sense of women as a class. No matter how political I think I am, I don't let what you have received as good because you are a woman be also received as good for me. . . . When I see a Hispanic getting credit, I somehow feel it, because there is a class-consciousness among Hispanics, but it's still not there with women."

3. Bell Hooks, *Ain't I a Woman: Black Women and Feminism* (Boston: South End Press, 1981), p. 153.

4. St. Paul Pioneer Press, October 3, 1983, given by the U.S. Census Bureau.

5. A happy exception to what seems to be otherwise an indisputably common rule has been the willingness of the dean, faculty, and board of the Episcopal Divinity School to admit openly gay/lesbian students and welcome and tenure an openly lesbian professor. We commend a careful study of this Cambridge seminary by those interested in what it means for a theological school to put its institutional life on the line, repeatedly, on behalf of justice. Three of Mud Flower's members have worked in this school. Like many women throughout the United States, Mud Flower celebrates the Episcopal Divinity School. We fear also that, *because women do appreciate this seminary,* its fiscal future may be uncertain in a world/ church still under the control of men.

6. See Valerie Saiving, "The Human Situation: A Feminine View," *The Journal of Religion* (April 1960).

7. See Martin Heidegger, *Being and Time* (New York: Harper & Row, 1962).

Selected Bibliography

Sandra Hughes Boyd

Acosta-Belen, Edna (ed.). *The Puerto Rican Woman.* New York: Praeger Publishers, Inc., 1979.

Andolsen, Barbara Hilkert. "Agape in Feminist Ethics." *Journal of Religious Ethics* 9 (Spring 1981): 69–83.

———. "Racism in the Nineteenth and Twentieth Century Women's Movements: An Ethical Appraisal." Ph.D. diss., Vanderbilt University, 1981.

Aptheker, Bettina. *Woman's Legacy: Essays on Race, Sex and Class in America.* Amherst: The University of Massachusetts Press, 1982.

Aronowitz, Stanley. *False Consciousness: The Shaping of the American Working Class.* New York: McGraw-Hill, 1973.

Baraka, Amari. "Philistinism and the Negro Writer." In *Anger and Beyond: The Negro Writer in the United States,* edited by Herbert Hill. New York: Harper & Row, 1966.

Beck, Evelyn Torton. *Nice Jewish Girls: A Lesbian Anthology.* Watertown, Mass.: Persephone Press, 1982.

Beck, Peggy V., and Walters, A.L. *The Sacred: Ways of Knowledge, Sources of Life.* Tsaile, Ariz.: Navajo Community College, 1977.

Bell, Roseann; Parker, Bettye; and Sheftall, Beverly (eds.). *Sturdy Black Bridges: Voices of Black Women in Literature.* New York: Doubleday, 1978.

Bennett, Lenore. *What Manner of Man: A Biography of Martin Luther King, Jr.* Chicago: 4th rev. ed., Johnson Publishing Co., 1976.

Bohn, Carole R. "Women in Theological Education: Realities and Implications." Ed.D. thesis, Boston University, 1981.

Bowles, Samuel, and Gintis, Herbert. *Schooling in Capitalist America: Educational Reform and the Contradictions of Economic Life.* New York: Basic Books, 1976.

Brown, Rita M. *Rubyfruit Jungle.* New York: Bantam Books, 1977.

Buchanan, Constance H. "Women and Religion. Part One: Feminist Scholarship in Theology." In *The Women's Annual, 1980: The Year in Review.* Edited by Barbara Haber. Boston: G.K. Hall, 1981.

Bulkin, Elly, and Smith, Barbara. *Feminist Perspectives on Anti-Semitism and Racism: Two Essays.* Brooklyn, N.Y.: Long Haul Press, 1983.

Bunch, Charlotte, and Pollack, Sandra (eds.). *Learning Our Way: Essays in Feminist Education.* Trumansburg, N.Y.: Crossing Press, 1983.

Burke, Mary P. *Reaching for Justice: The Women's Movement.* Washington, D.C.: Center of Concern, 1980.

Cannon, Katie G. *From Womenwisdom Comes the Way: Walking Together.* Loveland, Ohio: Seminary Quarter, 1977.

———. "Responses to Theological Education and Liberation Theology Symposium." *Theological Education* 16 (Fall 1979): 19–21.

Carroll, Jackson W.; Hargrove, Barbara; and Loomis, Adair. *Women of the Cloth: A New Opportunity for the Churches.* San Francisco: Harper & Row, 1983.

Chicago, Judy. *The Dinner Party: A Symbol of Our Heritage.* Garden City, N.Y.: Doubleday, 1979.

———. *Through the Flower: My Struggle as a Woman Artist.* Rev. and updated. Garden City, N.Y.: Anchor Books, 1982.

Christ, Carol P. *Diving Deep and Surfacing: Women Writers on Spiritual Quest.* Boston: Beacon Press, 1980.

———. "The New Feminist Theology: A Review of the Literature." *Religious Studies Review* 3 (Oct. 1977): 203–212.

Christ, Carol P., and Plaskow, Judith (eds.). *Womanspirit Rising: A Feminist Reader in Religion.* New York: Harper & Row, 1979.

Clark, Linda; Ronan, Marian; and Walker, Eleanor. *Image-Breaking, Image-Making: A Handbook for Creative Worship with Women in Christian Tradition.* New York: The Pilgrim Press, 1981.

Cobb, Jonathan, and Richard Sennett. *The Hidden Injuries of Class.* New York: Random House, 1972.

Collins, Sheila D. *A Different Heaven and Earth: A Feminist Perspective on Religion.* Valley Forge, Pa.: Judson Press, 1974.

———. *The Economic Basis of Racism and Sexism*. New York: Theology in the Americas, 1980.

———. *The Familial Economy of God*. New York: Theology in the Americas, 1979.

———. *Theology in the Politics of Appalachian Women*. New York: Theology in the Americas, 1978.

Collins, Sheila D.; Golden, Renny; and Kreutz, Eileen. *Half a Winter to Go: Poems*. Chicago: Sunburst Press, 1976.

Comitas, Lambros, and Lowenthal, David. *Work and Family Life: West Indian Perspective*. New York: Doubleday, 1973.

Cornwall Collective. *Your Daughters Shall Prophesy: Feminist Alternatives in Theological Education*. New York: The Pilgrim Press, 1980.

Daly, Mary. *Beyond God the Father: Toward a Philosophy of Women's Liberation*. Boston: Beacon Press, 1973.

———. *The Church and the Second Sex*. 1st ed., 1968; 2d ed. with new feminist postchristian introduction, 1975. New York: Harper & Row.

———. *Gyn/Ecology: The Metaethics of Radical Feminism*. Boston: Beacon Press, 1978.

———. *Pure Lust: Elemental Feminist Philosophy*. Boston: Beacon Press, 1984.

———. "The Spiritual Revolution: Women's Liberation as Theological Re-Education. *Andover-Newton Theological School Quarterly* 22 (March 1972): 163–76.

Davaney, Sheila Greeve (ed.). *Feminism and Process Thought*. New York: Edwin Mellen Press, 1981.

Davis, Angela. *Women, Race and Class*. New York: Random House, 1981; Vintage Books, 1983.

Davis, Lenwood G. *The Black Woman in American Society: A Selected Annotated Bibliography*. Boston: G.K. Hall, 1975.

Davis, Marianna W. (ed.). *Contributions of Black Women to America*. 2 vols. Columbia, S.C.: Kenday Press, 1982.

Doely, Sarah Bentley (ed.). *Women's Liberation and the Church: The New Demand for Freedom in the Life of the Christian Church*. New York: Association Press, 1970.

Edwards, George R. *Gay/Lesbian Liberation: A Biblical Perspective*. New York: The Pilgrim Press, 1984.

Eisenstein, Zillah R. (ed.). *Capitalist Patriarchy and the Case for Socialist Feminism*. New York: Monthly Review Press, 1978.

———. *Feminism and Sexual Equality: Crisis in Liberal America*. New York: Monthly Review Press, 1984.

———. *The Radical Future of Liberal Feminism.* New York: Longman, 1981.

Elmendorf, Mary Lindsay. *Nine Mayan Women: A Village Faces Change.* Cambridge, Mass.: Schenkman, 1976.

Elsasser, Nan; MacKenzie, Kyle; and Trixier y Vigil, Yvonne. *Las Mujeres: Conversations from a Hispanic Community.* Old Westbury, N.Y.: Feminist Press; New York: McGraw-Hill, 1980.

———. *Teaching Guide to Accompany Las Mujeres.* Old Westbury, N.Y.: Feminist Press, 1981.

Emmet, Dorothy. *The Moral Prism.* New York: St. Martin's Press, 1979.

Farley, Margaret Ann. "Justice and the Role of Women in the Church: Thirteen Theses." In *New Visions, New Roles: Women in the Church.* Edited by Lora Quinoñez. Washington, D.C.: Leadership Conference of Women Religious, 1975.

———. "Sources of Sexual Inequality in the History of Christian Thought." *The Journal of Religion.* 56 (April 1976): 162–76.

Fiorenza, Elisabeth Schüssler. *Bread Not Stone: The Challenge of Feminist Biblical Interpretation.* Boston: Beacon Press, 1985.

———. *In Memory of Her: Feminist Theological Reconstruction of Christian Origins.* New York: Crossroad, 1983.

Fortune, Marie M. *Sexual Violence: The Unmentionable Sin.* New York: The Pilgrim Press, 1983.

Frederickson, George M. *White Supremacy: A Comparative Study in American and South African History.* New York: Oxford University Press, 1981.

Freire, Paulo. *Pedagogy in Process: The Letters to Guinea-Bissau.* Translated by Carman St. John Hunter. New York: Continuum, 1983.

———. *Pedagogy of the Oppressed.* Translated by Myra Bergman Ramos. New York: Seabury Press, 1973.

Gearhart, Sally. *Wanderground: Stories of the Hill Women.* Watertown, Mass.: Persephone Press, 1979.

Gilligan, Carol. *In a Different Voice: Psychological Theory and Women's Development.* Cambridge, Mass.: Harvard University Press, 1982.

Giroux, Henry A. *Ideology, Culture, and the Process of Schooling.* Philadelphia: Temple University Press, 1981.

Giroux, Henry A., and Purpel, David (eds.). *The Hidden Curriculum and Moral Education: Deception or Discovery?* Berkeley, Calif.: McCutchan, 1983.

Golden, Renny, and Collins, Sheila D. *Struggle Is a Name for Hope: Poetry.* Minneapolis: West End Press, 1982.

Goldenberg, Naomi Ruth. *Changing of the Gods: Feminism and the End of*

Traditional Religions. Boston: Beacon Press, 1979.

―――. *The End of God: Important Directions for a Feminist Critique of Religion in the Works of Sigmund Freud and Carl Jung.* Ottawa, Ont.: University of Ottawa Press, 1982.

Gómez, Alma; Moraga, Cherríe; and Romo-Carmona, Marianna. *Cuentos: Stories by Latinas.* New York: Kitchen Table, Women of Color Press, 1983.

Grant, Jacquelyn. "Black Theology and the Black Woman." In *Black Theology: A Documentary History, 1966–1979.* Edited by Gayraud S. Wilmore and James H. Cone. Maryknoll, N.Y.: Orbis Books, 1979.

Greenlee, Sam. *The Spook Who Sat by the Door: A Novel.* New York: R.W. Baron, 1969; Bantam Books, 1973.

Grimke, Angelina Emily. *Appeal to the Christian Women of the South.* 1836. Reprint. New York: Arno Press, 1969.

―――. *Letters to Catherine E. Beecher.* 1838. Reprint. Freeport, N.Y.: Books for Libraries Press, 1971.

Grimke, Sarah Moore. *An Epistle to the Clergy of the Southern States.* New York, 1836.

―――. *Letters on the Equality of the Sexes and the Condition of Woman, Addressed to Mary S. Parker.* 1838. Reprint. New York: B. Franklin, 1970.

Grimke. (See also below, under Theodore Dwight Weld.)

Hafkin, Nancy, and Bay, Edna. *Women in Africa.* Stanford, Calif.: Stanford University Press, 1976.

Hageman, Alice. *Sexist Religion and Women in the Church: No More Silence!* New York: Association Press, 1974.

Hardesty, Nancy. *Women Called to Witness: Evangelical Feminism in the 19th Century.* Nashville: Abingdon Press, 1984.

Harrison, Beverly Wildung. *Making the Connections: Essays in Feminist Social Ethics.* Edited by Carol Robb. Boston: Beacon Press, 1985.

―――. *Our Right to Choose: Toward a New Ethic of Abortion.* Boston: Beacon Press, 1983.

Heidegger, Martin. *Being and Time.* New York: Harper & Row, 1962.

Heyward, Carter. *Our Passion for Justice: Images of Power, Sexuality, and Liberation.* New York: The Pilgrim Press, 1984.

―――. *A Priest Forever: The Formation of a Woman and a Priest.* New York: Harper & Row, 1976.

―――. *The Redemption of God: A Theology of Mutual Relation.* Washington, D.C.: University Press of America, 1982.

Hodge, John L.; Struckmann, Donald L.; and Trost, Lynn Dorland. *The Cultural Bases of Racism and Group Oppression: Western Concepts,*

Values, and Structures That Support Racism, Sexism and Elitism. Berkeley: Two Riders Press, 1975.

Holbrook, Sabra. *The American West Indies: Puerto Rico and the Virgin Islands.* New York: Meredith Press, 1969.

Hooks, Bell. *Ain't I a Woman: Black Women and Feminism.* Boston: South End Press, 1981.

Hughes, Langston. *The Ways of White Folks.* 1934, 1962, 1979. New York: Knopf.

Hull, Gloria; Scott, Patricia; and Smith, Barbara. *All the Women Are White, All the Blacks Are Men, but Some of Us Are Brave.* Old Westbury, N.Y.: Feminist Press, 1982.

Hunt, Mary Elizabeth. "Feminist Liberation Theology: The Development of Method in Construction." Ph.D. diss., Graduate Theological Union, Berkeley, Calif., 1980.

Hurston, Zora Neale. *Dust Tracks on a Road: An Autobiography.* Philadelphia: Lippincott, 1942.

————. *Mules and Men.* Philadelphia: Lippincott, 1935. Reprint with new introduction. Bloomington, Ind.: Indiana University Press, 1978.

————. *The Sanctified Church.* Berkeley, Calif.: Turtle Island Press, 1981.

————. *Their Eyes Were Watching God: A Novel.* 1937. Reprint. Urbana, Ill.: University of Illinois Press, 1978.

Isasi-Díaz, Ada María. *"La Mujer Hispana: Voz Profética en la Iglesia de los Estados Unidos."* Informes de Pro Mundi Vita, Rue de La Limite 6, B-1030 Brussels, Belgium. No. 28. 1982.

Jackson, George. *Soledad Brother: The Prison Letters of George Jackson.* New York: Coward-McCann, 1970; Bantam Books, 1970.

Joseph, Gloria I., and Lewis, Jill. *Common Differences: Conflicts in Black and White Feminist Perspectives.* Garden City, N.Y.: Anchor Books, 1981.

Kalven, Janet, and Buckley, Mary I. (eds.). *Women's Spirit Bonding.* New York: The Pilgrim Press, 1984.

Katz, Jane B. (ed.). *I Am the Fire of Time: The Voices of Native American Women.* New York: E.P. Dutton & Co., 1977.

Katz, Michael B. *Class, Bureaucracy, and Schools: The Illusion of Educational Change in America.* New York: Praeger Publishers, Inc., 1971.

King, Martin Luther, Jr. *The Words of Martin Luther King, Jr.* Selected by Coretta Scott King. New York: Newmarket Press, 1983.

Lavrin, Asunción E. *Women in Latin America: Historical Perspectives.* Westport, Conn.: Greenwood Press, 1978.

Lerner, Gerda (ed.). *Black Women in White America: A Documentary History.* New York: Vintage Books, 1972.

Lindsay, Beverly (ed.). *Comparative Perspectives of Third World Women:*

The Impact of Race, Sex and Class. New York: Praeger Publishers, Inc., 1980.

Little, Kenneth. *African Women in Towns: An Aspect of Africa's Social Revolution.* London: Cambridge University Press, 1973.

Lorde, Audre. *The Black Unicorn: Poems.* New York: W.W. Norton & Co., 1978.

————. *Chosen Poems, Old and New.* New York: W.W. Norton & Co., 1982.

————. *Sister Outsider: Essays and Speeches.* Trumansburg, N.Y.: Crossing Press, 1984.

————. *Zami, a New Spelling of My Name.* Watertown, Mass.: Persephone Press, 1982.

Lowe, Marian, and Hubbard, Ruth (eds.). *Woman's Nature: Rationalizations of Inequality.* New York: Pergamon Press, 1983.

Lynn, Robert W., and Fletcher, John C. *The Futures of Protestant Seminaries: A Conference for Seminary Trustees.* Rev. ed. Washington, D.C.: Alban Institute, 1982.

————. *Why the Seminary? An Introduction to the Report of the Auburn History Project.* New York: The Project, 1979.

McAllister, Pamela (ed.). *Reweaving the Web of Life: Feminism and Nonviolence.* New York: New Society Publishers, 1982.

McFague, Sallie. *Metaphorical Theology: Models of God in Religious Language.* Philadelphia: Fortress Press, 1982.

Maitland, Sara. *A Map of the New Country: Women and Christianity.* London: Routledge & Kegan Paul, 1983.

Marable, Manning. *How Capitalism Underdeveloped Black America.* Boston: South End Press, 1983.

Medicine, Bea. *The Native American Woman: A Perspective.* Austin, Tex.: National Educational Laboratories Publishers, 1978.

Miller, Casey, and Swift, Kate. *Words and Women: New Language in New Times.* Garden City, N.Y.: Doubleday, 1976.

Mirande, Alfredo, and Enríquez, Evangelina. *La Chicana: The Mexican-American Woman.* Chicago: University of Chicago Press, 1979.

Mollenkott, Virginia Ramey. *The Divine Feminine: The Biblical Imagery of God as Female.* New York: Crossroad, 1983.

————. *Women, Men and the Bible.* Nashville: Abingdon, 1977.

Moraga, Cherríe. *Loving in the War Years.* Boston: South End Press, 1983.

Moraga, Cherríe, and Anzaldúa, Gloria (eds.). *This Bridge Called My Back: Writings by Radical Women of Color.* Watertown, Mass.: Persephone Press, 1981.

Morgan, Robin. *The Anatomy of Freedom: Feminism, Physics, and Global*

Politics. Garden City, N.Y.: Anchor/Doubleday, 1984.

———. *Depth Perception: New Poems and a Masque*. Garden City, N.Y.: Anchor/Doubleday, 1982.

———. *Going Too Far: the Personal Chronicle of a Feminist*. New York: Vintage Books, 1978.

———. *Lady of the Beasts: Poems*. New York: Random House, 1976.

Morton, Nelle Katherine. "Preaching the Word." In *Sexist Religion and Women in the Church: No More Silence!* Edited by Alice L. Hageman. New York: Association Press, 1974.

———. "The Rising Women Consciousness in a Male Language Structure." In *Women and the Word: Toward a New Theology*. Edited by Anne McGrew Bennett, et al. Berkeley, Calif.: Graduate Theological Union, 1972.

———. "Towards a Whole Theology." In *Sexism in the 1970's: Discrimination Against Women*. Edited by Pauline A. Webb, et al. Geneva: World Council of Churches, 1975.

Murray, Pauli. "Black, Feminist Theologies: Links, Parallels and Tensions." *Anglican Theological Review* 60 (Jan. 1978) and *Christianity and Crisis* 40 (1980): 85–96.

———. "Black Theology and Feminist Theology: A Comparative View." In *Black Theology: A Documentary History, 1966–1979*. Edited by Gayraud S. Wilmore and Janes H. Cone. Maryknoll, N.Y.: Orbis Books, 1979.

———. *Dark Testament and Other Poems*. Norwalk, Conn.: Silvermine Publishing Co., 1970.

———. "The Liberation of the Black Woman." In *Our American Sisters: Women in American Life and Thought*. Edited by Jean E. Friedman and William G. Shade. 2d ed. Boston: Allyn & Bacon, 1976. Also in *Voices of the New Feminism*, edited by Mary Lou Thompson. Boston: Beacon Press, 1970.

———. *Proud Shoes: The Story of an American Family*. New York: Harper & Row, 1956, 1978.

Naylor, Gloria. *The Women of Brewster Place*. New York: Viking Press, 1982; Penguin Books, 1983.

Nelson, James B. *Between Two Gardens: Reflections on Sexuality and Religious Experience*. New York: The Pilgrim Press, 1983.

———. *Embodiment: An Approach to Sexuality and Christian Theology*. Minneapolis: Augsburg, 1978.

Neverdon-Morton, Cynthia. "The Black Woman's Struggle for Equality in the South, 1895–1925." In *The Afro-American Woman: Struggles and Images*. Edited by Sharon Harley and Rosalyn Terborg-Penn. Port Washington, N.Y.: National University Publications, Kennikat Press, 1978.

Niethammer, Carolyn. *Daughters of the Earth: The Lives and Legends of American Indian Women.* New York: Collier Books, 1977.

Noble, Jeanne L. *Beautiful, Also, Are the Souls of My Black Sisters: A History of the Black Woman in America.* Englewood Cliffs, N.J.: Prentice-Hall, 1978.

Pellauer, Mary. "The Religious Social Thought of Three U.S. Women Suffrage Leaders: Towards a Tradition of Feminist Theology." Ph.D. diss., University of Chicago, 1980.

————. "Violence Against Women: The Theological Dimension." *Christianity and Crisis* 43 (May 30, 1983): 206, 208–12.

Persell, Caroline H. *Education and Inequality.* New York: Free Press, 1979.

Pharr, Susan J. *Political Women in Japan: The Search for a Place in Political Life.* Berkeley, Calif.: University of California Press, 1981.

Plaskow, Judith. *Sex, Sin, and Grace: Women's Experience and the Theologies of Reinhold Niebuhr and Paul Tillich.* Washington, D.C.: The University Press of America, Inc. 1980.

Plaskow, Judith, and Romero, Joan Arnold (eds.). *Women and Religion: Papers of the Working Group on Women and Religion, 1972–73.* Missoula, Mont.: Scholars Press, 1974.

Pogrebin, Letty Cottin. *Family Politics. Love and Power on an Intimate Frontier.* New York: McGraw-Hill, 1983.

Randall, Margaret. *Cuban Women Now.* Toronto: Canadian Women's Educational Press, 1974.

Rich, Adrienne Cecile. *The Fact of a Doorframe: Poems Selected and New, 1950–1984.* New York: W.W. Norton & Co., 1984.

————. *Of Woman Born: Motherhood as Experience and Institution.* New York: Bantam Books, 1981.

————. "Toward a Woman-Centered University." In *On Lies, Secrets, and Silence: Selected Prose, 1966–1978.* New York: W.W. Norton & Co., 1979.

————. *A Wild Patience Has Taken Me This Far: Poems, 1978–1981.* New York: W.W. Norton & Co., 1981.

Richardson, Marilyn. *Black Women and Religion: A Bibliography.* Boston: G.K. Hall, 1980.

Richardson, Nancy. "Authority and Responsibility in a Liberal Feminist Perspective: A Study in Ethics and Education." Ph.D. diss., Boston University, 1985.

Richardson, Nancy, and Robb, Carol. "Politics and Theology of Ministry with Women." *Radical Religion* 2 (1975).

Richardson, Nancy; Timmell, Sally; Eames, Ashley; et al. *Taking the Next Steps: A Booklet for Groups Working Against Racism.* Women's Division, Board of Missions, United Methodist Church, 1972.

Rodgers-Rose, LaFrances (ed.). *The Black Woman.* Beverly Hills, Calif.: Sage Publications, 1980.

Romero, Oscar A. *A Martyr's Message of Hope: Six Homilies.* Kansas City, Mo.: Celebration Books, 1981.

―――. *May My Blood Be a Seed of Liberty.* Colombo: Centre for Society and Religion, 1983.

―――. *Romero, Martyr for Liberation: The Last Two Homilies of Archbishop Romero of San Salvador: Theological Analysis of His Life and Work.* London: Catholic Institute for International Relations, 1982.

―――. *Voice of the Voiceless: The Four Pastoral Letters and Three Other Discourses.* Maryknoll, N.Y.: Orbis Books, 1985.

Rubin, Lillian Breslow. *Worlds of Pain: Life in the Working Class Family.* New York: Basic Books, 1976.

Ruether, Rosemary Radford. *Liberation Theology.* New York: Paulist Press, 1972.

―――. *New Woman/New Earth: Sexist Ideologies and Human Liberation.* New York: Seabury Press, 1975.

―――. Sexism and God Talk: Toward a Feminist Theology. Boston: Beacon Press, 1983.

―――. *To Change the World: Christology and Cultural Criticism.* New York: Crossroad, 1981.

Rubin, Lillian Breslow. *Worlds of Pain: Life in the Working Class Family.* New York: Basic Books, 1976.

Ruether, Rosemary Radford, and McLaughlin, Eleanor (eds.). *Women of Spirit: Female Leadership in the Jewish and Christian Traditions.* New York: Simon & Schuster, 1979.

Russell, Letty M. *Becoming Human.* Philadelphia: Westminster Press, 1982.

―――. *The Future of Partnership.* Philadelphia: Westminster Press, 1979.

―――. *Growth in Partnership.* Philadelphia: Westminster Press, 1981.

―――. *Human Liberation in a Feminist Perspective: A Theology.* Philadelphia: Westminster Press, 1974.

Saiving, Valerie. "Androcentrism in Religious Studies." *Journal of Religion* 56 (April 1976): 177–97.

―――. "The Human Situation: A Feminine View." *Journal of Religion* (April 1960). Reprinted in *Womanspirit Rising: A Feminist Reader in Religion.* Edited by Carol P. Christ and Judith Plaskow. San Francisco: Harper & Row, 1979.

Sanday, Peggy Reeves. *Female Power and Male Dominance: On the Origins of Sexual Inequality.* Cambridge: Cambridge University Press, 1981.

Sargent, Alice (ed.). *Beyond Sex Roles.* St. Paul: West Publishing Company, 1977.

Scanzoni, Letha. *Sexuality*. Philadelphia: Westminster Press, 1984.

Scanzoni, Letha, and Hardesty, Nancy. *All We're Meant to Be: A Biblical Approach to Women's Liberation*. Waco, Tex.: Word Books, 1974.

Scanzoni, Letha, and Mollenkott, Virginia Ramey. *Is the Homosexual My Neighbor? Another Christian View*. San Francisco: Harper & Row, 1978.

Schaef, Anne Wilson. *Women's Reality: An Emerging Female System in the White Male Society*. Minneapolis: Winston Press, 1981.

Sennett, Richard, and Cobb, Jonathan. *The Hidden Injuries of Class*. New York: Vintage Books, 1972.

Shange, Ntozake. *A Daughter's Geography*. New York: St. Martin's Press, 1983.

———. *For Colored Girls Who Have Considered Suicide/When the Rainbow Is Enuf*. New York: Macmillan, 1977.

Shimer, Dorothy Blair (ed.). *Rice Bowl Women: Writings by and About Women of China and Japan*. New York: New American Library, 1982.

Sims, Janet L. *The Progress of Afro-American Women: A Selected Bibliography and Resource Guide*. Westport, Conn.: Greenwood Press, 1980.

Smerdlow, Amy, and Lessinger, Hanna (eds.). *Class, Race and Sex: The Dynamics of Control*. Boston: G.K. Hall, 1983.

Smith, Barbara (ed.). *Home Girls: A Black Feminist Anthology*. New York: Kitchen Table, Women of Color Press, 1983.

Smith, Lillian Eugenia. *Killers of the Dream*. 1949. Rev. and enl. ed. New York, W.W. Norton & Co., 1961 and 1978.

Sölle, Dorothee. *Beyond Mere Obedience*. New York: The Pilgrim Press, 1982.

———. *Choosing Life*. Philadelphia: Fortress Press, 1981.

———. *Political Theology*. Philadelphia: Fortress Press, 1974.

———. *Revolutionary Patience: Poetry*. Maryknoll, N.Y.: Orbis Books, 1977.

———. *Suffering*. Philadelphia: Fortress Press, 1975.

Spender, Dale. *Man-made Language*. London: Routledge & Kegan Paul, 1980.

Spretnak, Charlene (ed.). *The Politics of Women's Spirituality: Essays on the Rise of Spiritual Power Within the Feminist Movement*. Garden City, N.Y.: Doubleday, 1982.

Starhawk. *Dreaming the Dark: Magic, Sex, and Politics*. Boston: Beacon Press, 1982.

———. *The Spiral Dance: A Rebirth of the Ancient Religion of the Great Goddess*. San Francisco: Harper & Row, 1979.

Steady, Filomina Chioma. *The Black Woman Cross-Culturally*. Cambridge, Mass.: Schenkman Publishing Co., 1981.

Suchocki, Marjorie. *God-Christ-Church: A Practical Guide to Process Theology.* New York: Crossroad, 1982.

Thistlethwaite, Susan Brooks. *Metaphors for the Contemporary Church.* New York: The Pilgrim Press, 1983.

Thorne, Carrie, and Henley, Nancy (eds.). *Sex Difference in Language, Speech, and Nonverbal Communication.* Rowley, Mass.: Newbury House, 1975.

Trible, Phyllis. *God and the Rhetoric of Sexuality.* Philadelphia: Fortress Press, 1978.

————. *Texts of Terror: Literary-Feminist Readings of Biblical Narratives.* Philadelphia: Fortress Press, 1984.

Truth, Sojourner. *Narrative of Sojourner Truth: A Bondswoman of Olden Time.* Boston: Published for the Author, 1850, 1875. Enl. ed. Battle Creek, Mich.: Review and Herald Office, 1884.

Vetterling-Braggin, Mary. *Sexist Language: A Modern Philosophical Analysis.* Boston: Littlefield, Adams and Co. 1981.

Walker, Alice. *The Color Purple.* New York: Harcourt Brace Jovanovich, 1982.

————. *Good Night, Willie Lee, I'll See You in the Morning: Poems.* 1979. Reprint. San Diego: Harcourt Brace Jovanovich, 1984.

————*Horses Make a Landscape Look More Beautiful: Poems.* San Diego: Harcourt Brace Jovanovich, 1984.

————. *In Search of Our Mothers' Gardens: Womanist Prose.* San Diego: Harcourt Brace Jovanovich, 1983.

————. *Meridian.* New York: Harcourt Brace Jovanovich, 1976.

————. *Revolutionary Petunias and Other Poems.* New York: Harcourt Brace Jovanovich, 1973.

————. *You Can't Keep a Good Woman Down: Stories.* New York: Harcourt Brace Jovanovich, 1981.

Wallace, Phyllis A. *Black Women in the Labor Force.* Boston: M.I.T. Press, 1980.

Warford, Malcolm L. (ed.). *Colloquy: Conversations with the Faculty, Union Theological Seminary, 1976–1977,* New York: Office of Educational Research, 1977.

Wasserman, Miriam Wolf, and Hutchinson, Linda. *Teaching Human Dignity: Social Change Lessons for Every Teacher.* Minneapolis: Education Exploration Center, 1978.

Way, Peggy Ann. "An Authority of Possibility for Women in the Church." In *Women's Liberation and the Church: The New Demand for Freedom in the Life of the Christian Church.* Edited by Sarah Bentley Doely. New York: Association Press, 1970.

———. "Visions of Possibility: Women for Theological Education." *Theological Education* 8 (Summer 1972): 269–77.

———. "Women as Possibility." In *Women and the Word: Toward a New Theology.* Edited by Anne McGrew Bennett, et al. Berkeley, Calif.: Graduate Theological Union, 1972.

Weidman, Judith C. (ed.). *Christian Feminism: Visions of A New Humanity.* San Francisco: Harper & Row, 1983.

Weil, Simone, *Gateway to God.* 1974. New York: Crossroad, 1982.

———. *Oppression and Liberty.* Amherst, Mass.: University of Massachusetts Press, 1973.

———. *Simone Weil Reader.* Edited by George A. Panichas. New York: McKay, 1977.

———. *Waiting on God.* 2d ed. London: Routledge & Kegan Paul, 1979.

Welch, Sharon. *Communities of Resistance and Solidarity: A Feminist Theology of Liberation.* Maryknoll: Orbis Books, 1985.

Weld, Theodore Dwight. *Letters of Theodore Dwight Weld, Angelina Grimke Weld and Sarah Grimke, 1822–1844.* Edited by Gilbert H. Barnes and Dwight L. Dumond. New York: Da Capo Press, 1970.

West, Cornel. *Prophesy Deliverance: An Afro-American Revolutionary Christianity:* Philadelphia: Westminster Press, 1982.

Wheeler, Barbara G. "Accountability to Women in Theological Seminaries." *Religious Education* 76 (July-Aug. 1981): 382–90.

———. *Report on a Study of the Resource-Research Associates Program in Women's Studies . . . Harvard Divinity School.* Cambridge, Mass.: B. Wheeler, 1978.

Wilmore, Gayraud S., and Cone, James H. (eds.). *Black Theology: A Documentary History 1966–1979.* Maryknoll, N.Y.: Orbis Books, 1979.

Woodson, Carter Godwin. *The Mis-Education of the Negro.* New York: The Associated Publishers, 1933.

Young, Marilyn B. (ed.). *Women in China.* Ann Arbor, Mich.: University of Michigan, Center for Chinese Studies, 1973.

Zapata, Dominga María. "The Role of the Hispanic Woman in the Church." *New Catholic World* (July/Aug. 1980), 172.

Zaretsky, Eli. *Capitalism, The Family and Personal Life.* New York: Harper & Row, 1976.